CASSIUS

Book of Avenzyre II

GB MACRAE

CASSIUS

BOOK OF AVENZYRE II

Avenzyre awaits you — GB MacRae

Fannar Press

New York

CASSIUS by GB MacRae

ISBN-13: 978-1546738817

ISBN-10: 1546738819

Acknowledgements:

CJ Henderson, Bud Webster, and Allen Wold—thank you for all your wisdom and kind words.

To the editors at Reed, Hart, & Mandarino—you've been wonderful.

Thank you, Mark, for being so awesome.

And a big thank you for the continuing support from my friends and family.

Stories also available:

AWAKE, Book of Avenzyre I
Fiona
The Perfect Girl for the Price of Horsehair
Ethel's Bane
Precipice
A Night in the Garden

Available Soon:
ARISE, Book of Avenzyre III

Pronunciation Key (short list)

Amarynth—AM-a-rinth
Alezare—al-eh-ZAH-reh
Avenzyre—av-en-ZY-r
Alynderan—a-LIN-der-an
Cassius—KA-shus
Connylia—KON-e-lee-ah
Currain—Kur-AIN
Dournzariame—Dorn-zar-ee-a-ME
Gallylya—Gal-li-LEE-ah
Gellia—Ge-LEE-ah
Lorkiegn—LOR-kee-en
Quenelzythe—Ken-EL-zith
Rellyarna—rel-EE-arn-a
Sian—Shawn
Saquime—Sa-KEE-meh
Tintagel—tin-TAH-gel
Tunnaig—TUN-ag
Xianze—Zhan-zeh
Xzepheniixenze—Zef-en-ee-ZEN-zee
Zephronia—Zeh-fron-NEE-ah
Zyendel—Zy-EN-del

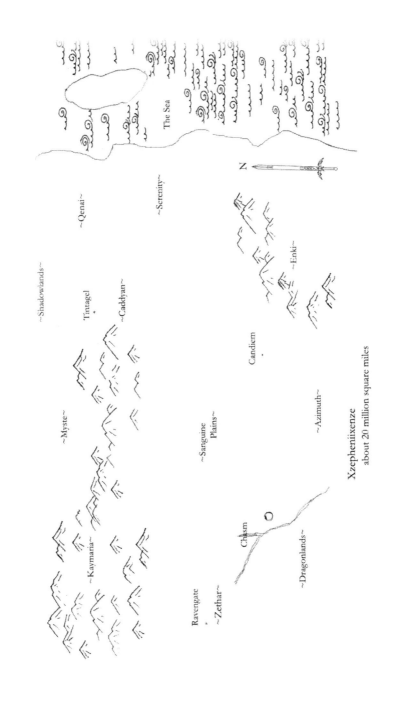

The Sea

~Qenai~

~Serenity~

~Shadowlands~

Tintagel

~Caddyan~

~Enki~

~Myste~

Candiem

~Sanguine
Plains~

~Azimuth~

Ravengate

~Zethar~

Chasm

~Dragonlands~

Xzepheniixenze
about 20 million square miles

N

1

Dawn was finally breaking after a wild night of
kidnapping and castle burning. It pleased Gellia that the women
were sleeping again; their blubbering was starting to wear on her
nerves. She supposed she'd never realized that someone could be
happy in Fuarmaania, and they were. They didn't know anything
different, and couldn't dream of anything else.

The three women slept in the back of the wagon,
exhausted from their abrupt departure. The two princes she
helped rescue took turns driving or resting. Gellia exchanged
smiles with them often, and they knew well enough to know her
thoughts. She had been away in Zephronia for far longer than she
realized.

Gellia listened to the creaking of her saddle, and started
to finger comb Amarynth's black mane. Her bond horse,
Amarynth, was more patient about their slow pace than Gellia.

They'd stopped once a few hours ago to rest the team of
horses and take turns visiting the bushes. As Gellia watched the
women settle back into the wagon she wondered what choice she
had. Either save them from the castle or let them burn. Cresslyn
and Corrah had been the ones to show her kindness in that awful
place. Cresslyn's roommate, Alexandria, wasn't even from the
kingdom, but Gellia wasn't about to leave her behind. As
unhappy as they were, Gellia couldn't have let them burn. And
burn they would have.

The elder prince and heir to the throne, Lucifer, had the lines of the horses. Her old horse, Tempest, was showing his fatigue while the younger horse was faring well enough. Gellia rode alongside Tempest and patted his dapple grey neck and tried to give him strength with her magic. It seemed to help. She reminded herself that he was a big reason why they had to go slow. The wild gallop with the wagon the night before must have been difficult for him.

"He's a fine horse," Prince Lucifer said. "Especially for one his age."

"Thank you," Gellia replied. She'd had many good years with Tempest when she'd lived in Fuarmaania. She was actually surprised the king—her stepfather—hadn't slaughtered him out of spite. At least now she could take him with her to a better place to live out his days in good care.

Corrah, Gellia's former nurse, was snoring in the back of the wagon, and it was clear the girls were asleep as well. It was the longest journey of their lives, which seemed silly now that Gellia had spent so many days in the saddle in recent months. "Lucifer, how were you captured, and why? Do you know?"

He ran a hand through his dark, messy hair. "There was a spy, someone who told King Hugh that Sen Dunea was harboring you. Apparently after his humiliation of you running away he was determined to have you back. Of course, you'd been taken by Zephronia at the time. Everyone knows about our hunting trips, and there was a plot. Our men were killed and we were taken."

"I'm so sorry, Lucifer."

"It's the way of war. I suppose we were lucky to live. And thankfully for Cassius' magic we were made fit enough to travel."

Gellia felt dreadful for her friends. They were good men and not deserving of such treatment. It made her all the happier the king and the castle were destroyed.

"We were just so happy to see you," Lucifer said. "You look well."

"I've had a much easier time than you have, I'm sorry to say."

Lucifer shook his head. "Well it's over now." He glanced back over his shoulder at the sleeping women and his dozing brother. "Did you call the dark haired one Cresslyn?"

Gellia nodded. "She's a bastard of my stepfather..." She smiled as she realized what he was about.

"Fuarmaania is yours now," Lucifer said.

Gellia laughed. "I don't want it, and I don't care if I'm the rightful heir. I abdicate. I renounce the throne of Fuarmaania, and I don't care what happens to it. Take it if you want. You'd do far better than the former king."

"I just might," Lucifer said with a nod and smile.

They watched the two wheel-ruts that was the winding road and were silent until the sun was high. The women were starting to stir once more. It seemed dismally slow travel with the wagon, but they were finally in Sen Dunea. The first time Gellia had traveled there she and her mentor had taken back paths through the wilderness. She wondered when she'd see him again, and what he was up to.

Lucifer barely had to pull the lines and the horses stopped. They were at a roadside well where two roads joined. "I think we should have a rest," he said. "We're well across the border."

Gellia nodded. "I think it's a good idea." Not for very long, though, she thought. She dismounted her beloved Amarynth and left him to his devices and paused to admire him. She would never tire of doing so. His black coat shined, his cresty neck arched so elegantly, and his sturdy legs tapered to feathers and large rounded hooves.

The princes hopped down, Mervrick helped his brother unhitch the horses and bring them to water. Gellia petted Tempest and scratched his withers. "Old friend," she said. "It will be all right. You'll have good care when we reach the King's City." He still seemed bright, just tired. She gave him a good pat.

Corrah poked her grey-haired head above the side of the wagon. "Milady," she whispered.

Gellia had never seen her without a wimple. "Corrah, it's all right. Come get a drink. Wrap yourself in a blanket. The princes will go find us something to eat." She spoke to the princes in their native language and they obliged her. The Fuarmaania language felt so awkward and choppy now, not like the flowing poetry of Xzepheniixenze.

Corrah and the young ladies came to drink and wash their faces. They were still tired, still damp from the rain, and barely dressed by their standards. There had been no time for much of anything but escape.

Cresslyn was sitting on the back of the wagon when Lucifer approached her with a leaf full of berries. He offered them with a smile, but Cresslyn was suspicious.

"They're not poison," Gellia said. "Eat them. You need strength. We have a long way to go."

Everyone ate the berries and felt better for it. Shortly they were on their way again. On the next stretch of journey Gellia translated for everyone, explaining how far they'd come, and how far they'd yet to go. She also tried to explain to the women that they were not in danger. It was a difficult point to prove. Fortunately Lucifer was gregarious and kind. Eventually tentative friendships were formed.

***

"Dogs? You like dogs?" Cress asked Lucifer, who smiled and nodded. Mervrick said something in Sen Dunean from the driver's seat and Lucifer waved his hand at him, Gellia was sure he blushed.

"Hunting dogs," Gellia informed her old friend. It was faster than repeating words and making shapes with hands and noises to describe things. "They have brilliant hunting dogs as swift at the wind."

"We used to go on hunts," Alexandria said. "I'm not a very good rider but I tried..." Gellia thought it was nice that Alexandria also was trying to join the conversation.

It was the second day of travel—a beautiful morning. Gellia smiled at the sun, stretched her arms towards the sky with a deep sigh. She gave her wild black curls a toss. They were tangled from being in the rain, but she never felt so glorious. The road welcomed her, the smell of the forest rejuvenated her.

"We were worried about you," Lucifer said to Gellia.

Gellia replied in Sen Dunean. "I was too. I was worried about Skip as well."

"He's quite the bundle of energy," Mervrick said. "He was ready to look for you on his own."

Gellia laughed to herself. "I'm privileged he is so loyal to me."

"We weren't sure what do to, but our father told us that Lord Cassius would return soon and that there was nothing we could do until he did," Lucifer said. "We were of the understanding that those who took you were far beyond our power."

"That's true as it turns out," Gellia said and smiled. "I would not have wanted you to come for me, it would have meant your deaths, and I was not in any immediate danger. I was treated quite well." She chuckled. "You should have seen me when I woke up there; I took a few of them down before I met my match."

"You've changed, milady," Corrah said, looking up at Gellia from the wagon. "I barely recognize you."

Gellia thought for a moment. She supposed they were all becoming reacquainted with her. Maybe Corrah was right, for Gellia had more experiences in the past few months that she ever had her entire life in Fuarmaania. "Corrah, I've met a relative of mine. I don't expect you to know her..." Corrah would *never* understand meeting one's immortal, many-times-great grandmother. "But she's very nice."

"I didn't know anyone was still alive from your mother's side of the family... What have you been doing since you left besides turning wild? Have you become a brigand's wife?"

"Corrah! I have better ways to spend my time," Gellia said. "A husband would slow me down." She'd spent her entire former life covered by the shadow of betrothal, marriage was the last thing she wanted.

"What are you talking about?" Cress asked. "Not that I have much of a hope anymore, but what's better for a woman than marriage and children?"

"At this point my life? Plenty," Gellia said. Cresslyn, although she still carried the same ambitions, had grown into a woman. Gellia's months away made it all the more obvious.

Cresslyn examined Gellia and thought a moment before she spoke again. "One time one of the ladies asked the baron how he could deal with your foul moods and strange ways and he told her that compared to all the other women he knew you were a lamb."

Gellia laughed. "I've met some strong-willed women, lately."

They finally crossed paths with other travelers, ones who looked rough from days on the road—or perhaps they were bandits. Nevertheless, they passed by with little more than a glance at Gellia and without a word. Lucifer looked at Gellia and raised his eyebrows. If they were bandits, it was Gellia's presence that dissuaded them.

Alexandria, who'd been thoroughly spooked by such rough people, murmured, "...Ah, oh my goodness what am I going to do? We're out here alone..." It brought on another wave of anxiety from the other two who had been frozen in the wagon. Alexandria quietly sobbed into her hands.

Corrah spoke. "You've taken us away from our home Gellia, and everything we know and now we're going to be prisoners of barbarians, is that what you want?" She brought the blanket she was wrapped in closer to her chin. "Who knows what will happen to us now. Four women alone with barbarians."

Gellia nearly groaned. "I'm glad the princes don't understand much Fuarmaanian because you would have offended them," Gellia said. "You don't know how much nicer it is in Sen Dunea. It's a lovely place—warm and bright—and will have good treatment."

"You tell them, princess," Cassius called from up the road. He and Nighthawk waited for them to catch up. The other women's faces lit up when they spotted him in all his dark glory. As was his habit lately, he was dressed entirely in black, and as his horse and his hair were the same color, it was difficult to tell where man ended and horse began. Gellia smiled at their natural magnificence.

"So he hasn't tamed you, yet?" Corrah asked, but quietly.

Cassius pushed his long hair from his face, raised his nose. "Tamed, no. I don't aim to tame, just to educate, nurse." He gave her the smirk Gellia had come to enjoy.

Even as seasoned as she was, Corrah blushed. Between him addressing her so familiarly and the idea of the princess she raised was now traveling with a man who was not her husband did her in. That and every female in Fuarmaania secretly admired him.

Gellia was ecstatic to see him. It had only been two days, but she was starting to wonder, and she missed his conversation. *I don't understand*, Gellia spoke with her mind. *I thought there might be more to them than this. Now it seems we have nothing in common. Before at least we were all Fuarmaanians, now we don't even have that.*

Cassius turned Nighthawk and rode alongside the wagon. *You convinced yourself there was more to them—there isn't, I assure you. You used to think your happiness depended on finding a husband who'd tolerate you, now you know that isn't true.*

"Goodness, Gellia, I thought you hated him," Cresslyn whispered.

Gellia grinned at Cassius. "Maybe I still do, it doesn't stop me from using him for what he's worth."

Cresslyn was shocked at such bold words, spoken aloud for all to hear. Lucifer spoke to Cresslyn again, not that she could understand it, but she interacted with him just the same.

They seemed to get along rather well with the princes, Cassius said.

Don't tell the girls that, they'd do themselves in. They weren't nearly as standoffish as they had been, at least. It was difficult for them to resist a prince who was interested in them, barbarian or not.

You think they have enough strength to do that?
I suppose you're right.

For much of the day the women spoke more and more to the princes, even learned a few words of each other's languages. Cassius kept up the horses' strength so they could continue on, and produced nearly proper meals for the travelers. Bread, cheese, fruit, and very fresh, too. Gellia looked at him curiously. *Magic,* he said with a smirk. *Don't worry, it's very real.* He offered her a lovely looking pear. When Gellia bit into it she was euphoric. *I could produce a stately meal, but that would confuse their little minds,* he said.

Mine too, Gellia said. *I'm still learning about all this magic.* The sun was low in the horizon. Aloud she said, "There's still a way to go, you should try to sleep." The ladies looked at each other and tried to make themselves comfortable. Gellia was surprised at how easily they followed her command.

"It's your tone, your resonance," Cassius said in Xzepheniixenze. He seemed pleased. "You now you have the tone of a Xzepheniixenze noble. Connylia has done well."

The three women dozed in the damp wagon while the princes sat in the front seat, the horses plodded along. As she stared at the team she felt Cassius' magic rise once more, just a little. Tempest and the other horse seemed to come to life again, looked fresh and frisky. Lucifer looked to the baron, who gave a nod. Lucifer brought the horses up to a trot.

Gellia smiled. *Do you think I've changed?*

I've killed the old princess remember?

Do you plan on killing me *too?*

He cocked his head. *You're far too interesting.*

For some reason it seemed to be one of the things he actually meant. There were so many times that Gellia was sure he was just mocking her. This was complement. *That's good to know. It's one less thing for me to worry about.*

Yes, but you'll have to worry about everyone else trying to kill you.

What?

They'll see you as a threat.

Lovely.

But I protect my investments.

How chivalrous.

Hardly. You think I don't benefit from this arrangement?

Of course. I wouldn't want it any other way.

Really?

She smiled a little. *That way I have your protection.* Her mind voice chuckled. *And that way I know I won't owe you later.*

They rode in silence for a time and Gellia felt that there was something else Cassius needed to tell her. As night fell the city came into sight. It occurred to her riding at night in a small group was unheard of in her former life. It would have been far too dangerous. She supposed she could understand why the women were so nervous. *Amarynth spoke to me when we were in Dournzariame.* She scratched her mount's withers.

Really? He eyed Amarynth. *You must have been desperate.*

I was. He told me he would protect my mind from the Zephrons so I could sleep. He also said he wasn't going to talk to me much.

Cassius chuckled. *Yes, when Amarynth protects your mind I don't think even the goddesses could harm you.*

Gellia watched the sleeping women in the wagon.

I'm giving you a day to say your good-byes. Cassius said as he watched the moonrise.

She was nearly dozing. *What?*

You have one day to say good-bye to everyone and then we're leaving for Xzepheniixenze.

She looked up at him as a chill spread over her. *What about Skip?*

We're taking him with us.

Gellia looked at the women again and wondered if it would be better if she left them without saying anything. Maybe she would write them a note. She knew that she didn't want to stay around to see the tears. The king would take care of them as she asked him to. Perhaps she would merely say good-bye to the king and his sons, collect Skip and leave. *Can we leave sooner?*

If you wish. An owl appeared from the night and landed noiselessly on his wrist. Gellia watched as magic formed a sealed letter, and the owl took it, flew towards the castle.

Gellia shook her head. She learned something new about him every day.

Yes, I can speak to them. I don't so much these days, but it comes in useful.

So that hawk in the forest those years ago?

Yes, I summoned her for your benefit.

Gellia shook her head. She was sure some of the reason for the rush was Emperor Gallylya—he might look for them and that would put the Sen Duneans in danger, but knowing Cassius, it could be any other myriad reasons.

As they entered the sleepy city she breathed deep to remember the wonderful warm smell of it. The spice market there was beautiful and rich, and the entire city smelled of it. She even reminisced about her one day in the streets, when she met Saquime, her little Skip. She smiled. She couldn't wait to see him.

The gate of the castle was open for them, and a small army of stable hands and servants waited. The horses were unhitched and led away before the women were barely awake. There were servants with robes for their new guests, and the princes were greeted by their father with a warm embrace. The king thanked Cassius over and over.

Gellia busied herself with helping her old friends who were confused and afraid. "I'm right here," she said. "These are friends. You'll be well tended. Do I look afraid?"

Corrah's eyes welled while the other two cried. "You look more radiant than you ever have," she said. "You have a bloom."

"You'll be all right," Gellia said. "Let's get you inside and to your rooms, some good hot food into you."

They would share a room for the first few nights, and Gellia stayed with them while they changed into fresh clothes, (Gellia into her gambeson) eat, and settle in. Her presence did them good. "I think Prince Lucifer finds you charming," Gellia said to Cresslyn.

Cresslyn looked at her for a moment and her eyes regained the light Gellia knew. "You really think so?"

"Oh yes." Young men entered the room and started to assemble Gellia's armor. Of course, having men in the room sent the women to the other side of their table. Not that they were indecent. The women watched in awe as Gellia transformed further into a stranger. However, she did look stunning. Not that the women knew what to think of all this.

Gellia spoke again. "Forget all you've been told about Sen Dunea," she said. "They're good people, and you'll get the best treatment. You've seen how lovely the princes are."

"I rather like them," Cresslyn said. There was finally some of her usual perkiness in her voice.

Of course, Gellia thought. Prince Lucifer was attractive and polite and gave her attention. "Then you already have some new friends. The king is very nice, and I think you'll like it here," Gellia told them.

Corrah finally decided they could trust what Gellia was saying. Probably because Gellia now looked more like a general than a princess. Gellia's scale mail wasn't the best protection, but it was impressive to look at. "I think then it's time to sleep in real beds, eh, girls? They're very clean here… If you promise no harm will come to us."

Gellia nodded. "I promise."

"We'll see you in the morning," Cresslyn said. She followed Gellia to the door where she whispered so no one else could hear. "Have a good journey, dear sister." Gellia started to say something but Cresslyn shook her head. "I've never seen you so alive, so beautiful—I know you won't stay, not when there are so many adventures out there for you… I know you wouldn't leave us here alone if we were in danger, either. Write to me when you're able."

"I will, Cress." Gellia smiled a little and closed the door. She hurried to the yard where the grinning Skip, Amarynth, and Cassius waited with her Sen Dunean friends. Cassius was already mounted on Nighthawk. Gellia hugged the king and the two princes and smiled sadly. Something in her beckoned her to Xzepheniixenze, even though she knew she could be happy here in Sen Dunea, though she could be happy in Zephronia. After she embraced Lucifer he beamed at her and said, "We'll take exceptional care of them."

Gellia returned the smile. "Cress can't ask for a better match. I'm sure she'll make a dutiful wife, and I know you'll make your new lands flourish. …I'll miss you." Gellia withdrew and hopped on Amarynth, pulled Skip up behind her. Without another word they rode away.

2

"Hold still, Skip."

"I can't help it."

"Dammit Skip, I can't heal you if you don't hold still. I'm not good enough to hit a moving target." Gellia held her hand over the boy's shoulder. "You shouldn't have climbed that tree," she scolded. The energies radiated from her hand. Healing magic—at the present time—was not her specialty.

"I'm going to be a seeker. I have to learn how to climb things," he insisted. "I don't have the supplies to work on disquises…"

"A seeker? Imagine that," Currain scoffed. "You'd be a better mage." He often transformed to this, his man's form, on the journey. Currain was his name as a man. Gellia supposed a person named "Nighthawk" would be a bit strange. When he was Cassius' steed he couldn't give his not-always-welcome opinions.

"I don't have any magic," Skip said. "I could only be a spell-caster like my mother."

"That's not what *I've* been told," Currain muttered.

Skip ignored the older boy. "When you were gone all sorts of them came to visit and I decided that is what I want to be when I'm big enough. It's my calling. I'm a quarter human, so I think there's enough Xzepheniixenze in me to allow it. I know I'll have to work extra diligently."

Gellia shook her head. "Next time be more careful. If you break your neck Cassius will have to fix it and I don't feel like begging him to do it."

"Maybe he's sending you to the School of Seeker Arts," Currain said.

The boy's face lit up. "Really?"

"Hold still! ...tell me something," Gellia said.

"I'm not telling you anything," Currain answered.

"He's a bond horse, he's loyal to the death to Cassius," Skip said.

"And *you* shouldn't address him so informally, scamp," Currain snapped. "Of course I'm loyal, it's my job. Strictly speaking I'm not even supposed to talk to you lot—only when he tells me to."

"I hope I get a bond horse soon," Skip said. "I've always wanted one."

"How much longer to Xzepheniixenze?" Gellia asked Currain as he stared at his hands. Why he was so sullen she wasn't sure. She had the urge to smack him. She might yet.

"Oh, not far now. He knows all the secrets to get us to where we need to be more quickly."

"So where *is* he? Will you tell me that? There Skip, you're better."

"He's arranging things for our arrival," Currain said. "He didn't want to be interrupted by this nonsense."

Skip bounced away and hid in the nearby bushes. They were many days ride from the city, and hadn't seen anyone else since. Not that they were on a proper road. With a sigh Gellia sat on the ground; Currain joined her. Gellia brushed the bits of dried leaves from her clothes. "Will I like Xzepheniixenze?"

"Oh yes..."

"He's returned," Skip called from a nearby tree.

The black stallion (formerly a man) next to Gellia whinnied as Cassius appeared. "Let's be on our way," Cassius said.

"So are you going to tell me what's in store for us?" Gellia asked as she mounted up. She was more excited than she'd ever been. Going to Xzepheniixenze was why she had trained for so long, and what her ancient family lore promised.

"Us?"

"Skip and I." They followed on an old hunting trail, one hardly used it seemed. The dry bushes and prickly fir trees rustled around them and snagged her clothes and tack as they passed.

"You can do what you wish."

She wished that for once he would choose to be one way or another, not friendly one moment, distant as the moon the next. "Do you mean...."

"Exactly what I said." He quickly started her lessons again. He wanted her to practice every waking moment, even if it was small tricks. Finally he was teaching her destructive magic.

"Can I do anything with my magic?"

"Anything that you can think of within the limitations of your gifts and your body's durability."

"I learned a lot about that in Zephronia." It was a painful lesson to learn, but the information was priceless.

"Congratulations."

"When I think about it, I think my magic is what called the Zephrons to Sen Dunea... I was trying to move the clouds and it was only a few moments later when the Zephrons appeared. I know you told me not to do anything we hadn't tried yet. I'm sorry."

"I wondered what you were up to," he said. "It was lucky it was just the Zephrons who took you. Your signature is unique and strong." He didn't tell her that some of the seekers who appeared in Sen Dunea were not his but the emperor's. They felt her magic and rushed to investigate only to find Sen Duneans. It was fortunate the blond haired, righteous Zephrons found her first.

"I have something to ask you. I don't suppose it was much of anything but I was curious." She dodged a low branch. She realized then he was using his magic to avoid being hit by the trees. It was so elegant. She wished she could do the same.

"Yes?"

"While I was in Dournzariame I noticed lights in the sky. They were very beautiful, but I had an odd feeling..."

Cassius glanced back at her. "Lights in the sky?"

"At night, on several occasions, I saw lights in the sky in the distance. I'm not crazy, I know what I saw."

"I believe you," he said. "I never expected you to see such a thing, although I should have."

"What do you mean? No one else seemed to care—are you telling me that it's unusual?"

"Not unusual, but rarely does anyone notice them, there are so few who have the ability to begin with, certainly not mages who are barely trained such as yourself."

"Why? What was it?" She took a tighter grip on the reins and Amarynth took the bit and jerked them from her hands.

Her teacher didn't answer her for a few moments. "Well," he paused. "Your rudimentary understanding of the mystic does not allow me to explain all its complexities." He sighed. "Have you ever noticed strata on a mountainside?"

"Yes," said she.

"Sometimes there are bumps in the strata, or other flaws. Magic is the same, layered over and through the world. The lights you saw were the upper levels grinding against the lower levels—it is a very dire event on a large scale. I cannot express to you the magnitude of the situation and you cannot understand it without much research, but it is not something to forget about."

Perhaps that was why she felt so uneasy when she saw the lights. Gellia was silent for a while, watched Skip as he scouted ahead of them. Nothing but woodland noises was around them until Cassius' voice cut through the chorus. "I have something for you."

"Oh?"

Nighthawk stopped, Amarynth stopped next to him. "Something for a mage who knows her limitations." From a saddlebag on the stallion's flank he produced a fine wooden box. He opened it before her to reveal a perfectly round purple pendant on an intricately designed silver chain. The purple stone was centered in a narrow ring of emeralds held together by a silver setting; the entire necklace rested on a cushion of velvet. Gellia picked it up and rested it in the palm of her hand into which it perfectly fit. In the sunlight it sparkled and gleamed and the flawless cuts in the back of the stone reflected light from every direction.

"It is not your average jewel," Cassius said. "With it, you can draw more energy without destroying yourself."

"I don't know what to say."

He continued. "No one can take it from you and live."

"Why?"

"I put a curse on it. If someone other than yourself takes it they must return it to you or die—death among other amusing things." He smiled. "*That* jewel is priceless, one of a kind. I forged it with magic from blood-stones of two different dragons, one blue, one red."

Gellia looked at the marvelous pendent in awe. Dragon blood-stones? It almost vibrated with magical potential. Cassius lifted it from her hand and placed it around her neck without touching a hair on her head. She placed her hand the smooth surface as it rested against her heart. She started to feel it work— with every breath it seemed to grow stronger, started to pulse with a life of its own. The horses started walking again.

"Well, now that you have the fundamentals you can use any one of your talents—perhaps not efficiently—but well enough to accomplish what needs to be for now. When we reach my castle I'll show you where the practice room is so you can work with your magic with little disturbance. You need to be a diligent student."

It was a peaceful and boring ride, with nothing much to look at but trees and Skip's occasional appearance. She was tired, achy and was sick of asking Cassius for help mystically to make her feel better. Once night fell and they were still riding, Gellia wondered if she would snap and start yelling at her mentor. Luckily he'd been moving them on towards a tiny homestead.

First the dogs barked, then the resident appeared with a pitchfork. Cassius dismounted and spoke to him, and an agreement was reached. The barn was available to them for the night. Gellia had never been so thankful.

She was quick to get Amarynth settled in, and spent little time getting herself cozy in the straw. Skip hunkered down nearby and the two of them were asleep in moments.

It was still dark as she began to awaken, but the goats were bleating to be milked. When she looked around she saw Skip was gone. She rose, filled with fear, until Amarynth mind spoke to her. *He's gone with one of the seekers to school,* he said. *He's safe, you needn't worry.*

Where's Cassius? She asked.

Outside. He'll be in momentarily. It's time to get going.

Thank you. After she collected her wits and her few belongings she tacked Amarynth. She really wanted to ask how much longer they would have to travel, but knew she wouldn't get a decent answer. She also wanted to ask why he didn't use his magic to get them there, but again…

So Gellia did as she needed to and she and Amarynth left the barn. The last weeks had been so trying she nearly wanted to return to the easy life of Dournzariame and her friend, Connylia.

Cassius was just mounting up as she saw him, and she did likewise. Who knows how long it would be before they rested again. Why did it have to be this way? Had he run out of money? Was he hiding from someone? What about a stately breakfast? That would be nice right about now. But no, instead there were apples. She would throw one at him if it would do any good.

They traveled down a narrow path until it was just dawn, then Gellia saw movement ahead. It was still dim, and if the man before them hadn't moved she likely wouldn't have seen him at all. When he did she realized there was a small shack nearby. She cursed herself for not paying more attention, but she was still desperately tired.

He gave them a nod, started to lead them just a bit further down the path until they came to an old stone archway. There was no evidence of a wall anywhere, just the arch. When Gellia was nearer she could see the forest through the arch trembled and shimmered as if it was a surface of a lake.

What is it? Gellia asked Cassius.

A portal. A fairly secret one, and one that only goes in one direction. Be prepared. It's going to be much brighter on the other side.

He didn't give her much time to prepare, and either did Amarynth. They went through.

She shock she endured upon crossing the threshold would forever be etched in her memory. The desperate few breaths she took felt like the first of her life, and she sensed she was surrounded by an existence that embraced every part of her. It was so very bright, so very colorful it nearly blinded her. Amarynth's calm presence and support kept her from fainting away.

☙ 17 ❧

Gellia blinked, held fiercely onto her stallion's mane. When she finally regained her wits she realized she was starting to feel euphoric, and her eyes focused on her surroundings. It was so sunny, so bright, and it shown through the trees surrounding her. Trees with twisted limbs heavy with clumps of flowers. Pinks, crimson, lavender, white. There were patches of plants and flowers on the ground around them, and plush green moss. Petals rained down on them as the fragrant breeze swept through. Songbirds twittered and chirped in the canopy.

Gellia held out her hand to catch some of the falling petals, and finally saw Cassius sitting on Nighthawk several paces away, watching her. "I'm sorry," she said. "I lost myself."

He shook his head and she was unable to read the expression on his handsome face. "Welcome home, Zapheny." Nighthawk pivoted and they started walking through the forest.

Gellia smiled despite herself, breathed deeply, raised her hands to touch the lower branches and let the petals fall upon her. She was nearly in ecstasy. I'm here, I'm here, her mind kept saying. How could she have ever doubted? How could she have doubted herself when she was so drawn to him when they first met? No, it wasn't romance. It Xzepheniixenze calling to her, beckoning her to join it. Even Amarynth seemed more relaxed. Gellia giggled a little, wanted to dismount so she could roll in the moss and flowers.

No, this rapture didn't continue for long, but the feeling of belonging remained. Fuarmaania and Sen Dunea were distant memories now. She trotted Amarynth to ride alongside Cassius, who looked at her with a sidelong glance. "Are you sober?" he asked.

She nodded, beaming. He smiled too. She realized she didn't remember ever seeing him smile like that before.

They came out of the trees and into the light of fields over rolling hills. There was a road in the near distance, and in the great distance she saw was a city. A massive city. There was a castle in the center, elegant spires cutting through the sky.

The landscape seemed to take her into its verdant existence as Gellia did the same to it. It had longed for her return. A world of color and light. It seemed that every blade of grass or leaf was beautiful. Even the air smelled beautiful. Gellia could feel the magic pulse through the life of the land, allowing free access to whoever needed it. Her magic was part of this, *she* was part of this. She could feel the presence of every living thing around her, the energies as it flowed around her.

The past was a dream—it didn't exist but for Zephronia. Zephronia was part of this somehow as well. Gallylya had come here to destroy. Connylia had come here to...? Gellia wiped her wet face and Amarynth shook his head and snorted. "Why didn't you tell me?" she asked. She watched a dragonfly with blue-green-gold iridescent wings land on her horse's mane.

"You wouldn't have listened." He watched her for a few moments.

"I was foolish."

"*I* wouldn't have trusted me."

She looked to the sky; it was a shade of blue she never saw before. The sun was bright and warm, no, suns. There were two; a smaller one was closer to the horizon.

"It holds less magic that it used to," Cassius said. He and his stallion made their way down the road.

She urged Amarynth faster. "Are there fairies?" Gellia asked.

He chuckled. "Every creature in your books has lived in this place."

"But no dragons."

Again he chuckled. "There are still a few breathing but you wouldn't recognize them if you saw them. They stay hidden as well as they're able."

Gellia could understand why living in Fuarmaania would be so intolerable for him, and now truly understood why she found it intolerable as well. "What is that city over there?"

"Candiem. The Lorkiegn clan. They're not allies."

"Whose side are they on?"

"Their own. That's where Saquime is right now for training—they won't give up the opportunity to make another seeker.... we aren't going there, we have too much to do. Those plans will come into play later."

"How far away is your castle?"

"A month's riding distance but we aren't going to ride. I'm having one of my mages portal us most of the way."

"So that your cousin, the emperor doesn't know you're in the area?"

"Perhaps."

"For some reason I can't wait to meet him."

He gave her a sharp glance. "Yes you can. He's not someone you should want to meet, and if you never do be happy about it... take King Hugh, make him more popular and better looking, less class, and give him immense power."

It gave her a chill, she felt the deeper meaning of his words in her very soul. "Sounds like someone who needs to be overthrown." Gellia looked over the surrounding fields and saw a few ruddy-faced, fair-skinned people working with an ox. Farther down the road there were several well-kept peasant houses. "Is everything perfect here?"

"Not by the idealistic standard of which you're thinking."

In the distance were greyish mountains, she could sense them with her magic like she had been there before, but could not see them with her eyes. "What are those called?" They seemed to change shape, as if viewing them through rippling water.

He understood to what she referred. "We won't be going there—they're another few weeks farther from where we're going. Nicely done."

"I feel something else." It was distant, just a whisper of magic that called to her in an almost inaudible shimmery voice. It knew her name. Gellia's breath grew heavy as she listened to its fragile song. The crash of the ocean waves… It was the dim heartbeat of Xzepheniixenze, only dormant magic now, that reached into the earth and far into the firmament. Gellia blinked rapidly as it overwhelmed her senses, she tried to keep steady in the saddle. "Cassius," she managed to say. "Help me." Her magic started to overtake her.

His power rushed to her aid before Nighthawk could even halt. It blinded all her senses until she regained control.

"You aren't ready for all that," he said calmly, although he was surprised at the magnitude of her mystical wanderings.

Gellia gripped the pommel of her saddle, afraid to let go until she had regained her wits. Her hands ached. "I don't know what happened."

"I was wondering how you would react once you arrived." He turned Nighthawk and started down the road again. "Best get you to Tintagel." What she could never appreciate was Xzepheniixenze felt different now that she was in it. Any of the old mages would feel it. They were likely in their distant castles wondering what they were feeling.

The cobblestone road turned towards the city, but they took a gravel road towards the mountains. Gellia was pondering if she would see any strange creatures in their near future, trying to distract her mind and calm her pounding heart. The roads were quite impressive. They were remote, yet the road was more than two wheel ruts. A wagon with a team of horses approached them. Were they Xzepheniixenze too? As the bay team passed, Gellia stared at the two drivers of the wagon—a man and a woman. Both simply dressed, both healthy complexioned with fawn colored hair. The two people stared back up at her, but avoided looking at Cassius as the horses ambled by. She smiled at them, and to her surprise they smiled back, they seemed surprised as well. Gellia turned to watch her companion. He didn't even look at the other travelers. "I thought everyone would look the same here."

Cassius glanced over his shoulder at her. "They didn't have that much Xzepheniixenze in them if any. Not everyone is purebred."

"Do you think they knew I'm an outsider? They were looking at me so strangely."

"That's because *you* were looking at *them*. It isn't very often that someone of your obviously good breeding pays peasants any mind."

Gellia thought about what he said for a moment and continued to survey her surroundings. She couldn't take enough of the scenery in to please her. She wanted to live it all; see everything.

Cassius was mumbling to himself. "...ugh, these wretched... disgustingly awful smelly..."

"Do you think we can take the long route to your castle so I can see more of the empire?"

"Certainly not. Not when I am so degraded.... No magic can save me."

Gellia smiled a little and almost giggled. Two peasants passed by and he was all upset about his looks. "You're so vain."

"Vain? I like cleanliness. The first thing I'm going to do when I get back is take a bath for the rest of the afternoon... there's our portal. Let's go, I have doubts about just how long he can keep it."

Before them, between two great trees, was a glowing arched doorway. It turned from orange to yellow to green in blotches and the other side couldn't be seen. It wasn't as pretty as the last one she'd been through. Once more she braced herself—she wasn't sure she'd ever get used to going through them.

"I know, it isn't very well made, but I can pull us through if it collapses," Cassius said. He and Nighthawk disappeared into the colors. She clung to her horse's mane and trusted him as he continued steadily into the magical doorway. First the stallion's head disappeared, then his neck, and Gellia wanted to crawl over his rump to escape but closed her eyes and froze as they passed through. It was that weightless feeling again then nothing.

"Open your eyes you silly girl," Cassius said.

Gellia blinked. They rode through an evergreen forest on a wide cobblestone road. The gate closed behind her in a puff of iridescent smoke. "Interesting choice of location," Cassius muttered, "and rather poor craftsmanship, which is why you're now dead."

The trees around them seemed to turn gold wherever the sun touched them. Every so often there were standing stones with beautifully carved dragons sitting on top. Gellia watched the highlights move along the branches as they rode until they came to a clearing. The castle in the distance was the most magnificent she'd seen. It sat on the surface of the lake, and although the stones that made it were black, it was difficult to tell where the castle ended and placid blue water began. The backdrop was rounded mountains covered by more conifers. Parts of the castle gleamed brightly. She heard Cassius sigh. Nighthawk swished his tail and jigged. They were home.

As they traveled the gently winding road surrounded by brilliantly green grass, Gellia felt that she was being watched. She was probably given good reason to feel that way. The surrounding forests were probably crawling with seekers. As they neared, she was better able to see the details of the castle.

Cassius spoke. "Be warned, Tintagel is not a palace, it's very much a fortress."

"I understand." Never for a moment did she take her eyes off their destination. Her stomach was full of butterflies.

Tintagel was entirely dark stone polished to a mirror finish; its walls gleamed brilliantly in the sun, casting large blocks of light into the forest. It sat off the shore of a lake that seemed the usual blue green, but its ripples glittered brighter than she had ever seen before. The closer they became the more Gellia realized just how great the castle was. She always thought she was closer than she was, yet they continued on. Tintagel was imposing, overwhelming. Even as stone she could feel its power.

A long bridge led them to the gate, with drawbridges and archways before the landing. Light reflected by the water flashed on the smooth sides of the black fortress. The bridge was at least twenty paces across and the shiny black stones below their horses' hooves were free of soil or blemish. All the archways and railings they passed were curved and twisted in an almost musical gracefulness.

Cassius spoke, his voice just a touch quieter than a conversational tone. "If you hear disembodied voices in the night don't be afraid, it's just the castle talking to itself. Some can hear it, some can't."

"You're teasing me."

"If you hear it, you'll know that I'm not."

At the gate there was a large platform where there were several statuesque guards. Their armor was polished, their boots clean, their long black hair tidy. They did not look at her and Cassius.

The doorway was massive, and the metal of the portcullis scraped as it was drawn up into the wall—the portcullis itself was a work of art. Cassius muttered something about having the noise fixed. Not that Gellia paid much attention to those details, for she was fixated on the brilliance that was Tintagel.

The horses took them into a stable yard that could hold an army. Two teenaged boys ran to them and stood by their horses, but didn't take the reins. Gellia and her liege dismounted and she said nothing. The castle had stolen all her thoughts.

She had to run to catch up with her baron, who was marching up the wide flight of stairs to the main entryway. "What is this place made of?" she asked. Gellia could almost see her reflection in the polished stone.

"Magic and black onyx. It was a long process but the result was worth it. One likes a striking castle." He was becoming annoyed with her excessive revere.

The stone around the door was carved with what she assumed was his family crest—a dragon. Tintagel's ornately carved, dark green door opened by itself. Gellia took a deep breath and walked into her new home. As best as she could, Gellia stayed at Cassius' heels. She didn't want to get lost as they passed by numerous corridors that seemed to be made of shadow and cool light. Giant, black stone dragons held up archways, their eyes green jewels. There were silver torch holders on the walls but no torches in them and the floor was black, with silver and emerald inlay, all highly polished. Some pillars were plain and black while others were also decorated with silver inlay—she tried to figure out the pattern. She spotted several guards here and there, but not a single person she'd recognize as a servant. They strode into a room so large it completed her feeling of overwhelm. The ceiling arched up into a graceful pattern she could barely see because of the beams of light from windows high above.

Cassius paused a single stride and people rushed into the cavernous chamber, all with something to say. She could tell he was already annoyed. At least a dozen or so impressive people passed her, leered their disdain at her. Cassius among them, continued is resolute pace, never broke stride as the rivers of courtiers flowed around him. They all disappeared down a corridor. Gellia, like a pebble under the waves, was only carried along a short distance before she was left behind. Alone. Her legs trembled, but she tried to keep her composure. It was so quiet.

"Mistress," a soft female voice spoke behind her.

Gellia turned and found a curtsying young woman.

"I am to take milady to miladyship's rooms," she said. She could only have been seventeen or so, possibly half Xzepheniixenze from what Gellia could tell. For a servant she was exceptionally well dressed, more so than the royalty of Fuarmaania—and better behaved.

Gellia followed her servant through the corridors and tried to pay attention to how everything looked so she could return without becoming lost. The walls of the corridors were black and smooth but there was still plenty of light. It wasn't dark and dismal as she thought it would be and yet there wasn't a single torch lit in the place. It could only be magic, Gellia thought. There wasn't a spec of dirt anywhere, everything was polished and clean, no clutter to be found.

On their way they passed several other people, courtiers perhaps, busily doing whatever it was that they did. Next to them Gellia felt rather plain, for every noble person she had seen was exquisitely dressed, their hair elaborately styled. None of them paid her much attention; they probably dismissed her as another servant, a slovenly one at that. When Gellia thought about it, she must have looked dreadfully filthy. She tried to subtly adjust her hair.

They traveled through endless passages and beautifully ornate rooms and Gellia examined artwork and architecture. Tintagel was perfection. She carefully reached out with her magical senses, not very far, to feel the castle. Its history was great, although she couldn't see its details. The magic was woven through the bastion, the most beautiful tapestry she could imagine. It was pure genius—a creation she couldn't dream of doing herself. "How beautiful," she said. Perhaps she would appreciate it even more as she learned the rest of her power. But if she were fully human, its true splendor would be lost. Perhaps at first she'd been overwhelmed by its color and grandeur; she realized now it was a calm and orderly place and oddly relaxing.

Finally they stopped at a great door that was opened by waiting servants. Gellia took the first few steps into her new room while her attendants hurried about. It was huge. On the walls hung colorful tapestries of unicorns and roses and scenes of parties. The opposite side of the room had two large arched doorways to a long balcony. The doors were open, circulating fresh air through the room. At one end sat a colossal bed with thickly carved posts reaching the high ceiling that supported the canopy. From that hung layers of sheer, sparkling curtains accenting the jewel tone bed covers, purple being the most common color. An array of fine furniture was placed around the room, all with velvet cushions and fluffy matching pillows. Tall candelabras were peppered about, silver like the ones in the halls, with crystals hanging from the arms. Several vases of flowers were placed here and there and on a lovely desk where there were also implements of correspondence. Finely woven rugs covered most of the floor. He said it wasn't a palace but it had more frills than Dournzariame. She even had her own musicians who were currently playing soft music from a corner.

Gellia saw another door and headed towards it. Servants moved silently about, came in and out of yet another room on the same wall as where she was headed. Between the two doors was a fireplace, a fireplace easily as tall as a person and several people wide. In the side room Gellia found nothing. It was as large as her room in Fuarmaania. "What's this one for?"

A girl answered: "For ladyship's attire, that's the other task we were ordered to do—fit milady with clothing."

"Oh."

"But a bath first, if milady pleases." The girl motioned to her and led her past the musicians and into the final room. In the center was a huge circular bath set into the floor. Water bubbled up from the bottom of the bath. The room had many candelabras, but the large windows on the end of the room cast enough light at this time of day. She wondered if candles were more for ambience than anything else, for she was certain the room would be magically lit like the rest of the castle.

As Gellia stood there dumbly, one of the attendants started to unbuckle her belt, another helped her with her armor but when started to unbutton her gambeson Gellia blushed and looked around at the women in the room.

The girl smiled sweetly as she worked at the laces. "No need to be—modest—milady."

Gellia shucked off her worn underclothes and hurried herself into the hot water. Her servants started to tend to everything from her hair to her skin to her toenails. Never had she been so pampered and thoroughly bathed.

"Could you inform me of the schedule here?" Gellia asked. She remembered that she shouldn't have worded her question as such. If they called her 'milady' then Gellia should treat them like servants, even if they were more refined than nobles she once knew.

"There is no set schedule, milady. Some stay awake at night; most are awake in the day. There's no real meal schedule unless there's a special occasion. Food is usually brought to the chambers. We perform on our lords' and ladies' whim so we don't have a schedule to speak of either—it's for milady to set. We were told milady is accustomed to a different situation and have been trained especially."

"What are your names?" Gellia asked.

"Of course, milady…" She started to tell her, and Gellia knew she would never remember them, not that she should have to, she realized. There were twelve in total, women and a few men.

"And you're all assigned to me?"

"Yes, milady."

When Gellia rose they wrapped her hair in a towel and dried her. There were lightly fragranced oils but no perfume. After slipping her into a chemise they ushered her into the main chamber where a lovely fire burned in the fireplace. They then measured her everywhere. One of them brought in a dress for her to wear. "Milady, this is a gift from one of the ladies, until garments made."

"That's fine," Gellia said. They slipped her into the layered garnet silk gown and gave her shoes to match, brushed and styled her hair and put on some simple jewelry.

"We're to tell milady that she is free to go where she wishes but to ask that if milady leaves the castle to stay close by. We also ask forgiveness for any transgressions we might accrue while learning milady's wishes." The group of servants filed out the door, musicians excluded.

Gellia assumed they would come running if she called, and was pleased there was no more talking. If she had to hear 'milady' one more time she'd scream. Yet it was the way it had to be, she supposed.

She wondered if one of them could guide her through the castle so she wouldn't spend a lifetime being lost. Well, it could only be as difficult as Dournzariame, which was by her reckoning, much larger. But that was a palace with gardens and numerous courtyards and a city surrounding it. Tintagel seemed remote, and although the surroundings were beautiful, they were wild and natural.

Gellia wandered to the huge balcony and looked into the world beyond. Below her was the crystal clear lake—so clear she could see to the bottom. Past the lake lived the rest of the glimmering forest, and farther there were mountains in deep hues of blue, purple and scarlet. Even farther, she could sense a glittering horizon, from what she could only imagine. The air smelled crisp and sweet. It suddenly dawned on her that *he* always smelled a like this forest. How magical. Gellia was strangely aware of everything; the air around her seemed to be living, the castle pulsed with consciousness. Even the water below seemed to be alive. Especially the lake. For a moment she wondered if it was looking up at her.

Gellia stood there until dusk, didn't care if she wasted time. And when the wind announced the coming of darkness, soft, airy music came from behind her. She turned, expecting her attendants to be playing their instruments but instead found that a wind chime hung near the door. It too was made from silver, all etched with scrolling and hanging from fine silver chains. One of the attendants spoke from the door. "We were told to put it there, milady, if milady doesn't like it we can take it away."

"No, that will be fine."

"When milady is ready to come in there's some food we brought and we'll dress milady for bed."

"Thank you." She might be hearing 'milady' in her sleep. Gellia turned to the landscape again to watch the twin moons rise over the mountains. The larger moon was at half, the smaller just a sliver. Of course the legendary black moon was nowhere to be found.

Below her the gold tinted trees turned to black, silver and blue. Tiny lights floated through the forest. Mesmerized and rather intoxicated with life, Gellia stared out into the familiar darkness and smiled.

3

Down the hall, past the room with all the twisted pillars and to the left? Or was it to the right? Or not as far as the pillar-room and down the hall with the windows? No, the hall with the windows went the opposite where she needed to go. This was it: through the pillar-room and to the left, then all the way down the corridor and left, then down the stairs forever through the servants' corridor (it was a shorter route) and down some more stairs to the kitchens.

The kitchens were wonderful places that were always bustling and filled with wonderful smells. Gellia helped herself to some bread and a succulent peach (a fruit which she just discovered) and journeyed back through the castle eating her breakfast on the way. It crossed her mind that someone such as herself who had a small army of servants probably shouldn't do things like visit the kitchens or serve herself, but it was an excuse to wander.

She hadn't seen much of anyone so far that day other than glimpses of servants as they hurried here and there, and the spectacular guards. She wondered about the slight variations in uniforms and weapons. Part of her wanted to stare at them as if they were statues or paintings, but she couldn't bring herself to be so bold.

One of the servants told her the audience was being held and most people went to watch. Of course, she thought that if it were anything like Gallylya's court they would be bored to tears. But from the way the servants spoke, it could be a spectacle. Unfortunately Gellia hadn't woken up early enough to catch it from the beginning and she wasn't about to show up in the middle—how rude.

When she woke that morning her attendants dressed her in black from head to foot. Black was the most accepted color for wardrobe here, and being that it nearly took an enchantment to dye things black, it was practically a competition to see who could make the blackest cloth. The dress was brocade satin with a short train. It was fancier than she ever wore previously and yet it seemed simple compared to what she saw in Tintagel so far. Even so, she felt more like a princess than she had in ages. They had left her hair long and bouncy, minus a few delicate silver hair chains that Gellia was quite taken with.

They conservatively applied kohl to break her into the habit, for cosmetics were worn by both men and women of Xzepheniixenze. And of course she wore the necklace Cassius gave her, she felt naked without it.

Gellia passed through a huge connecting room, still admiring the architecture on her way. This room had windows in the ceiling made from what seemed to be cut glass that cast tiny rainbows at her feet. Footfalls came from the corridor across from her. She looked up to see a Xzepheniixenze approach her. He was very tall. Gellia wanted to stand there and stare as if she had never seen a Xzepheniixenze before but instead she kept moving, forgot her admiration and tried to remember her etiquette. She passed him doing her best to appear unapproachable but shortly after he was behind her, his footsteps stopped and Gellia knew this person wanted to at least have another look at her. "*Don't let them intimidate you,*" Connylia said so many times. Gellia stopped and turned. He watched her as she stood there as proudly as she could muster. He was a mage, she could feel it.

"What are you called, little one?" he asked, his voice like silk.

Gellia gazed up at his face in the light. He looked weary, his eyes were almost silver rather than violet, and his waist length ebony hair was streaked with white and smoky grey. His face was without blemish, long and thin, but attractive just the same. Somehow he seemed younger than he really looked.

She realized she had no title, no surname she wished to share, and no name added to the end of hers to describe her accomplishments. "Gellia," she said. It was so plain and small.

"Ah, I thought that's who you might be. Welcome to Tintagel. I am Sian, one of the baron's mages. I'm sure we'll meet again." He bowed then turned and quietly departed.

That wasn't too painful, Gellia thought. If others were like Sian it wouldn't be difficult to get along with everyone. She continued on her way, pleased to have met someone who seemed of some importance. Xzepheniixenze didn't seem as bad as Connylia said they were.

The audience must have ended for Gellia heard voices echoing down the different corridors. Maybe now she could find out just what went on in the average day. While she walked down a long arched corridor a well-dressed group passed her. It seemed they were very involved in some subject of controversy but her presence distracted them. All of them were impeccably dressed in what surely must have been their best with jewels and elaborate braids in their hair. Gellia felt quite short next to them, for most of them were far taller than she—even the women. In Fuarmaania she had been a giant but certainly not here. And *everyone* was beautiful.

Gellia made her way through the throng careful not to cause a fuss if she could help it. She finally came to the mostly empty audience room. It looked very much like a throne room, honestly. It seemed that the center of magic lie in that room.

It was rectangular, a great door on one end and the throne on the other; opposite sides were corridors to many different places. Each corridor was shaped into an arch, with pillars separating them, pillars carved into agile-looking black dragons. Below her feet the floor was etched in a continuous battle scene, which she lost herself in. Mages, knights, horses and an array of familiar and unrecognizable exotic creatures scampered through the shiny black floor. It almost told a story, and Gellia followed it across the surface until she was well into the room. Cresslyn with her artsy ways would have loved to see it. Gellia could only imagine what the girl would say. A long letter to Sen Dunea would be in order, that was for certain.

Someone watched her.

Gellia quickly righted herself and looked at the few people left in the grand room. There were six of them, all stood together in a semicircle to watch her. Not knowing what to do and not able to judge what they thought, Gellia raised her nose a little. Five men, one woman, all looked stoically at her. One of them had very long, snowy white hair and was very pale. The others looked something like Sian with grey in their hair, if they hadn't gone completely grey. All of them wore similar black clothing. One spoke. "Come here, girl."

Gellia didn't like it at all.

"Maybe you should read her before you pass judgment," the white haired one said. At a glance he looked bored. His icy eyes regarded her with what Gellia took to be restrained curiosity.

The others stared down at her. Another man spoke, she wasn't sure whom. "Just what do you think you're doing here?"

"Perhaps looking for someone to take her in?" the woman purred.

"I don't know, she doesn't look to be all badly put together, in fact I don't think I've seen anything quite as exquisite, even for a half breed."

The woman approached and Gellia froze, felt the woman's prodding mind. "She has a bit of magic," she said, "or a bond horse," she added, tossed her long dark hair. "She looks too young to have her mind this well protected."

"Unless."

"Unless *he* taught her," Snowy said.

Gellia could smell the perfume from the woman's hair. "It must have taken ages to curl your hair like a 'Phron," she scoffed.

It was the first time Gellia heard *that* name for Zephron in a regular conversation. It was not a polite word. Gellia stood her ground. She had a feeling that if she ran it would end poorly for her. Perhaps if she just tried to be uninteresting…

"Perhaps. Perhaps someone with DuVray in their blood, like a Zapheny," Snowy added and smiled. He looked closer at Gellia. "*That* is a fabulous jewel you're wearing." Gellia felt he knew everything, perhaps even more about her than she did, but he wasn't going to tell the others. Or perhaps he was just guessing.

"As if there is a Zapheny left."

One of the other men spoke. "What in the world is Zapheny?"

Several looked irritated as much as Xzepheniixenze would show; a few looked slightly confused as the last man who spoke. "You must be terribly young," someone said. Gellia had a very difficult time deciding who spoke when. They all looked so similar and their voices carried oddly through the room. She tried to pick out characteristics and assign them as names. So far she only had Snowy and Lady. Maybe Zyendel was correct about Xzepheniixenze all looking the same. She wondered if she could see what their magic looked like but was too afraid to try.

"I'm bored, let's take her to the pit," a man said.

The others spoke amongst themselves for a moment. The white haired one just looked at her in a way that reminded her of Cassius. Gellia planned her escape. Whatever that "pit" was, she wanted no part of it. She took a step back. She *could* use her magic but she didn't know what these people could do—chances were they were far better than she. The magic here felt different than what she was used to as well, she wasn't sure if she knew how to handle it for an attack.

"I want no part in your festivities," Snowy said.

"Let's go," one of the men waved his hand and castle guards came towards Gellia, who gathered energies in defense.

Gellia could feel a flood of familiar magic fill the chamber. It was calming and exhilarating all at the same time.

"*That*—would be unadvisable." His voice was resonant and calm like the ringing of a temple bell.

Cassius! Gellia looked around almost frantically for him until he made his way through the group.

"You know what I recommended," murmured Snowy. He was the only one who didn't bow like a cowering dog. Gellia didn't bow at all.

Cassius looked more spectacular than she had ever seen him, and he had a vibrancy about him she didn't remember. The mages seemed almost to shrink from him as they waited for a command. It gave her great pleasure to see them cower as they did, although they tried not to lose their haughtiness.

The guards moved away as their lord spoke. "Nathair, you are quickly becoming my next amusement." Cassius said while he studied his glove. "I'm feeling generous today. You might have one more chance." He turned to gaze at Gellia. "As Mephibosheth has already guessed, this is Princess Gellia." He said it like she was of great importance, like she was someone to be admired. It was the first time she'd ever heard Cassius say her name and it felt strange to her, like he gave it a quality no one else could. "Since no one remembers manners I'll do the introductions. This is Mephibosheth," Cassius motioned to Snowy. "He is my least incompetent court mage. Your assailants are Nathair, Pethuel, Agravain, Meliot and Irina. The others have gone off on business already while these decided not to do what they were told and stand about to flatter each other, for it is a favorite pastime of my mages to lie to one another."

Gellia started to open her mouth to speak. *Straighten up.* Cassius hissed into her mind. *Have you forgotten everything you've been taught?*

"I met Sian in the corridor," she announced. Gellia tried to look more regal. The cool stares of the mages didn't seem quite as frightening.

"And he recognized you?" Cassius said, rubbed his chin and looked at the mages. "How ingenious of him."

"We apologize," Mephibosheth said as he glanced at the others. Gellia thought it strange that this one was apologizing when it was the others who treated her unkindly. He didn't act as if he were the type to do a good deed. The other mages owed Mephibosheth for taking the hit for them. Cassius wasn't appeased, Gellia could tell, but the others seemed to relax. Gellia wondered if she was the only one who noticed.

"I have better things to do than stand here and watch you stare at each other." He marched back through them; his cloak trailed behind him shimmering in the sunlight. It was then Gellia realized just how long Cassius' hair was, nearly floor length. Wasn't there something about telling one's age by their hair? Her stomach turned. He wasn't thirty five as she'd guessed before. No wonder why he'd laughed. No, he was many centuries old. She steadied her breathing and tried to collect her thoughts.

The other mages followed obediently, Mephibosheth gave her a final glance before bringing up the rear. Gellia watched them all go, wondered just what the white-haired mage thought, and why he looked the way he did.

Once they were out of sight Gellia's knees unlocked and shook. She must have looked like such an imbecile. Gellia was sure she still did as she stood there in the middle of the room all by herself. Pull yourself together, she told herself. Being all wobbly in the knees every time one of them approached her just wouldn't do. She certainly couldn't hide in her room for the rest of her life.

Once more Gellia wandered through the corridors, taking note of anything that would mark her way. Again, most who passed her tried not to pay her any attention. She was not someone who had a certain demeanor like Cassius, not yet. Sometimes she wondered if he was able to walk into a room and have people cower before him since childhood.

Gellia meandered until she saw a door that looked like it led outside. She could use some air, and the tiny stream of warm light under the door beckoned her. As she opened the door she was greeted with a sweet fragrance and the light was almost blinding. It was a large courtyard, filled with thorny bushes of the most perfect roses Gellia ever imagined. She stepped out onto a walkway under another level that enclosed the yard. Spiral columns with archways bordered the walkway and the garden; climbing rose vines crept up most of them, the blooms almost glowing in the warm sunlight. Perhaps it was a fortress, but it obviously didn't lack the finer things, Gellia thought. She wondered what a Xzepheniixenze palace would look like. Oddly, she felt she might already know.

She walked down a little stone path, the stones themselves were round and had carved designs on them. At every bush she touched the flowers, and occasionally smelled a few. Red, pinks, white, yellows, peach, coral, and every color in between each had its own bush in the garden. Each plant was well cared for, not a single wilted bloom or leaf could be found anywhere. Gellia wished she could take a few back to her room. Bees and butterflies fluttered leisurely around the garden, and a tiny old woman hobbled in from a side door. "Oh," the crone said and stopped to stare for a moment.

Gellia straightened her dress nervously. "I didn't mean to—" she began.

"Oh, don't be excusing yourself to the likes of *me* milady," the old woman said, "I've just come to do my work, I'll stay out of your way."

"I was just leaving,"

"Stay if you want, no one really comes here much. I'm surprised that you actually took the time to visit, but I must say you look natural amongst the roses if you don't mind me saying it."

"Oh. I don't really have that much to do so I thought I would take a look," Gellia said.

The crone smiled. "I'm sure you have plenty to do, you just don't know it yet." She had white hair pulled into a braid that dragged on the ground and wore a blue frock with an apron. Her face looked wise and kind as she shuffled through the garden adjusting branches. Gellia wasn't sure how to act and didn't want to make a fool of herself or seem 'weak' as Cassius put it. Servants were known for gossiping after all, but the old woman intrigued her.

"I hope you didn't pick any," the woman said.

"No."

"These aren't supposed to leave this courtyard. His lordship is quite irritated when the roses leave the garden. Not much to ask, really. He's a generous employer."

She smiled. "I understand."

Gellia strolled over the paths a bit longer, breathed in the sweet scent of the roses and thought of how much it comforted her. This could be her new favorite place to spend time. But she knew she had other places to explore yet and took her leave. As Gellia closed the door the crone murmured to herself that there wasn't a single bud to be found, all bloomed for the visiting magic.

It was quiet in the corridor when she returned inside. What did everyone do all day? She wandered through the tunnel-like passages until she ended up in a large room with too many options for direction. Now which way? Which way seemed to be the most exciting?

"There you are."

Gellia turned and found that two men approached her from who knew where. Immediately she felt apprehensive, for she recognized them as people who could only be more court mages for they had a way about them that was similar to the others. Just how many of these people were there? They walked towards her as she tried to decide if she should run or stay and try to have a conversation. They were strangers to her, Gellia realized; different from the ones she already met.

"You are our new project?" one asked. He didn't take his eyes off her.

What was she supposed to say? Gellia didn't really know what part she was playing at Tintagel. Project? How did they know who she was?

"She's already been harassed by the rest of you, why don't you go grovel at your master's feet?" A feminine voice called from behind Gellia.

Now what? The castle was so large, how did this woman already know what happened earlier? The two mages scowled, a truly disturbing sight.

"Why don't you do me a favor and I *might* decide to return it," the woman said.

The two mages strode away, Gellia never took her eyes off them until they were out of view. She didn't trust any of them, or anyone else really. Only after Gellia was sure they were gone did she look for her defender, who stepped from the shadows.

"How does it feel to be in the favor of the most powerful man in Xzepheniixenze?" she asked as she approached. The woman was taller than Gellia, of course, and had all the attributes of a courtesan.

"I don't understand."

"Is that all you can say?" She walked a circle around Gellia, not the tiniest bit ashamed of how she was looking at her. "I suppose you're too new to know who I am, so introductions then. I'm Vellura." She said the name as if the name itself was a title.

"I'm Gellia."

Vellura looked bored. "Really? I never would have guessed." She had a look about her that men must have loved,

Gellia thought. That and the fact that Vellura wore only a few layers of silk, a dress that revealed her legs as she moved. Her red lips smiled at Gellia. "You are a quiet little mouse, Gellia," she said.

But Gellia barely heard what she said. She was working other things out. "The emperor likes me?" Gellia asked.

"Oh, what I said? The emperor is *not* the most powerful man in Xzepheniixenze... you're very sweet and naive like a little peasant girl from the country. Don't mind the mages. They never last long; in another few years or maybe less there'll be new ones. They live very precariously... Save Mephibosheth, he's a laster." She winked but the joke was lost on Gellia.

"Why are you being nice to me?"

Vellura smiled again. "Honestly I'm wondering what he sees in you. I see now that you are *quite* the sight to behold even if you are a child." Vellura's gaze rested on Gellia's pendant and remained there for some time.

"Who?"

"Baron Vazepheny of course, silly child."

Gellia didn't know why she was calling her a child; Vellura herself didn't look much older than Gellia. "You know him well?" Gellia asked.

Vellura showed Gellia a certain smirk. "I'm not sure if you'll make it here, Gellia."

"Why do you say that?"

Vellura shook her head. "So many reasons, Gellia. And it's a waste of his time to continually rescue you. There must be something very special about you."

Gellia spoke but with more force than even she herself expected. "I'm me."

Vellura looked a little shocked and perhaps confused. "Well, I've been told I have to show you a few places and I certainly have better things to do with my time than look after you. Let's be going, shall we?"

As she followed the striking Vellura, Gellia didn't let her naiveté be in the way of realizing this woman was undoubtedly Cassius' mistress. She hated herself for being jealous. She noticed after a moment that Vellura was also a mage. It probably added to her professional life.

"Life is never boring in Tintagel," Vellura said. She ran her hand across the shoulders of a hapless guard they passed, but he didn't stir. Some of the men servants hazarded another glance. "… and I never tire from trying to cause trouble with guards. I must say these are the most resistant." She looked over her shoulder to see if the guard reacted at all.

How could any man resist her? Perhaps some of the ladies in Fuarmaania fancied themselves seductresses but everything Vellura did was sensual. The way she moved, spoke, her glances—she was constantly working.

"How old is he?" Gellia asked. She watched Vellura as the courtesan looked down corridors as they walked; Gellia supposed it was to scout for business or people to toy with.

"What does it matter? Who really knows? Mephibosheth's been around for some four centuries and I know he's older than that. Thinking of chasing after him yourself? Good luck. You won't find an icier person, especially to an indecisive, inexperienced, little mouse-girl like you." She sighed. "He's tremendously difficult to please, but there is no greater trophy." She looked at Gellia through her eyelashes.

Gellia started to feel homesick for other lands. Zephronia or Sen Dunea—and she also missed Skip.

Vellura continued to saunter down the corridor. "I have to show you the two most important places in the castle, at least in his opinion." Little did Vellura know that Gellia was already distracted with her own thoughts. They walked into a very large room with very high ceilings and Vellura continued her tour speech but Gellia didn't pay much attention. "...You can find out almost everything..."

Gellia tried to clear out the confusion as she blindly followed the woman. There were tall people all around her. In Zephronia she felt caged but now that she was free she realized that not only was it a cage but it also a shelter… And why did she dislike this woman so much? Was it her beauty? Her haughtiness?

"...That's the section with history and...."

What happened to her? Gellia stayed in the empire for a week and fell apart. She felt a pain in her leg and tripped, landed face first onto a table. After she scolded herself for being so foolish, Gellia picked herself up and hoped Vellura wouldn't laugh at her. She certainly didn't dare look around at people who were likely staring. It was certainly a loud enough noise to attract attention.

The table was in an odd spot in the middle of the room and cluttered with literature. It looked as if an entire shelf's worth of books had exploded. Gellia traced her finger over a leather cover before she picked it up and opened it. It was too familiar. She didn't notice the staring librarian across from her.

Vellura spoke, "Those old things arrived recently. Look in what poor condition they are. He has a penchant for literature, that's for certain." When Vellura went to pick one up, the librarian stepped closer and grabbed her wrist, glared at her. Vellura withdrew her arm and was released, didn't challenge the librarian.

"These were *mine*," Gellia whispered, not even noticing the exchange between her escort and the librarian. "I've read most of these." How did they get here? What was this all about? She glanced at the librarian then back at the books to do a rough count.

"What do you mean?" Vellura grumbled.

"I've read it before." She didn't see all of them though, these weren't the ones she considered more valuable, but she didn't want to discuss it with Vellura. "Don't we need to be going?" Gellia asked. She didn't want to leave them there, but at the moment she had no choice. As far as she was concerned they were still hers and she'd protect them from people like Vellura if she could help it. As she looked back at the librarian she saw him fend off someone else with a mere look. Perhaps they would be safe for the time being. Gellia would still worry, though.

The courtesan smiled as only a courtesan could. "Come Gellia, I have to show you where to practice magic before it's your bedtime."

Vellura explained the rules of what was often called the laboratory. It was a cavernous, mostly empty, domed room that was magically sealed off to protect those outside its walls. Gellia wondered if she could find her way back here on her own. It might be very useful for her if she could spend some time practicing.

"If the doors are sealed it's unwise to enter," Vellura said. "Although I'm sure he enters whenever he feels the desire." She watched Gellia for a moment. "I have an appointment."

Gellia nodded but didn't answer. Vellura sauntered from the room without another word. It was eerie to be there alone. She didn't remember the last time she was somewhere this quiet. She walked through the room and looked at the graceful lines of the walls, the archways that all crossed at the top of the room like a skeleton. She was at the far wall when she heard voices and turned to see if someone wanted to use the room. No one stood at the door. There was a tiny light on the other side, though. Gellia walked towards it, tried to read it with her magic but found nothing. As she neared she saw it was a tiny white sphere of light, no bigger than a grape, which floated chest-high in the air. She heard the whispering again and turned. No one was at the door. Suddenly she felt sad but it was not her own sadness. She wondered what was wrong. The light slowly wove back and forth but did not fly away. "What are you?" She asked and reached out to touch it. It wasn't solid, but it was warm. "What is it?" She felt something in her magic flutter; someone was near. She turned quickly to see who it was but only caught a glimpse of something from the corner of her eye, by the time she looked it was already gone. It had been silver and light, large, and despite her good sense was sure it was either a person or a unicorn but her mind couldn't decide which.

4

"...And then he said..."

"I did not. You're a liar."

Cassius tapped his fingers on the arm of his chair and watched the two men shoot nervous glances at him. His mages wandered through the crowd as the two lords bickered in the center of the room. The moment Cassius opened his mouth to speak the room fell silent. "Do you think me daft?" he asked. "Did you think for a moment that I would believe this ruse? And you had the audacity to bring such an insignificant dispute to my court? Meanwhile your peasants are being attacked by marauders."

"My lord…" one of them said.

"At least your deaths will be of no consequence, but you *have* wasted my time."

"But my lord…"

Cassius glanced at few large knights who escorted the two treacherous lords down one of the corridors as the baron nodded for the next visitor to come in.

"This is it?" Gellia asked. She and Vellura had picked out a vantage point early that morning. Gellia watched Cassius from the edge of the crowd. Oh yes, he dressed conservatively when he visited Fuarmaania. Every lock of hair on his head was braided with silver threads—it must have taken days to finish the work—or with magic. His face was stern as he listened to whoever had the floor. Gellia tried to imagine what he thought.

And as she suspected, his audience chamber was very intimate. His very throne-like chair was raised so he could be eye level with those who came to see him, and they were never far enough away that they couldn't look him in the face and know exactly when they were judged. It was the first time she'd seen such an audience. Her step father had little use for such gatherings, but he was intoxicated most of the time anyway.

"Mostly. Mostly reports and announcements and such things. I know it doesn't look all that impressive, but little do most know that he reads all their minds and finds out the details of the province," Vellura said. "His mages don't really do much but keep everyone nervous. The baron is completely self-sufficient. He doesn't miss a movement of anyone in the room. If he feels like it he can read the minds in the castle, but I don't think he feels the need to do that unless something catches his attention." She raised her head and gazed at him. "Rumor has it he pulls the strings of every noble this side of the empire." She smiled. "But unlike many he doesn't tell his courtesan everything."

"No one reads *his* mind?"

"No one would dare. Not that they could."

"Oh," Gellia resisted fidgeting with the hem of her tunic. Connylia always scolded her for doing so. Conny. If only she were as elegant as her friend. On the bright side, at least Gellia recognized that she fidgeted and could correct it.

"If you're bored we can leave, little mouse girl."

Gellia started to sneak her magic up to their liege until Vellura demanded a response.

"What do you say, little one? I see him enough; I don't need to watch him verbally eviscerate fools."

Gellia did her best to hide her disdain for Vellura. "If you want to go I'll be fine." Perhaps this was a good time to exercise telepathy, Gellia thought. Perhaps not on Cassius—not today. It was obvious the room whirled with magical energies. Everyone tried to spy on everyone else. Non-magical people rarely had any defense against it.

Gellia reached out and let her magic's tendrils sift through the hundreds of thoughts to find anything of interest. A few of Cassius' mages watched her. One of the guards thought of a pretty girl. There were seekers everywhere, thoughts moving like lightning, but she could not see them and certainly didn't find the ones who were talented enough to hide their thoughts.

"I'm leaving," Vellura whispered to Gellia.

"Bye."

Sian watched her intensely with his magic although he looked at his liege. Gellia wondered what it was about her that interested them all. She was sure that compared to them her life was not that much of a mystery. Cassius brought her here to be a student: there was no riddle about that. But these mages who seemed to be so powerful came to Tintagel for what reason exactly? What was their purpose for being there?

We all are here for the same reason, Sian mind spoke to her.

Gellia jumped. Had he heard her? And if he did could others? She started weaving shields around herself.

No, only I can hear you, and only the surface, Sian assured. *It is a rare occurrence when two are harmonized to the point that we were for just a moment. I wasn't about to let that opportunity escape.*

She wasn't convinced.

So, you do *have magic. I think Mephibosheth already knew. I don't probe as a hobby like he does and everyone else who knows anything about you has been very secretive.*

Why are you talking to me? she asked. And what 'everyone'?

Why would any of us talk to you?

She felt him smile at her as she made her answer. *Because you want something.* Gellia watched him from across the room. He still didn't look at her. She could hear his voice but his mouth wasn't moving. Could she trust that it was really was him?

Of course.

Gellia tried not to look stiff. *What is it?*

You needn't worry, child, I'm not going to harm you. I am more tactful than some of the others. I don't have a reason to harm you, do I?

It if suited your mood I'm sure that would be reason enough. Gellia wove the walls thicker around her and pushed him out. His mind voice was so different from that of her liege; it was thin and plain, not quiet or squeaky, but light like mist. Connylia's voice was certainly strong, and Cassius' was a vivid and rich. At least with her shields no one would come in, and her thoughts wouldn't leave unless someone picked a fight.

Sian looked at her and smiled. She could tell his action attracted the interest of the other mages. Her mind started to race as her Xzepheniixenze instincts came to the front. Sian *wanted* to attract the other mages. Since she pushed him away he brought her the unwanted attention. He knew it would make her uncomfortable. He didn't even have to mind speak to them, the smile was enough. In fact it was probably a better idea not to speak to them for they would be more suspicious. Gellia forced herself to breathe. Her heart raced but some part of her liked the stimulus. She realized she too could play these games with some practice.

Cassius' voice swirled around her mind and she let him in. *What sort of nonsense is it that attracts the complete attention of my mages?*

She caught a glimpse of his smirk before it disappeared. She didn't need to answer. It was the first time she truly appreciated his communication.

The problem on the floor was resolved and the next was called to come into the room. Gellia felt a strange feeling in her stomach. Was it magic? A few people around her perked up and she glanced to the nearest court mage who seemed tense. She didn't have time to look at Cassius. A great bellow echoed through the hall and there was a scuffle in the doorway. A blur of a man sped into the room holding his hands in front of him, the energy crackling around him. Before she could blink the man cast a globe of raw energy at the throne. People scattered, some screamed, Gellia had no place to go, trapped in the crowd. But the ball of energy was enveloped in a sphere-like barrier, which shrank and quickly disappeared.

The man stood dumbly in the center of the room. Cassius hadn't moved an eyelash. His face hadn't changed from its forbidding look and not a hair on his head had been disturbed. Everyone collected themselves and waited. The doors closed and the would-be assassin sweated.

It seemed strange to Gellia that someone other than a seeker would try to assassinate another. Wasn't that often a seeker job? Cassius' brow wrinkled in the slightest way. "You aren't going to tell me who you are, are you?" he purred. "No proclamation? No announcement of my affronts?"

Gellia felt her knees weaken as the air shifted. The intruder did nothing but stare up at the baron, panting. It seemed the man was caught in some sort of catatonic state; he could not tear his gaze from that of their baron.

What's going on? She asked Sian, hoped he would answer her.

She speaks when she has use of me…He's reading his thoughts. This should be amusing.

Why?

Besides the exquisite way he peals open someone's mind? He's angry with Nathair and he has something to destroy.

She still didn't quite understand, but she wasn't going to admit it. With a glance around the room Gellia saw that the other mages seemed somber. As she looked at them she found Nathair by the fact that his hair was turning white as she watched. His eyes were closed, he looked braced against something.

A globe appeared around the would-be assassin, bolts of energy came from all around to fill the globe with smoke and green light. Gellia was fascinated, entranced. Nathair cried out, but when she looked for him he was gone, only the space he'd occupied was there. The globe released, and a small pile of ash fell to the ground.

Cassius' expression had not changed. He motioned for the next person to be brought in. Gellia watched the courtiers, who seemed to have moved on without another thought of what had transpired.

The doors opened and four terrified people walked through. The porter announced them; there were no titles before their names. Gellia noticed the scoffs of the courtiers but she was intrigued. There were three men and one woman, each dressed in well-used clothes and covered in dust, none of them purebloods. They bowed—not properly—but their attempt was valiant. "Sire, we have come from far away to ask your help," the man said, his voice shook and no more words would come for him. He watched the servants finish cleaning the floor.

If it were Fuarmaania, the king would have them beheaded for bothering him, and perhaps the emperor would too, but they were facing a baron using the etiquette for royalty. The woman spoke. "Sire, please forgive us but we were told to come here. The duke rides upon us for sport, kills us by the dozens, takes our animals, taxes us so we cannot live then turns us into slaves when we cannot pay…"

Gellia heard the murmurs around her, the snickers. Cassius' voice filled the throne room; the sound of it seemed to vibrate the peasants. "What brought you to the conclusion I would help you against a noble of higher station than myself?"

Gellia thought fiercely to herself: I will help them if you will not. They have great and admirable courage to come here.

The peasants looked at each other. A different man spoke, very softly. "The legend of your lordship's generosity is well known. Your lordship is the only remaining hope we have."

Cassius smiled a little. "Your duke is young and reckless, not having the grace of his predecessor nor the understanding of how the world works."

Their eyes started to show more life. "Sire knows?" the woman asked.

"Yes. Yours is the town by a lake, in the outer ring of the Plains. I believe the locals call it Lake Kolyrai."

Their surprise was apparent, and their awe. Gellia smiled.

"Yes, I will help you. I'll even give you fresh horses for your return home. In fact, I'll take care of this misunderstanding myself." Cassius rose to leave. The peasants hugged each other, weeping.

In a blink Cassius disappeared amongst his courtiers. She wished she could speak with him, but that looked impossible. It seemed that whatever her relationship was with him, it was never going to be the same. It was difficult for to admit, but she missed him and the times they had together.

Vellura said Gellia was in his favor. Did that seductress really think this was favor? Not that Gellia wanted to have the relationship that Vellura had with him. Gellia thought he was going to teach her and now he ignored her. But maybe he was…

***

Gellia walked the corridor alone, her suede slippers noiseless on the floor. It took her a few weeks, but she learned her way around and was able to spend her time studying and not worrying about being lost. This library was a dream come true; she was happy to spend much of her waking moments there. It was quiet and she rarely saw other visitors. The main chamber was tall and wide, the shelves were laid out in an easily navigable pattern, but once beyond that main room there were rooms set all around it. Some had a few stairs, some could only be accessible from the second tier in the main room. Some of the rooms were round, some were long. Gellia was determined to learn all about her new friend, the library, so started to spend much time there, out of the way. And here in Tintagel no one thought it odd, and no one bothered her.

She made her acquaintance with the librarian, Soren, and although he wasn't the friendliest person, they seemed to have an understanding. Gellia guessed that Soren had been informed of her, for she had free access to all the rooms and books in the library. Indeed, all the books from the Fuarmaanian library were protected by guards. She would have loved to take books to the rose garden, but the restricted books had to stay in the library. There was, however, a cozy reading nook that she improved with a comfortable chair and a small table. The nearby window gave enough light for reading. Soren had given her a quizzical look when she had the servants move the furniture in, but said nothing.

Gellia dove into books written by her great ancestor. Now that they were in Xzepheniixenze they changed in some way, and more information came to light. She read one of Quenelzythe's several journals, nearly in tears of delight. In it Quenelzythe spoke of her duty, of the magic of Xzepheniixenze, and the importance of being a good leader. Much of it was riddled with elaborate sentences and archaic words she barely understood.

She spent many hours reading in her beautiful chair, often near the sunny window. When her eyes were tired she could look at the beautiful stone and woodwork through the room. Her heart sighed at its glory. Depending on which room, the ceilings were also elaborate. This place was built by someone who treasured books, and it gave her a new appreciation for her host. Like the rest of the castle, his signature was everywhere. Perhaps craftsmen did most of the hands-on work, but his magic helped it happen.

It was another sunny day and Gellia kept busy. In the morning she had her daily ride—not a wild gallop across the country, but in the riding arena for more structured practice. She found there was in fact a riding instructor there who was more than happy to help her refine her position and push her limits as a rider. Every morning brought her there. Even though one had a bond-horse, one still needed to know how to ride.

After the lively ride and a freshening up and change of clothes, Gellia went to the library once more to study. She walked along the shelves in the section of information on magic. Soren had given her a tour of the library early on, and seemed willing enough to help her find the right book if she was looking for something specific. She found the book she was looking for and pulled it from the shelf. It was a smallish book compared to many, and easy to glance over while she was standing there. Its leather cover was supple and free from cracks, its binding solid, its pages fresh. This was Cassius' library, all books were pristine, even the very old ones.

She heard some voices nearby but didn't bother to look. After being in Tintagel for a while Gellia learned to sense bad things that were about to happen, although sometimes she didn't exactly trust the instinct. This time she really didn't care; she just built a barrier around herself. The words before her were too interesting for her to be bothered.

It was about magic pendants—yes—she had one. Cassius gave it to her. Even though they had to be perfect, not all were created alike. The number a mage carried could change but quality was still a big factor. They were usually worn like jewelry but also often set into weapons for most mages also knew hand to hand combat.

Her heirloom sword, Xianze, had jewels in it, Gellia thought. Cassius always wore jewels. His mages too. She started to wander through the library with her nose in the book.

Without one a mage was more likely to burn himself out. That was what happened with Nathair, but *he* didn't do it. Somehow Cassius had learned to use other *mages* to spare himself. How did he ever figure out how to siphon energy through others? As far as she knew one could only draw through stones and through oneself. This book said nothing of siphoning through others, only that it could happen with some bond horses if the need arose. She would have to look for a book about siphoning through others next. Once more she headed to the solace of the restricted library.

...So Cassius had killed one of his mages. Yes, the memory haunted her. If that was common enough, why did anyone want to become a court mage? Obviously Mephibosheth was well used—that's why he had the white hair. But what was the advantage of withstanding the abuse? ...What was that? She felt a flick of magic and her barriers were shattered.

"Power," Cassius said.

Gellia turned and looked at him, her heart still pounded from the assault. His execution was so flawless...

Cassius stood not far away, looked for something to read himself. "You were wondering why mages come to me."

"Why are you speaking to me?" she hissed after composing herself.

"Ah! You are still a shrew I see."

"You're amusing as always," Gellia scoffed.

"How odd it is that you are spineless to everyone else but I, and I'm the one everyone fears the most." Cassius pulled a book from the shelf and opened it. "Imagine that," he muttered.

It was one of her books, the one with the drawing tucked in it. She'd nearly forgotten about it. "Oh, that. My sword is in that picture," Gellia said. She wanted to look over his arm, but certainly didn't want to be that close to him.

"You're correct. That is Connylia's son, Quenelzythe's sword."

Giving in, Gellia approached him and looked over his arm, but was careful not to touch him.

"Two swords were commissioned when there was enough money earned to do so. Xianze, and Elezare. Quenelzythe's was Xianze, which is why it is now yours."

"And Elezare?"

He smirked and raised an eyebrow. "You've seen Elezare, but you didn't know it had a name at the time."

Gellia looked at Cassius and felt almost as if she saw him for the first time. "So how old *are* you?" He and Quenelzythe were childhood companions? That's how Cassius knew where the secret room was; he knew it when Quenelzythe first built the castle. He knew her family for centuries. The Welcoming Festival. It was to welcome *him*. Why hadn't she realized it before?

He concentrated for a moment.

"Don't tell me you've forgotten your age." She couldn't decide if he really couldn't remember or if he mocked her.

"Exact numbers aren't important to most people." He placed the book back on the shelf. "Come with me." He walked away and she hurried after him.

"After who knows how long, you've finally recognized the fact that I'm here." She was surprised she could keep sassing him. The more she learned about him the more she wished she knew less.

"I rescued you from the mages."

"Not quite. I would have defended myself but I wasn't sure how'd you react to me killing them." It was partly true...

"Funny, you would have won. None of them really have that much experience with their own magic—even less than you," he said. "Ignorance is much easier to control, and they are willingly ignorant of their magic. That way they don't instinctively fight me." They passed Vellura who was coming from another corridor, she followed. Cassius and Gellia ignored her. "You could kill them for all I care. As long as you don't bother with Mephibosheth. I rather like him."

"Good. I don't mind him either, and I don't mind Sian really. They were all quite disconcerting at first, but I think I'm used to them now." She might have said it to convince herself rather than convince him.

"They said you avoid them."

"I've been doing some research on my family. There are some parts that I'm not sure about though," She hoped he would follow her change of subject. They lost Vellura in a group of courtiers.

Cassius smiled. "If you don't fear *me* you certainly don't need to fear *them.* Yes, Connylia was Razhiede's mistress and Gallylya *did* kill Razhiede despite his sister's regard."

Gellia was almost shocked at his frankness. "Is that why she's so—disturbed?"

"I suppose. I've never understood Zephronian sensibilities. I suppose the fact that Gallylya banished their son from Dournzariame didn't help, not that it stopped us."

"Us?" She took a few quick steps to catch up again. She cursed her shoes for her inability to keep up with his pace.

"Yes, Quenelzythe and I were associates. How else did you think I knew my way around Dournzariame?"

"You'll have to tell me about all your exploits some time," she said, and perhaps she could learn some insight to her great ancestor. Vellura had caught up again, possibly through her own magic, apparently desperate for who knows what.

"There are too many to tell. Here we are. Goodbye Vellura," Cassius opened a door and directed Gellia through before he closed it in Vellura's face. Gellia felt oddly pleased with Vellura's abrupt dismissal.

Her pleasure was short lived. Much to Gellia's dismay, the room was filled with all of the court mages. "Good to see you're all here," Cassius greeted.

The cold faces stared at Gellia and she felt a winter storm had begun in the office. They didn't like her—that was for certain. If they thought she was so much lower than them then why did they hate her so?

Cassius walked to the end of the room and sat at his desk. So this was the famous office, Gellia thought. She didn't want to look around for fear she would make eye contact with one of the mages. They stood on either side of her, formed a corridor of gloom that led to their liege. They still stared at her. Gellia tried to look confident. "Well," Cassius said. "I've called you all in here to tell you I'll be leaving for Ravengate. Surprise, surprise..."

"To explain the destruction of Ulamra?" one of them asked, Gellia wasn't sure which one.

He smiled. "Amongst other things," Cassius said. He played with a trinket on his desk, not paying the other people in the room much attention. "...I'm leaving Princess Gellia in command."

Gellia's stomach threatened to depart, and she felt much, much smaller as the mages started to frenzy. She wished desperately to melt into a puddle and slip away through the almost nonexistent seams in the floor.

"What? She's not fit to run this place!" Una blurted. The other mages stared at their master, some spoke at once and not very clearly.

"Una is correct, she isn't worthy of licking our boots." Someone said from the back.

Cassius spoke, his voice took a stronger resonance. "How dare you question me. My decision is final."

Gellia tried to keep her dignity, did not flinch at all the words. The one called Una still looked angry and Gellia could feel Cassius' magic rise.

"I apologize, your lordship," Una said softly.

"I leave her with full power over Tintagel including dispatching any of you who displease her." He dismissed them with an abrupt flick of his hand.

The twelve mages filed from the room giving Gellia dirty looks as they passed. She just stood and watched Cassius ignore them as he sat behind the great mahogany desk. The door closed behind her. "I can't believe you've done this to me," she said.

He sorted through some papers. "You won't have to do much. The castle runs by itself. All you have to do is hold an audience now and again. You like working with peasants, don't you?"

"Hold audiences by myself? I've barely even been there to watch. What am I supposed to do? Let *Vellura* help me?" She slammed her hands on the desk.

He ignored her rage. "She'd enjoy that. No, Vellura isn't a leader. This is your test, princess. Fly or fall to your death. You haven't a millennium to figure it out. You are mortal. You have a limited time in this world to accomplish things—to grow into who you're supposed to be. If you're coming with me you have to learn how to adjust quickly, how to take command."

"I'm going to rule with you?"

"What, you want to rule on your own?"

"We're going to take over Xzepheniixenze?"

He smiled a little. "Where have you been?"

"And Zephronia?"

"Only if *you* want to. I have no use for it. Gallylya will need dealing with no matter what happens."

"It still doesn't make me feel any better about you leaving me here." Gellia was silent for a moment, watched him open letters. That was something else that would need tending to when he left. She mused to herself. "Still, this is much better than even my prince could have offered, I suppose."

He was slightly distracted by a letter, but still spoke. "Yes, well, like all your betrothed, he had the shortcomings of humans from the Outlands. Percy in particular was a weakling, his whole family was made of weaklings."

"You knew him? Or are you just assuming..."

"Knew him? Only briefly, thankfully. Don't tell me you haven't figured that out." He refolded the letter and started to look through other correspondence.

"What are you saying?" She felt uneasy, more so than when the mages assaulted her. She sat down in a nearby chair.

"I only knew him for as long as it took to send him to the afterlife," he muttered. "Your other betrotheds were only slightly more competent."

Gellia felt faint "You killed them?"

"It was quick," he assured. "And he must have been honored considering it was I who dealt with him and not a seeker." He read through a paper and muttered. "It took me days to recover from dealing with such filth."

"How could you do that? Percy was the only one I liked." How long had he been skulking around Fuarmaania? She knew he did the deed himself, for sending someone else would leave a trail of evidence. Why didn't he take her a child? He must have been waiting for her to mature, and wanted her to have access to the library. That had to be it.

"Do you really think I was about to lose you to an imbecile like him?" Cassius said.

Gellia gathered her rage. "Yes, then you would have to use your magic to fetch me and everyone would know what you're up to because I would have put up a fight. But to keep your plans like you wanted you killed innocent men... You should have just kidnapped me and left him alone."

Cassius launched to his feet. "No one is innocent, princess," he growled. "And I'm offended you think my plans were that simple. I see your Zephron heritage is rearing its ugly head. All upset about losing a mediocre means to a slightly less miserable end in some backwater heap of compost where they copulate with their cousins…"

"…And then you think nothing of killing someone who has spent their life serving you. Power or not I don't know why…"

"They come here *willingly*, princess. The mages have everything they could never have otherwise. Wealth, stature, consorts, power, protection, everything. And yes, they might die for one reason or another but they know that when they come here. They don't serve me because they want to be nice or from loyalty. They want to be here so they can use whatever resources I may have. Some of them last longer here than they ever would out in the world."

"Protection until it suits your whim to let them perish." Gellia, even though angry, was still cautious of this newly discovered side of Cassius. But if he chose to fight—she wouldn't die with a whimper—she would cause as much havoc as possible. The magical energies swirled around them. She felt a mystical tug and braced herself. Cassius appeared directly in front of her.

"You can't tell me you came here simply because you want a companion. You came here for myriad gains," he snarled. "How dare you sit there and act like a Zephron. Taken on some of Gallylya's inflated righteousness, have we? Perhaps I left you there a bit too long. Perhaps I should send you back to him. I'm sure Zyendel would enjoy your company."

Outside, the mages waited and listened. They could only understand every few words, the rest was muffled by the thick door. "Do you think he'll kill her?" Abaddon asked another mage as he stood near the door. "I don't think I've seen him this angry."

"We should be so lucky," Gareth said.

"Angry isn't the word for it," Mephibosheth told them.

"What do you suppose this is all about?" Meliot asked.

"I don't know." Mephibosheth shrugged, strained to listen. "You may think he tells me more being the eldest of you lot, but I know just as little. Unless I've missed my guess he's trained her himself, that's why we can't sense much from her."

Gareth smiled. "It doesn't matter to me what he's doing but I will say that if he tires of her I'll take her. I've never seen the like."

Mephibosheth shook his head. "You're a fool, you know that? One thing is for certain, I've never seen him so patient before, or put so much effort into someone. You all would be intelligent to pay attention. Think of it, if one of us was to be as impertinent as she is we would be lucky to be just dead."

…Gellia wasn't going to back down. "Don't make me seem like a monster," Gellia shouted, "*You're* the monster." Her fists clenched by her sides, Gellia glared up at the looming Cassius.

"Is it that simple to you? Is everything black and white?" His eyes narrowed. "You *are* Gallylya, aren't you?"

He meant it as an insult, but honestly she would be proud to be as loved and respected as Gallylya was.

Their mystical auras were swirling around them, mingling, during the stand-off. Gellia felt some strange connection she wanted to give in to. It flustered her further. "You're just evil, aren't you?" she sputtered. "I always knew you were." She came with him despite her opinion of him. She knew better, she knew from the first day she met him. She told everyone of his corruption and no one believed her. Still she came—no one forced her.

The rage on his beautiful face changed to something entirely different. His eyebrows rose in a look of disbelief and he backed up a step to look at her. His aura died away and the energy winds vanished as he laughed.

Gellia didn't know what to think but let her magic rest. Cassius sobered a little and continued. "I am only me, princess— no matter how others define me." He looked directly at Gellia and smirked. "I fight for what I believe in; I don't follow some idiot because I don't know what else to do. Nor do I destroy for the thrill of it. I hold my realm in the highest positive regard and will do whatever it takes to protect it. Xzepheniixenze is a very beautiful, very savage place requiring strict rules. These people don't learn from a slap on the hand. Anything the Zephrons don't understand they label for their convenience."

She didn't know what to say remembering when she defended dragons against Gallylya. Cassius wasn't lying to her, either. Somehow Gellia knew that he was being very truthful. The mood seemed to pass.

Yes, he had killed her prince and the others, but still Gellia looked to her liege, her teacher, with—fondness. And there was something else about him of which Gellia was unsure. There was something very special about this person, more than appearance.

"Connylia's coming to visit you—she should be here in the morning."

"What?" He started her out of her thoughts.

"She sent word with one of my seekers via our countess. I was just told this morning. She should be able to help you while I'm gone." He leaned against the front of his desk.

"I want Skip back," Gellia said.

"Send for him."

"So all this effort for me is what advantage to you?"

"When I return I hope you'll be transformed into another powerful ally."

"That's all?"

He look smug yet thoughtful. "And I promised Quenelzythe I would."

"You're the Moonseeker." The multi-faceted. Suddenly she had so many more questions and likely no answers. Quenelzythe wrote often of him. No wonder the journals were in a restricted part of the library. Not that the accounts of him were vast or unflattering…

"That was a very long time ago."

"What about the dragons?" From what Gallylya had told her and what little she read in the books she had so many questions. To think when she first read the books in Fuarmaania she thought they were fiction stories of a madman. In the times of rampant dragon slayers and Gallylya's band of professionals, Cassius and Quenelzythe had orchestrated ways of cursing dragons into objects to save them, with the idea of releasing them at a safer time. Why they chose to do this she didn't know. Quenelzythe was modest, but she felt his writings hinted that he had come up with the way to do so, and Cassius was his partner at the task. So many questions.

"Gallylya told you about the dragons," Cassius said and cocked his head. "I suppose he wonders where we hid them... does he have the dragon key?" He picked up the trinket on his desk again and tapped it against the wood.

"He said he had half and the other half is lost someplace."

A languid smile spread across his face. "Of course he did."

Gellia didn't want to discuss the Zephronian Emperor, just the dragons and their history. Her memories of him still haunted her. He instilled such awe, such fear. "Before you go, I have to show you something I just learned to do." She held out her hand. From her palm appeared a glowing ball of purple energy, tiny sparks popping out around it. "It's my magic, right here in my hand where I can see it, where others can see it."

Cassius watched her. She was so—childlike—but her magic was so very, very old. "I'll have to show you what I can do when I have the time."

"That would be very interesting to me," she said, looking at the tiny globe. "I can't really tell that about people yet—about how much magic they have. I can tell how much they're drawing though, sometimes."

"It comes with experience... well, Gallylya doesn't know everything, but I won't make you continue to speak of him."

5

"Is it time to wake up already?"

"Yes, Milady."

"Oh I don't want to deal with today... has the baron left yet?" She didn't know why she asked. He always told her she was leaving only a few hours before he did.

"I heard his lordship left in the night, milady."

"Of course." Gellia crawled from the luxurious bed and stretched. What a fabulous morning. The servants set fresh flowers around the room as they did every morning and the first sun brought a warm glow into the room before it had even climbed over the hills. As she sat up a woman started to brush the tangles from her hair. Breakfast was already in her chamber—her favorite assortment of fruit, and toast. It hadn't taken that long for her servants to learn her ways, and now they knew what she wanted and had it to her before she knew she wanted it.

"The rest of milady's wardrobe has finally arrived."

Soft music played in the corner of the chamber and some of the servants were taking care of Gellia's bath. She discarded her nightgown and slipped into the hot water. What would this day be like? What would it be like to be Cassius? Gellia smiled. "Are my clothes fabulous?"

"Yes milady."

"What should I wear today," she mused. "Not a dress. I wore one yesterday. Do I have any fetching doublets?"

"Yes milady."

After choosing an ensemble her attendants were quick to put her together. They were just finishing her up when someone knocked at the door. Her doorman opened the door, closed it, then announced, "Milady, his name is Tunnaig. He's one of the court mages in training."

Gellia had heard several terms for such a person. "A petty mage?"

"Yes, milady."

"Send him in," Gellia said.

The man was quick to enter. "Yes, I suppose that's what people like to call us." His hair was still black, his eyes still very violet, and he was dressed in all black as the court mages did.

"You look young. How did you become one of them?" Gellia asked.

"I was born near Tintagel. And I'm a very good potential telepath and I'm still older than you. Milady."

"How old?" She looked in the three mirrors her servants held up, turned to see all angles. Her servants brought her a marvelous hat to don.

"Forty."

"Is that your true age?"

His brow wrinkled just a bit. "Yes. I'm here to assist you, as I'm sure you've guessed. The court mages said they wanted nothing to do with this."

"I'm not surprised. What do you think?" Gellia twirled around to show off the elaborate clothing. She knew her servants would respond with admiration, but everyone else…

"Appropriate," Tunnaig said.

"Thank you." Gellia smiled. "What first?"

"We have to go to the office and meet with the mages."

Out of habit she smoothed her doublet but found it fit so well it didn't need it, so she straightened her hair. One last look in the mirror and she was ready to go.

The court mages stood around her like vultures; Tunnaig seemed unnerved as well. So Gellia sat where Cassius would have if he was there and stared into the room of annoyed mages. "They're supposed to report to you before you go out there, apprise you of anything out of the ordinary," Tunnaig whispered.

Gellia cleared her throat. "Well?" She was just going through the motions. She already knew the results.

"We have nothing to say," one of them said. Someone muttered that their baron was doing this to torture them. The rest glared at her from under their dark manes.

Of course they didn't. They wouldn't report to her. Gallylya's words echoed in her mind. *Playing princess.* Only the fear of Cassius kept them from killing her. If they could pin the act on someone else it would be done. "Then we're done?"

Tunnaig covered his face with his hands and said, "Yes," through his fingers.

As she walked the corridor towards the audience chamber Gellia pondered the difficulty of the task. When she entered the endless room with the seemingly hundreds of people staring at her she stalled, and Tunnaig almost had to prod her towards the dais. It looked much bigger than she remembered. What would happen if she bungled everything? Gellia stuck up her nose and strode to the marvelous onyx and green velvet chair and arranged herself as gracefully as she could.

Tunnaig mind-spoke and she accepted. It certainly wasn't the most impressive voice she'd heard. *Too late to tell you not to sit in the chair... He told me you have telepathy. Don't be afraid to use it on them... just nod at the doormen when you want someone let in. I think if you make eye contact with whoever you want and nod they do what they're supposed to... but I think he does it all with telepathy so I guess you could do that too... The mages might try to stir up the crowd against you.*

It would have been nice to have more information than this, but with Cassius' abrupt departure and unwillingness of everyone else it was how it was going to be. The throng stared at her with mixed emotions: curiosity, surprise, defiance, and amusement. *You aren't being much help, Tunnaig.* She rested her hands on the beautiful chair arms and nodded slightly to the doorman. It was a much more comfortable seat than she expected even if it was big for her.

The great doors opened and through them strode a very fancily dressed man carrying a gilded gold box. When he saw that a woman sat before him he faltered and glanced around. Gellia tried to make herself look impressive, tried to remember her liege's posture when he sat there.

The man cleared his throat. "I am Byxe from a small town in the north. I wish to offer this gift along with my gratitude for..."

It felt as though it took hours. People bearing gifts to please their baron. The longer she sat there the more she was understanding that he wasn't just a baron. It seemed to her that everyone who appeared came from towns Cassius helped. They came freely to thank him for the assistance he provided. He tended his peasants with great care and they adored him. It was only the other nobles who were troublemakers—the ones who had all the ambitions. For a very long time Gellia patiently listened to them until she decided it was done. After the last, she returned to the office to try to squeeze information from the mages but knew it would be a waste of time.

"There was nothing unusual," Una said.

"Other than you being there," Gareth added.

"Hm," Gellia was tired of their condescending ways. This would have to change if she was to retain control of Tintagel. She had spent a large amount of her precious time listening to homage and for what reason? Wasn't the real purpose of public audiences to see what was happening in the region? And now she was surrounded by smug mages while she figuratively tore her hair out. Someone knocked at the door. "Yes," Gellia muttered.

A servant peeked his head in. "Milady, there is a woman here who insists that she be let in immediately."

"Fine."

Seeing Connylia come through the door was no surprise to Gellia, but the mages were in shock. "So good to see you," Gellia said, trying not to look *too* happy.

Connylia was dressed in grey and black. Her blond curls were free and wild, her blue-grey eyes bright. The mages looked repulsed and enraged, and Connylia looked happy for it. "You're looking well, milady," she said.

Abaddon, apparently offended to the point of speaking, said, "Will the insult to this castle never end?" There were a few vocal agreements.

Gellia opened her mouth to speak but never had the chance. All at once Gellia's Zephronian friend was not as she remembered. Connylia had the posture of someone with great power, someone who wouldn't tolerate insolence. "You forget your place, mage," she said, and with a graceful sweep of her hand Abaddon froze where he stood. It would be difficult to tell for those who were unfamiliar with the race, but Abaddon seemed to age before their eyes. The other mages gasped and took a few steps back. "That's correct," she said, "I have *that* magic. Do not think for one minute that I won't use it against you. And don't try to threaten me with your liege's name because unlike you, I am not afraid of him." With another movement of her hand Abaddon was freed, but trembled with shock. She turned back to Gellia and smiled sweetly.

Mephibosheth prodded Abaddon who opened his mouth once again. Connylia cut him off. "I don't want to hear your pathetic excuses."

"He wanted to make an apology," Mephibosheth said. He looked from Connylia to Gellia and back to Connylia several times.

Connylia held up her hand. "Or you either. Don't think I can't call the wrath of the goddesses down on you? One word."

Mephibosheth tried to look collected but Gellia could sense the fear in him and she reveled in it.

Are they giving you a hard time? Conny asked.

You don't know the half of it and it's only the first day I'm in command.

I'm right on time. I'll help you.

"You can go," Gellia told them. And after the mages filed from the room she said, "You are amazing." In Zephronia they called Connylia insane, and she lived in solitude at the palace, hidden away by her brother, Emperor Gallylya. However, Gellia truly felt Connylia was brilliant, just horribly misunderstood.

"The Xzepheniixenze breed couldn't have changed *that* drastically over the centuries and I've certainly dealt with people more powerful than they. Not to mention my magical talents seemed to frighten even the boldest mage," Connylia said as she walked over to sit on the desk. "Are you ready to play?"

"What? What do you mean play?"

"You have the world at your fingertips with Cassius' name behind you. You're going to be challenged and worshiped, hated and admired. I've been doing some research on my way here. Would you like to hear about your host?"

Gellia perked up. "Yes!"

"Let's ride then. Have you even been outside the castle yet?"

"No, Conny, I haven't had the time."

"Oh Gellia. You haven't seen anything yet." She started out the door with Gellia on her heels. Conny seemed so comfortable, even more so than Gellia and, Gellia had been in the castle for some time.

"What if we lose our way?"

"We won't. Not only do I know Xzepheniixenze fairly well, but also our horses know it very, very well. They'll get us home from anywhere we end up." They turned down another corridor. "This place is so different from the last time I saw it... The nice thing about Tintagel is that it's fairly symmetrical so it's easier to find your way around than some of the larger castles."

"That's easy for you to say. This is at least ten times the size of the castle in Fuarmaania."

"Yes well, I spent most of my life in some of the biggest places in all the kingdoms. Where is your room? You should change."

Once they arrived at her rooms her servants rushed to dress her into something better for riding. Gellia was impressed with how quickly they were able to finish.

"...Let's see. We're at Mirror Lake and Tintagel, so north would put us in the Shadowlands." Conny said. "We don't want to go there—south is Griffins; northwest is Myste and west of that is Ravengate. We could go see Cassius, that's where he is, but I've never liked Raven and don't particularly want to see him, it's a very long way besides. Where would you like to go?"

"I don't know." Gellia felt those places were far, far away from the castle. She didn't know if Conny was being humorous or serious. "You've ridden so far already, are you certain you'd want to travel all that way? I haven't even seen the entire castle yet."

Conny laughed. "Well then we'll take the scenic route to the stable. Let's..."

A servant opened the door for Tunnaig, who was startled to see the Zephron woman. "Yes?" Gellia asked.

"Milady, I have word."

"Lovely," Gellia said. Well, even if the other mages were useless to her, at least she had Tunnaig, whose ambitions would drive him to work for her.

Tunnaig straightened his tunic. "Rumor has it that you are a cousin to the family who has recently come of age. Everyone wonders what his lordship has planned for you for he *never* allows someone to rule in his stead; it's created quite the stir. In fact news of you will probably spread quickly... I also heard this Zephron woman has some very rare magic." He cleared his throat.

"That's nice," Gellia commented. "Tunnaig, this is Princess Connylia from Dournzariame," Gellia said. "Tunnaig is—my advisor—I suppose you could call him."

"You're The Phoenix's sister," Tunnaig said to Connylia and his face turned white. "Everyone thinks you're dead."

"Yes. Do you study ancient history?"

"Yes,"

"Then you are more clever than the court mages," Conny said and smiled, "for I am famous for two reasons, that being the lesser."

He gave an abrupt bow. "I'll take my leave, milady…" Tunnaig said, he watched Connylia.

"Yes, go ahead. We're going out," Gellia told him.

There. He'll let the others know just how precarious their situation is, Connylia told her friend. *And the fact that you have allies in the Zephronian Capitol should confuse and worry them to no end. They'll be pondering for weeks. Always be unpredictable if you can help it. It's probably why Cassius welcomes me here.*

***

They rode for the rest of the day, watched the butterflies and grasshoppers scatter before the horses. The verdant field was vast and lovely. Although it was kept relatively short, the plants growing there were varying and lovely. There were many species of tiny flowers.

Tintagel was stunning in the distance, the towers shining in the sun with the lake glittering behind it, the evergreens created the frame of a fine picture. It became obvious that the forest was tended but not overly so. After being in the warm sun, the coolness of the shade was a welcome change. Gellia started to remember the simple bliss of the ride. Connylia was every bit the rider Gellia was, and they galloped, jumped, and swerved their way around the nearby countryside. It was the escape Gellia needed. It even seemed that Amarynth enjoyed himself.

"...And just like that he told me I was taking over for him while he was away, and left me. I have no real idea what he expects of me although he did say this was a test," Gellia said.

"He's likely training you for the future. You're mortal, you don't have time for nonsense, and he's a man of ambitions."

"He's taking over the empire," Gellia said.

"I wouldn't be surprised if he already has, just no one knows it yet," Connylia said. "I've heard he's been pulling the strings of the rulers for many, many years... I had forgotten how beautiful Xzepheniixenze was, how much I loved it."

Gellia looked at the ocean of wildflowers at their feet. "I didn't think I would adjust to this place as easily as I did. The heavens are very strange when I really think about it, but it's never bothered me. Two moons, two suns."

"You were meant to be here, that's all. You would have never been happy to live in Zephronia forever. No matter how much I wished you could—but that's for selfish reasons." She smiled.

"How did you escape?"

"I told Emperor Gallylya that I wanted to visit my old friend, the countess, and he agreed to let me go. I suppose he might be suspicious, but he has no idea of the countess' occasional connections to Xzepheniixenze. I promised I wouldn't be gone for too long, and he arranged an escort while I arranged a double for myself."

"I double?"

"Oh yes. One of my unicorns comes with me," she patted the black horse she rode. "And one stays behind in the likeness of me. It's just like old times." She smiled. "These unicorns in particular have unfathomable magical power, they just don't show it very often."

Once more Gellia had so many questions. Her entire life would likely be trying to find answers to them all.

Connylia stayed for a week before she had to steal away to Zephronia once again. In that time she continued to school Gellia, usually in the privacy of Gellia's suite or the laboratory. Between trying to figure out what she was doing, and lessons with Connylia, most days Gellia was exhausted to the point where she barely ate dinner, just went straight to bed.

Even though Gellia was sad that her friend left, she felt better about dealing with the mages. For since that time they treated her with more caution. She wasn't sure if it was the threat of Connylia visiting her wrath on them, the idea that Gellia knew someone from the Golden Age of Xzepheniixenze, the possibility that Connylia might be important to Cassius or that Connylia might call on her brother to stomp on them—everyone feared the Phoenix and the Vega Knights. Connylia said it was because all Xzepheniixenze children were threatened with those stories to make them go to bed at night. Go to sleep or the Vega Knights will get you. Whatever they thought was fine, for it made Gellia's life easier. It did make Gellia curious to why Cassius would allow Connylia to visit. Conny was the enemy, or at least the sister to the enemy. He didn't seem concerned that she might go back to Dournzariame and tell her brother everything. Gellia wondered if his association with Quenelzythe created some sort of close relationship with Connylia. Still, it seemed strange Cassius let her do as she pleased.

Audiences became more familiar, people started to recognize her, but she always had to read their minds to remember who they were until she eventually developed a system for remembering. She also became very adept at reading people's minds while she spoke, thought about something else, or kept an eye on the mages. Of course, it also became far clearer that the mages were not the only people to be distrusted. Many of the nobles who lived in or around Tintagel were also up to no good. Most had small ambitions; none were as great as Cassius' desire to rule everything. Or hers, she supposed. With Tunnaig's assistance though, she quickly learned their names and their games—*his* ambition was to be on Cassius' good side when he returned. And everyone was out to see just how much she would miss and how much she'd let go.

Then there was Vellura. Vellura appeared and disappeared when she wanted and was never much help once Gellia found a rhythm. Luckily Vellura wanted nothing but money to buy more jewels, and the lords and mages of the household were more than happy to give her plenty for services rendered.

It didn't take long before Gellia realized there were three worlds in Tintagel, even as it became smaller to her. There was the world of the nobles, the servants, and the military, and each tended to stay in their own world with rare crossovers, usually for carnal pleasure or minor favors. When she had a moment or was completely bored with what she was doing, Gellia stole glances of these other worlds to observe how the people outside hers lived. Much of it was fascinating to her. Even the stable hands had their own subculture.

Every so often she almost missed Fuarmaania, but she quickly tossed the memories aside. In Dournzariame life was easier as well, for even though she didn't have any responsibilities, she could trust others. That was not possible here, not possible now. She never realized how simple her life was before Tintagel. But change was often a challenge.

…Nights were the worst, there was no one to talk to, not even her servants who were probably some of the trust worthiest people in the castle. All she could do was lie on her bed and stare at the canopy, wondering what Cassius was doing and hoping he or Connylia could come back soon. *I wonder if I was pure Xzepheniixenze if I would have these problems*, she said to Amarynth, not expecting a reply. He was not a talkative bond horse. *Or if I'm lonely only because I'm half human.* She twirled a curl around her finger and looked out the balcony door to the stars.

Amarynth's voice came to her in a shimmer of starlight in her mind. *You're half human, but you would still have problems if you were full Xzepheniixenze, just not in the same way.*

So I'll be battling to fit in somewhere for the rest of my life, she said and took his silence as a yes.

…Correspondence was difficult as well. There was so much to be done and she barely knew where anything was in the office. Not the seal, not paper, nothing. It took her a whole day to find everything. She even cursed Cassius and promised herself she wouldn't feel guilty for pawing through the drawers of his desk. It was his own fault he didn't leave her with instructions. After every letter she wrote to her nobles she had to call for seekers to deliver them. Not regular messengers, for they were too inept at avoiding capture—it was always seekers. Of course, she didn't know this at first; one of them had to tell her when she questioned him.

Finally Gellia found the steward, who when he was not entertaining himself with the ladies, ran the household. His name was Kiore, and even though he seemed neglectful, he kept Tintagel running flawlessly. She found he was one of the most organized people she had ever met and understood why Cassius kept him. Cassius hadn't lied about Tintagel running itself. If fact, the castle had a system that interlinked through all of its different areas to make sure everyone was informed and performing well. Gellia was quite impressed. She left Kiore alone. She also found all servants were content—despite long hours of work—and received handsome wages. One of them told her they were honored to serve at Tintagel and meant it. She also learned which guards were which rank and who to order to do what.

The strangest development to her was she was certain a few of the visiting nobles were interested in her—perhaps in a carnal way being this was Xzepheniixenze and without marriage. Several exchanges with them and she came away wondering if they had been making advances towards her. She'd had little experience with flirtations in her past. One didn't flirt with a princess of Fuarmaania, one just made arrangements and married. They weren't so bold as to touch her, and certainly not touch her hair, but still…

A month passed and once again Gellia was blessed with another visit from her best friend. Gellia would have been more excited to see her if she had the energy. Connylia walked up alongside Gellia as she strode through the corridors, Gellia never paused for a moment. Now she knew why her liege was always in motion. "Your brother must think you're very fond of the countess," Gellia said, smiling.

Connylia sighed. "There's a good chance he knows where I'm going."

"You really think so?"

She shrugged. "It's possible… but enough about that. How is everything? Any better?"

Gellia beamed with pride. "If anything I appreciate all the nonsense his majesticness has to go through… I'm very happy to see you."

"You seem tired and in need of a holiday—but you look fabulous."

"Are you here to take me riding? I haven't had a chance to go out in a while."

Conny smiled. They walked along the row of archways, ignored everyone else around them even though many stared at the Zephron. Conny was still impressed by how elegant the castle was and said that it had more magic in it than she remembered when Cassius' mother was still alive.

"Have you ever been hawking?" Conny asked.

"I've been on hunts but the old king never kept a mews."

"We'll have to do that some time. It's quite amusing. I'm sure Cassius has a very lovely mews," she laughed.

"I'm sure Cassius has a very lovely everything. He has impeccable taste." Gellia laughed as well. "Or his attraction for things of quality, and desire to keep everything tidy."

Conny stopped them. "Oh dear look at this." She nodded towards a commotion.

"What?" Not all that far from them was a poorly dressed man having a desperate conversation with a courtier, a few guards waited nearby. Gellia immediately approached, Connylia by her side.

"…He isn't here now go away before I have you run through,"

"I need to talk to—"

"Who is this man?" Gellia asked the courtier. The man in question looked mostly if not all human, covered in filth, but she could tell that what he wore must have been his best even though it didn't fit quite right on his skinny body.

"Milady," the handsome Xzepheniixenze courtier said and bowed. "He is nothing. I'm getting rid of him right now."

"What does he need, Lord Haemar?"

Haemar looked surprised. "It's his own fault he missed the audience."

Gellia gave Haemar a look and he moved aside. "That is *not* the question I asked you. What is the problem, man?" Cassius' peasants were taken care of, this one looked destitute. He must have come a long way to be there.

The peasant spoke. "My town is starving. We're in a drought and all our crops have failed. A mage battle stopped the rains and now we're dying."

"He's lying," Haemar said.

"Did I ask you for your opinion?" Gellia said to Haemar then turned back to the peasant. "We will go with you to your village. If what you say is true we'll decide what is to be done." *We were going out anyway, right?* Gellia said to Connylia. On second thought, it probably wasn't the smartest idea, but it came out of her mouth and she would follow through.

Keep in mind it could be a trap. A trap and this man may not even know he is a part of it, Connylia said.

I know, but you're coming with me, so what do the two of us have to worry about? Gellia mentally smiled.

The very next morning a group from Tintagel left for the nameless village. Tunnaig insisted on coming along, and with him brought a small army. Having never been in such a fine procession, Gellia was quite tickled with the whole thing despite the purpose of their trip. The group started off through the still dew-laden countryside with the peasant man in the lead. Tunnaig rode next to her along with Connylia—who even though was Zephron, rode her fabulous black charger that several of the company admired. There were several jealous bond horses in the company.

The peasant rode with one of the knights and told the tale of his journey. He'd traveled with merchants, farmers, pilgrims, whoever would accept his presence. He ate whatever he gathered from the land, and tried to stay out of anyone's way. It took him so long to arrive at Tintagel he was afraid his village was done for.

Gellia often had doubts as they traveled, but she tried to distract herself with the beautiful surroundings. Mostly she was unsuccessful. Was it a trap? If it was, it was likely for Cassius, but Cassius wouldn't fall for a trap, so could it really be one? Or would she arrive and find she was vastly overfaced?

Tunnaig scolded her for the tenth time. "It probably would have been wiser to send a seeker."

"I enjoy going out," Gellia said. Cassius probably would have ended him right there for questioning authority, but she wasn't as motivated.

After a few days they left the shimmering evergreen forest and entered the plains of Xzepheniixenze, where oceans of flowering grasses swayed in the wind. *How painters must love this place*, Gellia thought, and breathed in the fragrant air. In the distance she saw towering mountains in pale tones of amethyst and sapphire. "Those are the mountains of Razhiede," Tunnaig said and pointed.

"Razhiede?" Connylia asked. "They've named mountains after him?"

"Of course, Razhiede is the god of wisdom, his temple lies in the heart of one of them—I'm not sure which mountain, though," Tunnaig said. "I've done much research on the subject, actually."

"Obviously not enough," Connylia said.

Tunnaig just looked at her, but didn't say anything about it. "On the other side of the mountains is this fellow's home. It will take us almost a month to arrive there at this speed."

"So be it," Gellia said. She hoped that realistically the mages wouldn't take over the castle. It wasn't hers, it was their fearsome liege's. Turn it against her perhaps, and she wouldn't have a place to live... She reminded herself she had to take things as they came. She wanted to help these people. It would be a long trip and she'd have to distract herself with other thoughts.

**

Amarynth picked his way down the rocky slope as the group descended into a large chasm. The path was narrow, but bond horses weren't flighty as their non-magical counterparts. Gellia rested her hand on the pommel of her saddle and made sure not to interfere with Amarynth's balance. There was no way her old horse, Tempest, would have traveled this path... She wondered how he fared.

The chasm had been carved out by an ancient river; a waterfall was in the near distance. Mists surrounded them, and the sun's light granted them rainbows. The rocks glittered with dampness, the moss clinging to them covered with dew. *I think this place must be heaven,* Gellia told Connylia. One side of the chasm held a ruin of broken archways and crumbling spiral columns. There seemed to be the remains of a road leading to what must have been the doorway, but it was not easily passable, not to mention no obvious way to reach the old road. A pair of eagles had a nest on one of the old arches.

Connylia connected with Gellia. *There have been times I've wondered the same thing... I meant to ask sooner, how were things going with the snobs?*

The mages?

Yes. I shouldn't assume the mages are the worst, really. All of them are arrogant in some shape or form... The fact that he draws energy through his mages is phenomenal. Not even in the Golden Age did people have such talents, and those days had many more powerful mages than now.

He's strange, that's all I have to say.

Connylia gave Gellia a look then sighed and smiled. *I imagine so.*

Well, Sian seems tolerable; he minds his own business and rarely spends time with the others. Mephibosheth makes me nervous but he treats me well and Tunnaig is tolerable. Everyone else hates me and certainly don't respect me. I suppose it's to be expected. She watched water droplets form on Amarynth's mane as they neared the falls. *I think some of the nobles fancy me.*

Conny smiled, tilted her head as she looked at Gellia. *Really now?*

Gellia tried not to blush and failed miserably. She felt so foolish. *I can't be certain, really. I'm not as familiar with how things work here.*

Well if they had mage talent they'd be attracted to your power, that's for certain. And even though you have human blood in you, you're astoundingly beautiful. Do you share their interest? In one or more?

Gellia looked to the distance and shook her head.

Don't be ashamed if you do, it's about time, really. If you like one, have one, then in the morning send him on his way. A tryst could relieve your stress. Humans use silphium, which would work for you, but Xzepheniixenze generally can control their procreation with a thought. I would recommend the silphium just to be safe. A tryst is likely the least scandalous thing you could do here. Wearing the wrong outfit for the time of day would be more scandalous.

Tunnaig spoke. "I've word that there's a town we can reach fairly soon," he said. "We'll stay there for the night if it suits you, milady."

"Fine," Gellia answered. She took a deep breath and was happy to veer of the previous topic.

When they came over the last rise from the chasm they followed the river though fields covered with wildflowers. Tunnaig pointed to a grove of shiny-leafed trees that were all that stood between them and the rising pillars of smoke of the town. Gellia was happy to see civilization again. Amarynth's ears pricked forward. The horse Connylia rode nickered.

"I guess they're looking forward to nice straw beds," Tunnaig said.

Gellia felt uneasy but said nothing to the others. A quiet came over the group and several of the horses snorted. She had a feeling there was much conversation between horses and riders. *Something's not right,* she said to Amarynth.

He agreed, and she hoped she was just overthinking.

They entered the forest, and through the trees they could see that things didn't look quite right. Conny said what they were all thinking but didn't want to admit. "There's too much smoke..."

Someone at the front of the group shouted and Gellia and Amarynth trotted through the remaining trees to find only devastation. The knights immediately broke into groups, one stayed with their lady while others scouted for any remaining danger. The town was nothing but a tangle of timbers and scattered bricks. Everything smelled of burning flesh and the coppery smell of blood. The horses snorted at the stench, and Gellia wished she could, too. As it was it took all her concentration to keep her composure.

Fires still burned. Bodies lay strew about like some giant monster tore through the town in a rage. Amarynth picked his way through the mess, undisturbed by the dark puddles and popping timbers.

Tunnaig had stayed close to Gellia, thankfully. "Who were these people, Tunnaig?" Gellia asked.

"They weren't anyone special, just farmers and some merchants." He seemed unaffected by the slaughter. "Just another village destroyed."

"Another?" Gellia said. She slid off her horse and wandered through burned buildings and into the main square. There was a pile she didn't need to look at to know what it was. The dirt streets were covered with dark stains, thatch and other debris. Hoof prints. The attackers were mounted. No other animal but for a lone wounded dog seemed to be still in the town. And it had been a large town, perhaps not very wealthy, but from the looks of the wrecked shops it had some of the finer things.

One of the knights came to tell her he'd found a dying girl who spoke her last to him. "She didn't know who it was," he said. "But she thinks a few of the villagers escaped. Many were taken as slaves."

Gellia nodded. She had no words as her mind still processed everything. These people must have had warriors in their community, didn't most? Some sort of defense? As she wandered she noticed many died from wounds that couldn't be treated, perhaps were even alive up until a few hours ago. Some of the bodies were still warm. Quick and messy; they must have been in a rush. Gellia returned to the town square. Conny looked over the pile. "It's odd that there are so many here, while the rest are scattered through the village," she said.

"I think you might know them better than I," Gellia said. "I haven't witnessed anything like this." These poor people. She felt sick. She was amazed at how calm Connylia was. Gellia felt that the only reason she hadn't fainted or vomited was because Amarynth was supporting her.

"I don't know what to tell you. I haven't kept up with local politics in many centuries." Connylia said. *Keep your composure.*

Gellia took a deep breath. It seemed any warriors this village had were outnumbered and slain on the borders of town. Gellia started to wander again, passed the peasant man, Murr, who was in quite a state of shock.

This was one of Cassius' towns, larger than any Fuarmaanian town. Some one of greater power than these people destroyed them. She rubbed her chin. "This happens often?"

"Often enough," Tunnaig said.

"It seems odd to me that his lordship would allow his villages to be attacked so regularly," Gellia said. "These peasants are well fed and well dressed. The buildings and streets were well tended."

Tunnaig shrugged. "He hasn't been home much for the last decade and none of his nobles would dare make a move without his command."

Gellia pursed her lips. "And we have no idea who's doing this."

"It could be any of the clans. They're always fighting amongst themselves," Tunnaig said.

Connylia watched as Gellia ruminated. *This would leave unrest amongst the people,* Gellia said to her friend. *Unrest can lead to dissention.*

Indeed, Connylia replied.

"This can't go on," Gellia said. "It must be stopped."

This seemed to shock Tunnaig. "What are you saying?"

"We're going to put an end to this," Gellia said.

"You know if you mention this to the mages they're going to laugh at you," Tunnaig said.

"I wasn't going to tell them," Gellia muttered.

One of the knights came to her and bowed.

"Yes," Gellia said.

The knight spoke. "Milady, one of the knights at the castle mentioned his home town was attacked a few months ago. He thinks the Lorkiegns were to blame."

"The Lorkiegns are all seekers, they would have poisoned the well," Tunnaig said.

"Who else opposes Tintagel?" Conny asked for Gellia.

Tunnaig's laughter mocked her. "Everyone? At one time or another."

"What about *my* village?" Murr asked. One of the knights threatened to hit the man for his insolence.

"Leave him alone," Gellia said. "How quickly can we get to your village?"

"It will still take many days." Murr started to whimper.

"I don't want to spend that," Gellia said.

"If we could go through the mountain—but the gods may strike down anyone who enters..." Murr told them and wrung his hands. "It's only eight days ride from here…"

Conny snorted. "Don't worry about it. Where's this cave?" Her beautiful mount kneeled, bowing his head, for her to mount. "Going under the mountain is the most direct."

"Yes," Gellia agreed, mounting as well. "Five of you stay here and build a pyre." She knew it wasn't many for such a large job but she couldn't spare any more than that.

Tunnaig shook his head.

***

Gellia was thankful for the strength and endurance of bond horses, even when one of them carried two riders. They kept a furious pace, trotting and cantering most of the way. Finally they came to Mountains of Razhiede. The path into them was narrow but easy enough to navigate. It was only when they neared the temple that they slowed to a walk.

The cave sat in the base of a mountain, the stone mouth carved into columns and statues of unicorns, vines and tree roots wrapped around it as if holding it open. Everyone looked at it nervously. Gellia stared dumbly at the entrance while she tried to sort out what she was feeling. Was superstition getting the best of her?

"No one goes in there," Murr said.

"If we aren't there to do harm we should be fine," Tunnaig muttered. "I don't think this has been a habited place in ages. Peasants are full of superstitions."

"This feels strange. I feel like I'm invading someone's privacy," Gellia told Conny. She'd never been in a place of worship, populated or otherwise. "We might as well go ahead," Gellia said finally. They were there, and they weren't going back. Going forward was sometimes the only thing she could do.

Murr shook his head. "I'm not going first."

None of the Xzepheniixenze volunteered to enter first. "I'll go," Conny said. "Cowards."

Amarynth spoke into Gellia's mind. *You should do your best to emulate Connylia,* he said. *She is not as calm and confident as she looks, yet she leads the way.*

Gellia acknowledged his words and wondered of the full story. If he was speaking to her there was significance.

Upon entering the darkness several mage orbs were created to light the way. Indeed, Xzepheniixenze were talented at seeing in the dark, but it was exceptionally dark. They could see the ribs of the tunnel. They were without decoration but elegant on their own.

The horses' hooves echoed against the stone walls as they walked along the leveled floor. They seemed to walk for hours, but she had no idea if that idea had merit. Gellia started to doubt her sanity, but it was likely from the close quarters. If she focused on Amarynth under her, she did feel a little better. *It will be all right,* he told her. She took up a lock of his mane for reassurance. She started to fear there would be a trap, a giant hole in the floor or something else deadly. *There are no traps,* Amarynth said.

No one was speaking; she wondered if they too were unnerved by the place. She had to say something, even if it was foolish. "Why would it take so long to get to your village any other way?" Gellia asked over her shoulder. She knew it was a silly question, but it sounded even worse when she said it aloud.

"The mountains. The way over them is long and full of dangers, but not as dangerous as going through here!" the peasant said. "We'll be lucky to get out alive!"

Some of the horses shifted nervously at his cries. The sound of the hoofbeats started to echo as they entered a large cavern. The light orbs spread out to illuminate the room. There was a grand statue in the center of the room with dusty offerings around it. The ceilings were high and covered with smallish stalactites. Despite its decrepit appearance it still seemed to have something stately about it.

Tunnaig spoke to Gellia but his eyes were curiously scanning the room. "No one's really been devout for many years. I think they used to tell stories to keep away the thieves."

Gellia said nothing and turned her attention to the statue. It was of a larger-than-life man dressed in regal clothes, who wore a crown that someone must have placed on his head. He was dusty but otherwise seemed in good shape in the dim light.

One of the knights was moving. "Don't touch anything," Gellia reminded everyone, for she didn't trust there was nothing in the room. Tunnaig shook beside her. "I thought you said you weren't—" Then she felt it too.

"There's something here," Tunnaig whispered, "what is she doing?" He meant Connylia, who rode closer to the center of the room. Her horse seemed weightless. "I'll admit it, I was wrong. I want out of here. Whatever it is it's not something I'm ready to fight." Tunnaig started to turn his horse. The air was heavy with magic, so much that the human peasant could sense it, causing him to panic.

"Are you turning into a coward, Tunnaig?" Connylia called over her shoulder. She dismounted and ignored the wailing of the peasant man and the insecurities of the mage. Only the knights seemed to stay strong as they waited for a command. Connylia whispered something, looked up at the statue.

Gellia felt energies rise up from slumber, permeate everything in the room. It was beautiful and welcoming, all the while being terrifying from the depth of it. Now the bond horses were upset, snorting and surely asking to leave.

Tunnaig and his horse hid behind Gellia and Amarynth, the only horse who stood firm. Gellia trusted Amarynth and followed his lead. Even though he wasn't talkative, she knew he was very old and wise and could be trusted. She could smell roses and the ocean. The statue glimmered with life. Gellia was frozen into place, and from sudden the silence, so were the others.

Connylia spoke in a language she hadn't heard yet; it was so distinct she would have recognized it if she had. Gellia whispered the command to her enchanted ring and waited to hear the translation.

Everything seemed to change around her. Gellia barely felt she was there, almost as if she were looking through a window into a mysterious scene. The others didn't seem to exist wherever she was. Gellia felt calm yet in awe.

The statue looked at Connylia as he spoke, but his voice came from all around. His hair was a soft grey like the stone but the rest of him took on pale colors. Connylia's words became clear. "...killed our Quenelzythe," Conny said, "and he took the key..."

He smiled in a way that melted Gellia's heart. "Worry not," he said. "Hope is not lost. Times change, we all change. Do not regret the past, think only of the future and the hope of balance once again." His gaze rose to rest on Gellia, who held her breath. "What have you brought me?" He smiled at her; it was warm and kind.

Gellia's face was hot and her heart skipped several beats. She wanted to run to him, bask in his light. His magic sang to her of great and wondrous things.

He continued, "The newest Zapheny." Gellia felt her magic unfold itself for him like it was no longer just hers but theirs. They shared the same magic. She felt touched by warmth, felt secure like being in a father's arms. He told her not to fear, to do her best to protect and guide their people and heal their land. Xzepheniixenze and the rest of the kingdoms were in great danger—danger they hardly knew existed as they fought one another. She needed to solve this. She didn't know how but she would find a way. That was his one wish of her and those after. She felt her magic change; as if he reached into her soul to places she didn't know existed and brought it to life. They were two points in a circle, he and Gellia. He promised that in the future she would stay with him for a time and he would reveal to her all the secrets of her birthright. For the first time Gellia's heart smiled, and Razhiede smiled back at her. When he turned away she still felt she was in a state of bliss.

He was still speaking to Connylia. "...And an old friend," his face became somber, "but I sense a change coming. Two generations, I think, for it to be complete."

Connylia looked in her direction. Gellia couldn't tell who she was looking at.

"You will be by my side once again soon," he said.

"I've waited this long."

"First you must do a dragon a favor," he said, his gentle smile renewed. "I leave you once again. My magic shall live again in others, as will *Her* magic." The energies around them died down.

...Gellia remembered this. This was a dream—one she had before in Fuarmaania. It was so peaceful. The castle grew up out of the shore, out of the waves of the ocean, and reached far into the heavens. She could smell the roses all around her and hear the waves crash in the distance. She was in a long gilded boat, glided on a wide stream through the gardens. Still she could hear his voice—the man she dared to believe she knew. *"When found, a new era will begin..."* The Key. It was within her but not within her alone. It was night, the moon shone down upon her castle, set it softly aglow. Tiny lights floated around her; she was in a rose garden inside the castle. There was a fountain and people. A regal Zephron woman, her beautiful lady in waiting nearby. The regal woman seemed nervous and someone stepped into the courtyard—a man she recognized from a memory deep her soul. She recognized the lady in waiting as Connylia, although she knew her as older. She couldn't breathe.

***

The ceiling was thatch. Her body wouldn't move. She was in a thatch hut. Her companions were sleeping around her but for Tunnaig, who read from one of his cherished books. "How did we get here?" Gellia asked. She was so groggy she might have been sleeping for a century.

"What? We rode, remember?" Tunnaig said without looking up from his book.

Somehow she managed to sit up. "But I—" She rubbed her head and tried to remember.

"You were talking in your sleep. Perhaps you were dreaming. It was a hard ride here, not stopping to rest."

"I don't remember arriving here."

"I do. You said you wanted to eat bark because you were so hungry. Which is good because that's all there is to eat here. That and dirt, milady."

The village, Gellia thought. The others couldn't remember—she knew it wasn't a dream. How was she missing so much time? The others were starting to wake, it was just before dawn. Gellia rose and pulled on her boots. She watched as the resident children drew pictures in the dirt floor and giggled.

"I had a friend who liked to draw," Gellia said to them.

The three children looked up at her with their dirty faces. "Donna pay them any mind," the mother said to her, "they'll stay outta yer way, m'lady. Thank yeh again for the water."

"They're lovely children," Gellia said. "Do you like this?" she asked, noticing one of the little girls was looking at a small sapphire brooch attached to her cloak. Gellia plucked it from the fabric and handed it to the child. "I have lots of them, you can have this one. I think I have one for each of you."

"Oh no, they canna take such…" the mother began; she vigorously rubbed her already dry hands with a rag. Gellia noticed the woman barely looked at Gellia, like the sight of her would burn the woman to a cinder.

"I insist. You've put a roof above our heads, call it a boarding fee."

The three girls compared the trinkets they were given with awe while Tunnaig frowned at her. Connylia walked through the door and Gellia quickly pulled a new tunic over her head. The knights shuffled past. "It is quite desolate," Conny said.

"Let's take a look," Gellia replied. They all went outside.

It was so dry. Dust clouds billowed behind people as they walked. Gellia sighed, surveying the parched, almost desert looking landscape. A few withered plants stood where there used to be a lush field. An emaciated dog sat under a chair, the starving children played in the dirt. "Magic can be so damaging," Gellia said to herself. "...I don't know how to fix this."

Tunnaig shook his head. "I don't think I could use my magic here, the energies are unstable and unpredictable. This damage can't be undone. They're better off moving someplace else."

Connylia spoke. "The mages who did this killed each other and left this mess—from what I found out from the locals. They have one laughable water source and they're living off old seeds and whatever else they can scrounge. So what are you going to do?"

Gellia spoke again. "They only thing I can really do is have supplies carried in. Unless they want to relocate." The surrounding countryside was at one point quite lovely. There were steps that used to hold crops, there were mountains full of dead trees. It really was a shame. She thought that if it went on much longer the entire place would be a desert; she wondered if the opposite could happen from mage damage and turn everything into a swampy wasteland.

"I don't think they'd survive the move," Conny pointed out. "They'd have to go quite the distance to find fertile land again, and it would probably already be taken."

Everyone looked at Gellia. It almost unnerved her. She wondered if Cassius could—no he *could* do something for them. But would he? He would have to have a reason to do so. Maybe it could be a favor to her? "We'll have supplies brought here until I can think up something else to do." She gave orders to a knight.

The next day they left for Tintagel. Connylia had to pull her horse away from the children of the village who were quite taken with him. "I suppose I would be the same," Gellia said and smiled. "He is wonderful." She noticed what kind eyes he had and how careful he was with the little ones as they ran through his legs and under his belly.

Connylia waved to the children. "Justin is an old and dear companion… this is how most react to him. Someday he'll serve you—when I'm gone I suppose."

Gellia looked at Connylia. "Don't say that. I want you to stay and be my friend."

Connylia smiled sadly. "I enjoy being your friend, but I don't want to stay."

They were about a day away from the village when Gellia finally brought up her dream. "…it all seems so real, so strange, but no one else has this memory so it must have been a dream…"

To this Connylia smiled and said, "You certainly are Zapheny with all your wonder."

On the return trip they went through the more traditional pass, and no one brought up the temple.

6

Upon her return Gellia found out about more villages being attacked. She was exhausted from the trip and was in no mood to think on such an affront. Action would be taken. Connylia had headed home as soon as they were out of the mountains, so there could be no help from her, and there was no word from Cassius. Gellia would have to deal with this mess on her own.

Gellia strode down the corridor, a dozen or so of the staff followed her and each waited their turn and tried not to step on her flowing gown. "I want seekers," she told no one in particular.

"Yes milady."

She passed two of the court mages but didn't look at them. It would waste her precious time trying to talk with them. Soon several seekers appeared around her from seemingly nowhere. Seekers, she thought. "There have been several towns attacked and I want you to find out who has been doing it. I want this done in a few days' time. Take as many seekers from Tintagel as you need." Connylia had told her seekers were some of the most useful people around and not to be afraid to make them work for her.

"Yes milady."

"I also want to know where all our troops lie. I assume there is an army?"

"Yes milady. There are several that are loyal to this house."

Tunnaig sped up to walk next to her. "Are you planning an assault?"

"If need be," Gellia told him.

"Do have the slightest idea what you're doing?" he demanded.

❧ 86 ❦

Gellia spun and came to an abrupt standstill. The people around her tried not to trip over her. "Are you questioning me?"

"I—"

"And how dare you address me so informally," she said.

"Milady," he began. "No one commands his lordship's generals but him." The other courtiers decided it was time for them to leave.

Gellia put her hands on her hips. "What are you so afraid of? I'll face any wrath that's dealt."

Tunnaig scowled at her but still took a step back. "None of us know where he found you or *why* he did. Obviously wherever you came from you were very sheltered. Death can be very welcome around here. He's not someone to be trifled with, certainly not by an upstart, who he for some strange reason, left in command. I'm surprised they even follow you as much as they do." Tunnaig looked at her with a building rage. Gellia could see it in his eyes. "I don't care who that Zephron you were with thinks she is, but it doesn't make you any more capable in this position."

"Tunnaig, unless you leave me this instant your wish for death *will* be granted."

He must have realized she was making a promise for he backed down.

***

The room was huge; high vaulted ceilings and a few windows were the backdrop for a massive topographic model of Xzepheniixenze. Gellia held her breath when she first saw it in all its glory. It must have taken years to construct. It sat on many tables, split into random looking pieces one could walk between. Everything was there before her, tiny modeled castles, forests, mountains, rivers, the larger towns, everything. For some reason it seemed familiar to her.

On three walls of the room were also paper maps of the empire and maps for several smaller areas as well as one for Zephronia with markers all over it. A large bookshelf contained rolled maps, a label under each. Zephronia, Yzelle, Sen Dunea; the list went on. For several moments Gellia wandered through the room, feeling the whole world was at her fingertips. Tunnaig stood in the doorway looking irritated.

Gellia moved around the tiny landscape, looking for Tintagel and finally found it. "We went here, to the village, yes?" she asked Tunnaig, pointing.

He sighed and walked over. "Yes, that's it."

"These flags—armies?"

"Yes."

"The green ones are ours?" She was shocked at how many green flags there were.

"Of course," he sighed again.

Gellia said nothing in reply and paid no attention to his obvious lack of faith in her. So, she thought, it was a month's ride to the village and that was south of them. The nearest army to Tintagel was north in the Shadowlands. Another army in the Mountains of Myste, another in Serenity, one past the mountains of Razhiede, one a week's ride from Candiem, one in the Dragonlands. Dragonlands? There were another dozen or so green flags spread around the realm. How many people was that? "How many people are there in each of these?" Gellia asked.

"I don't know," Tunnaig snapped. "I keep busy enough with my own business."

Gellia nearly groaned and looked at him. "Haven't you already left?"

"I don't have any choice but to follow orders."

"Leave before I'm forced to slap you. I'm tired of your complaints," she told him.

"Good day then."

Gellia didn't watch him leave. It seemed obvious to her that if someone was threatening the people Cassius protected then it was her job to take care of it while he was gone. If another clan was attacking and nothing was being done about it, eventually the people would turn against their ruler. She knew she had to do it. And after all, some of the reason he was barely home was because of her.

The door opened and a stalwart Xzepheniixenze strode in wearing black seeker armor. He didn't exactly look like the lithe type of seeker, but he was also not a mountain like so many of the soldiers. At first he didn't seem to notice Gellia but when he did he stopped and looked at her for a moment before he bowed and spoke. "I'm Sir Dallen," said he, "...and milady must be the woman who is stirring everyone up?"

"I am Gellia," she answered, she stood up straighter.

"That would be the name I keep hearing. Well, what may I do for you, milady?"

"Are things always this uneasy?"

"Usually, milady. Meanwhile you're planning your own assault?"

"As soon as I find out who's at fault."

"Milady, with as many seekers you have out there it shouldn't be a problem. I wouldn't be surprised if you find out who it is by nightfall." He smiled at her with fabricated warmth.

Gellia wandered through the room while she thought. Was she ready for this? And even this man measured her, she could feel it. He was some sort of officer, and one who knew everything about terrain and locations. Certainly more than she knew.

"It must be difficult to come from where ever it was you came from and fit in his place, milady," Dallen said.

She laughed a little. "It's worse when you weren't expecting it."

"You seem very sheltered, milady. Where did you come from?"

She smirked and said nothing.

He smiled. "Even *he* trusts me to a point, milady."

"I'm not him."

He shook his head. "Fair enough, milady. If you don't need anything else right now I'll tend to my duties."

She nodded.

* * *

Late that night Gellia sat in the office to sort through correspondence from all over the province. She wrote return letters and added them to the pile to go out. Servants brought her hot drinks and food on occasion to keep her conscious. It didn't seem unusual for them to be doing such things at such late hours. These weren't *her* servants—these were Cassius' servants. It seemed there were an endless number of his personal attendants, for she didn't think she saw the same face twice. All of them were older, too, some much older than she and they were very quiet and respectful.

"How does he do all this?" Gellia said to the empty room, "all these messages from every one of his lords and generals and seeker reports and he's barely ever home." She sighed and rose from the desk. It was true; he was baron in title only for he had all the power of any king. People of greater titles answered to this baron and he left all this work to *her*. She shouldn't complain. Would she rather be in Fuarmaania? Probably married to some horrible elderly man? Gellia turned and walked to the window to watch the rain hit the glass. This rain would last only a few days at most, not months like the rainy season back in...

Now she was making decisions that Hugh probably never had to make in the tiny country and he was the king. Gellia tugged at the buttons on her tunic and shook the heavy velvet garment off, tossed onto the corner chair. She sighed.

"Hello."

"Currain?" Gellia spun around. "What are you doing here? Why do you always sneak up on me?" She demanded, but not too harshly.

He smiled and tossed his hair. "He never takes me to Ravengate. He thinks I'll get into trouble there with the emperor's mare. Not that Ravengate is the only place he's visiting right now."

"I didn't see you in the stable."

"I've been outside the castle walls on holiday. I didn't even realize you were stuck with this job." Currain pulled up a chair to the other side of the desk and sat down with her. "I wondered why there were seekers all over the place. Then I heard through nobles' gossip that you're up to something."

"I don't know how he keeps up with all this. It's not really the writing because I don't have to write much but there is so many—"

"He doesn't sleep," Currain said, picked up one of the papers.

"What?"

"He doesn't need to sleep." He folded the letter and sealed it for her. "In the time I've known him he's maybe slept a few nights."

"How does he do that? People die without sleep."

"He's just that powerful. His magic certainly helps."

"He never ceases to amaze me," Gellia said.

"Me either."

Gellia picked up a pen and started scribbling return correspondence. "I'm certainly learning the nobles and a lot about the culture this way. ...So tell me, who usually gets this job when he's away?"

"No one, but he can also use magic to go through all the papers and write back in a matter of moments."

"I wish I could do that," she muttered.

Currain looked at her, a smile touched his face. "He's been doing this sort of thing for a very long time. Longer than I've been with him."

"So you really don't know much about him?"

The boy shrugged. "Not really. I have a limited access to his mind. If you *truly* wanted to beat more information out of someone you'd have to ask Julian."

"And he is?"

"That's right, you haven't met him yet. He isn't in the regular stable; he's in the stable in the center of the castle when Cassius is home. There are actually three of them. They're his permanent bond horses, and I think they must be at least as old if not older than Cassius. The other two look after an old friend of his." The two of them looked at each other; Gellia with disbelief and Currain with surrender. "Did you see this box?" Currain asked.

"What?"

"This box down here," he motioned to the floor.

"No, I didn't know there was—"

Currain picked the box up from the floor and placed it on the only clear spot on the desk. It was painted blue with gold scrolling and around was tied a gold satin ribbon. Gellia untied the bow and lifted off the top.

"Think he knows you at all?" Currain asked.

"A book?"

"A book of poetry by the looks of it."

Gellia picked up the treasure and opened it. A note was tucked inside the cover. 'Something procured from the Alasdairs. Enjoy'

The pages were all perfectly even and shiny with some sort of preservative. Every page was decorated with gold designs and fabulous pictures. As she looked at it Gellia decided that it must be magical for it almost whispered to her as she turned the pages, and the pictures started to look real.

"I better be going," Currain said. "I've distracted you long enough. But perhaps you should go to bed before long instead of continuing this?"

"Yes," she whispered.

Yes, bed sounded like a splendid idea; it had to be the very early hours of the morning. She had most of the paperwork done. She turned to look out the huge window and watched the stars. If she ever had time, she'd study a bit about astronomy. She heard a knock at the door. "Come in."

The guards opened the door and Sian glided through. "Oh, hello," she said.

"Greetings," said he. Sian came into the center of the room, smiled crookedly. His grey-black hair fell across the sides of his face like curtains.

"What brings you here at this hour?" She asked and shuffled some papers, made sure not to lose track of the letter she had been reading.

"Whether you believe it or not, I'm here to assist you." His voice was little more than a purr.

Gellia laughed. "Then something must be going wrong that if corrected it will make you look good. If that's the case then I'm listening."

"I always look good. I'm here to help keep you alive."

"So you're not like the other mages, then? I've already unearthed several—"

"Those plots were merely to gauge you, I assure you, and the mages who arranged them have ceased since your orders for the seekers."

"So you're telling me they stopped because the seekers I put to work will find information other than what they're looking for?" Gellia wondered what he was up to and couldn't help thinking about how odd Xzepheniixenze truly were. It seemed amazing she was half.

Sian raised an eyebrow. "Perhaps you've underestimated the baron's seekers, naïve one. They'll tell you anything of interest as well as give you the information you asked for. He pays them very well to be informed. With this many seekers you'll find out all sorts of interesting things outside the castle—as well as inside."

"There's a conspiracy inside the castle? Is that what you're saying?"

"I'm not saying anything other than the seekers are very talented and you shouldn't ignore anything they tell you. There are many nobles in this castle, not all live here permanently and many have interests in their own territories of course."

Gellia eyed him.

He looked at the papers on the desk. "…It must be difficult trying to keep things the way you want them when you have a small plot of land. But luckily, I suppose, there are many ways to change your situation, especially when there are so many helpful people out there." He looked at her coolly and folded his long fingered hands before him. Gellia noticed a signet ring and that he wasn't wearing gloves.

Gellia measured her words. "But helpful people are often out for their own gain, and don't care if it ruins the benefactor of such assistance," she said.

"Yes, but if one is desperate enough, fearful enough in his or her own situation, one might try alternate routes to assist them. Brute force, for instance. If someone thinks another has a greater force to assist, that other might be a lucrative alliance."

"True. But what if an alliance already exists between the one who is feared and brute force?"

He smiled and raised his chin. "There are those who feel strongly about their abilities and who forget just how far someone's reach is."

Cassius was away from home—the Lorkiegns knew this. But who was this other person Sian was talking about? Whoever it was she needed to find out soon, she had no idea there was such a leak in the castle. She cursed herself. "You know everyone in the castle?" Gellia asked, meaning the nobles, of course.

"Yes."

"Perhaps you should introduce me at some time."

"That would be nice, wouldn't it? But I haven't the time; his lordship keeps me busy in the library. Good night, milady." He turned on his heel and left Gellia before she could say another word. She rested her forehead on the desk. She had no patience for such things. But how could she make Sian tell her? He obviously knew. Did she have to play these games? She could see that this could be another reason why Zephrons hated the Xzepheniixenze so. Nothing was ever straightforward. Damn them.

She looked out the window again. Must be nice for Sian just to be in the library all day and not have to deal with anything… she straightened herself in the chair. Why would Cassius keep him in the library? Soren had enough assistants. Did he research something for Cassius? She rose from her chair, closed the book and put it back into the box to take it to her room. With a light orb floating nearby, she went out into the quiet hall. There were still people awake, more than usual, and more than just the servants.

As she crossed one of the larger rooms a figure came from the shadows towards her. Her magic readied, she waited for the person to come closer. "Milady," he said, bowed before her.

"What is it?" She brightened the globe. The youth before her was soaked to the bone, mud splattered on his face, on his clothes, in his braided hair. Servants stood nearby to clean up the water that gathered on the floor.

"Milady, the Lorkeigns are indeed responsible for the attacks. They're planning a small scale assault on another village not far from here. I saw the written orders…"

She stiffened. "Are you loyal to Tintagel, master seeker?" She did her best to appear menacing.

Even though it was subtle, the seeker seemed surprised, then nervous. "For the sake of my soul I would not betray his lordship for all the money in the world."

After seeing the look in his eyes at her almost accusation she nodded. "Come with me and show me where." Gellia led him off to the map room. Mentally she called for a servant and somewhat to her surprise, one appeared. "Find Sir Dallen and tell him to meet me."

Gellia flung the door open and lit the room with her magic. Everything was as it was when she left. The seeker pointed to the location.

Dallen walked through the door, armored and all. The drenched seeker repeated himself for his superior and continued for Gellia. The enemy had plans to attack Tintagel, not soon, but the grand scheme was in place, and they were bolder with a new powerful mage.

They all leaned over the map together. "What do you know about this person?" Gellia asked.

The seeker nodded. "Ziyad? He's powerful, milady. I think he's studied with the Rintaro. He's a weather manipulator from what I can tell. Word has it he joined with the Lorkiegns because he wants Tintagel for himself." He continued with more details, what family Ziyad was from, what accomplishments he had.

"Hmmm," Dallen said.

"I didn't hear them say it, milady, but I believe the assault on Tintagel will be the first of many, all trying to be planned when his lordship isn't here," the seeker continued. "Right now they rally from Candiem."

"*I'm* here," Gellia said and looked at Dallen. Could it be him? But he wasn't a noble, was he? "Well done, master seeker." …There were so many fronts on which to fight…

The two men straightened up. Gellia could read the doubt on their faces. "The Lorkeigns are powerful," Dallen told her. "But Tintagel has mystical defenses as well as physical. They would know this, would need a plan, talented mages and seekers, and optimally someone living here—"

"Hence all the seekers I've sent out. I'm more concerned about traitors already in the castle, trying to take Tintagel from within," Gellia replied. "What do we know about the Lorkiegn forces?"

The seeker went into everything he knew about the clan, their armies, their strengths and weaknesses. Gellia did her best to take it all in.

Meanwhile, Dallen couldn't take his eyes off her for he was sure he knew what she planned, but felt she would not tell him. She was young and rash, and he hoped she knew what she was getting herself into. He wondered how long she'd live.

They discussed the armies further, then the seeker moved close to her and whispered so she could barely hear him. If it weren't for his obvious apologetic stance she would have punished him for coming that close to her person. "Forgive me but I have heard whispers that there are some who would betray you, milady. Be warned."

It was hours later, and after much more discussion, when Gellia finally had it in her head what she was going to do. "Who do I contact to launch an assault?"

Dallen's face was easy to read, and not for good reasons. "That would be me, I suppose. At this time."

She took a deep breath. They'd discussed everything and anything and he knew her mind; probably knew what she would ask before she actually did. There was a town needing protection, and a clan that needed to be taken down. "Offer the enemy seekers anything they want within reason. I trust that ours will know the difference. The Lorkiegns will pay for their insolence. We need to move now, before other cities are attacked."

Dallen shook his head. "That's a long distance to cover in that amount of time."

"It's the way it has to be." Gellia stared at the map.

Tunnaig glared at her as he strode through the door. "You are completely mad. Candiem is a huge place with tens of thousands of people. Milady. And we don't have a mage of Ziyad's caliber."

She glared back at him. "Are you arguing with me?" Was it he who was plotting against her?

Tunniag stiffened. "No."

"Good. Now, I'm going to meet this army as it swings around Alasdaira. There's no way the Lorkiegn army can make it here while I'm on my way, and after I arrive that army will never make it here. Go now." She was likely making a huge mistake, and certainly felt she was in over her head. However, no one would be allowed to abuse her people. No one.

On her way through the corridor she eyed every person she passed. No, there would be no sleep for her this day. Gellia pushed away the drowsiness and headed directly for the library. To her surprise there were already many people there despite the early hour. Sian was easy to find, he stood in the first vast room. As she approached he looked up from his book and bowed. He reminded her of rain, everything about him, hair, clothes, jewelry seemed to always fall straight down.

She smiled. "It is my understanding that you are very familiar with the library."

"Yes I am," he said.

"Then would you be so kind as to show me a section of great interest?"

Sian smiled with a touch of deviance. *You're bringing me along?* "There are many fascinating books in this library but I think I know one that will interest a lady such as yourself."

What do you think to gain in return? Gellia asked.

It's a simple request, I ask you to practice magic with me.

Why would that benefit you? "I suppose if you know me that well, I should follow you." They started to stroll through the library, which seemed to be the pace of everyone there.

I have room for improvement, he said.

So he wasn't going to tell her. Well, there had to be more to it, but she wasn't sure how to extract it from him. *Then we'll practice together. Perhaps in time you will tell me what you plan with the skills you attain.* If this was a trap she would take it apart.

Sian led her through the rooms and corridors to a scarcely populated room. She recognized a noble who walked past them to leave. Sian sauntered along a row of books, ran his long fingers along the spines until he came to one in particular. He pulled it from the shelf and opened it. Gellia looked at him. "These are rather old," he said, "and very valuable." He handed her the book and took out another one for himself. "Only a few of this collection have been brought to the accessible library."

In the book she found familiar handwriting in the section he opened. It wasn't one of Quenelzythe's books, but it was from the Fuarmaanian library, one Quenelzythe's grandson had written. She looked up at Sian who gazed coyly at her from over the book he held. *Yes, I know who you are,* he said, *as do few, but unlike them, I understand.* He showed her a slip of paper that came from between the pages, then returned it and put the book back on the shelf.

Someone approached and Sian backed away, read the spines of other books several paces from her. Gellia stared into her book, noticed no one else was in the room but for she, Sian and now a seeker. The seeker pulled the book Sian had shown her, glanced in it and quickly closed it. He smiled at her then walked across the room and pulled several books from the shelves and went to a nearby table to read them.

Gellia wondered exactly what was supposed to be happening, and kept skimming her book for quite some time. Sian was across the room by then, looking into this and that. Finally the seeker picked up his books and strode from the room. He left one. Gellia looked around and saw no one but Sian, felt with her magic to be certain they were alone. She investigated the book he left. It was about Candiem.

Sian came to her. "Sloppy seekers. Never put anything away after they use it. What a disgrace," he said.

Gellia opened the book and found its pages easily parted for her to folded papers tucked into the seam. She took the papers out; Sian lifted the book from her and put it back on the shelf. "Riffraff. Well, it's time for you to go to court, I would imagine," he said.

Gellia tucked the papers into her tunic. She left him standing there and hurried to her room, luckily it wasn't far from the library. Once she blasted through the door of her chamber her servants bolted into action and she shucked off her clothes. They had an outfit already pulled for her. While they redressed her she opened the folded papers and read what was legible, she had to remind herself to breathe.

...The baron won't be back for another few months, now is the time to act. Without him, the castle will fall and there will be no reserves thanks to your efforts. Tintagel fights within itself, and with that child left in charge it is a fruit ripe for the taking... I've arranged for specific guards to be in place at certain times so your seekers will be able to infiltrate easily, although passing through the surrounding areas will be difficult with the number

of seekers she's put out...She's found out about the villages but it is too late... Her frantic precautions will not thwart our plans...

The seeker was to deliver it but he left it for her, he would be rewarded. Gellia's servants were finishing her hair, braiding it with silver chains and ribbons. When they were done she tucked the papers into her bodice, and left for the office to meet with the mages. As she thought more on the letter she started to grow angry. How dare he. Maybe Cassius wasn't there but *she* was. The bastard. Child indeed.

The mages were waiting in the office. "Well, she had the eventful night, didn't she?" Agravain said.

Mephibosheth paced through the office around the other mages, his steps slow and steady. Una tapped her foot on the floor. Tunnaig stood behind the desk, wondering where Gellia was. The mages were edgy, more so than usual. "Did you know about the villages and Candiem?" Lysithea asked Mephibosheth.

"Of course I did. Someone has to keep track of what goes on around here," the white haired mage said.

Several of the mages rolled their eyes. "Can you believe the number of seekers out there?" Gareth muttered.

"A little nervous, is she?" Kythera said.

"I think she's trying to steal Tintagel from under him," Agravain said. "Saying this fictitious conflict is the reason for such unrest so she can move armies farther away from the castle." Several of the other agreed.

Laveran shook his head. "She wouldn't be that foolish, would she? He would know better, not leave her in command, certainly not when he's focused at Ravengate."

Agravain scowled. "Unless he's trying to flush her betrayal out into the open, trap her in her own game."

Sian chuckled and pulled a lock of his hair down in front of his face to examine it. "Your imagination is running away with you," he said.

Laveran started to pace across the room. "Are we? No one knows exactly what she has planned and frankly I don't want to be a part of this mess when he returns."

"Whatever it is she has planned it won't work. He won't stand behind an upstart," Una said.

"So we stay out of it and stay safe from his wrath," Meliot said from the corner. "Just as we planned originally."

"Our original plans are already gone. Remember all the seekers out there," Gareth muttered. "You think she knows? You think she knows about how the things work?"

"Nervous, Gareth?" Mephibosheth asked. "Perhaps this war is an excuse to retrieve all the information she can about everyone."

"You overestimate her. She is a child with a powerful sword," Sian said. "She may be able to lift it but she cannot wield it." Mephibosheth ceased his pacing and stared at Sian who ignored him. "She's more likely to stab her own foot." Sian looked briefly at Tunnaig as the other's attentions rested on him. "Besides, why wonder what she has planned when her shadow is right here? Foolish of her to tell everything to someone who is trying to become one of us."

Everyone turned to Tunnaig. He opened his mouth to speak although he hadn't decided on the words to say. He had a choice to make and considering what little information he had they would most likely torture him in disbelief. They stood silently and watched him. Sian smiled at him from the back of the group.

"Stop your bickering," Gellia said as she charged through the doors. The mages parted for her as she made her way to the desk. She didn't sit down. "Do you have anything to say to me?" They all looked at her silently. *Sian, I need more information.* She hoped he would tell her more of what they were discussing before she entered. Tunnaig could barely cover his look of terror as he cowered behind her.

How wise, Sian replied.

"I will give you a warning," Mephibosheth said, "for perhaps you don't understand—don't think you can treat his place as a toy, it will not be tolerated."

Gellia noticed some tense looks Mephibosheth and Sian exchanged. "Why the concern? I don't plan on letting you take any of the blame for my decisions."

Sian chuckled into her head. *I'll see what else I can find out.*

"If there's nothing else, we best be off," Gellia said. The mages left the room, and Gellia tucked the intercepted letter into the top drawer of the desk before she too went into the hall. She was curious when she found Mephibosheth and Sian remained outside the office having a conversation.

"...the baron was a child once, as well," Mephibosheth said, but stopped when he saw her.

The two mages exchanged glances; the white haired mage gave a look to Sian that surely would have killed someone of lesser strength. They moved away in opposite directions. Something began to dawn on Gellia. Cassius said that all the mages desired power above all else. Mephibosheth was the most powerful of the court mages, certainly because of title, perhaps because of magic. What was Sian's position?

The throne room was abuzz from the newest rumor, but no one could confirm exactly what was going on. Probably because they couldn't believe it. Gellia did hear whispers of her complete incompetence. Whoever came to speak to her sensed the tension as well, and many were distracted by the unrest. Early on she spotted the noble she saw in the library. He watched her closely. She tried to ignore him so he wouldn't catch on and bolt.

Shortly after they started, a seeker came to her with a message: a bird was sent from Tintagel. The seekers wondered if she wished them to keep the bird or to let it go—it bore the seal of a certain noble. She told them to let it go. There was already one message that wouldn't get through to the Lorkiegns. They needed to think their plans would work if she was going to catch them. If they thought her incompetent then...

Sian captured her attention. He was moving through the crowd towards the noble in question. Mephibosheth watched him as well. She looked away and tried to only see things out of the corner of her eye. The white haired mage didn't need to know of the alliance between she and Sian. And it was shaky at best. It occurred to her perhaps she should just gather evidence and use it against this traitor, but not accuse anyone until Cassius' return. If she were to let it out about this noble she wasn't sure what else would come of it.

The people who stood before her wondered if she would protect their village from marauders that attacked a town near them. Gellia smiled. "Shortly," she told them.

Sian tapped on her mind barrier and let her listen to his conversation at the edge of the throng. "I understand you're a man of many ambitions," Sian said.

"Aren't we all?" He asked.

"Ah, yes, that is why I speak to you, Lord Idris. I am ambitious and need your assistance. I know you travel far and wide and know many people whom take in such people as myself."

Lord Idris didn't take his eyes off Gellia. "You're a mage in the court of Tintagel. Those who are under his power aren't always welcome elsewhere."

"Under his power? Hardly, and I tire of my position. I realize my potential now; it is far too great to waste in this place. I, sir, am a weather manipulator amongst others talents, and an asset to any court or army. I would be of great use to anyone trying to say, wage a war with someone else. Think of how much I could slow down other armies or create floods or cyclones..."

Idris was silent for a time and Sian was patient for a while then spoke again. "And *he's* not here, is he? The girl sits in his place, a child of disputable heritage who has many years to reach her half-century. Hundreds of betrayals could occur while she sits there, and she would never know the difference. If your question is loyalties, just look at her and think of us."

Gellia forced herself not to look nervous as Sian spoke. She could do this. She would win, she kept telling herself. This was how it worked, she realized. This was how it happened for her liege. A mage was working for her like he did for their liege.

Idris pursed his lips and smiled a little. "It might be suitable for you, they could use someone of your talents at court, or so I've heard. Meet with me later tonight in the library." Idris moved away, Sian looked up at her.

It's amazing, isn't it? Sian asked.

What exactly do you mean? Gellia replied.

How arrogant he is. Anyone with half a mind knows the penalty for betrayal, although one could say a lack of intelligence is also at fault here.

Gellia waited for the person before her to leave then rose and strode from the room. *I have to get out of here, Amarynth. I must go with the armies and leave this place. Open war seems far easier than dealing with all these people.*

Amarynth spoke, a soft rumble in her mind. *You're tired, that is all. Sleep and you will feel better.* She had the distinct impression Amarynth was against war, it struck her as extremely odd.

Tunnaig spoke as he strode beside her. "I don't know what you're up to, but I can't help you if I don't know."

"Perhaps if you know you'll be more of an obstacle to me than you are an asset," she said. "I will do what I feel I must." It was true. No matter what they said she had no choice but to attack Candiem, it was apparent now, especially when there was no sign of their baron returning. Whatever he was doing in Ravengate couldn't be disturbed. She couldn't manipulate her way through this whole thing, she didn't know enough of the people involved or have the right connections, but she couldn't stand by and watch them destroy her people.

Later that night after some rest, Gellia watched her servants pack her for travel. Even later than that, a seeker came bearing papers Sian collected from Idris. They were contracts to a secret alliance with the Lorkiegns and the underlings of Tintagel. It was plain that they wished to take Tintagel from within while destroying its lands. If its territories were in shambles there could be little organization, just desperation. But what Gellia felt was desperation created heroes. Gellia took a moment to scurry to the office, and place the newest documents in the desk drawer. She sealed it magically. Sian didn't seem to think there would be any consequences for not returning them to Idris, that or he knew he could handle them himself. There is so much to do, she thought, and scarcely enough time to breathe.

***

"Dear me," the emperor said.

Cassius silently laid another card on the once beautiful table. He could only imagine the origins of the stains that marred it, and he certainly wouldn't use his magic to find out.

"My cousin, this message tells me that one of your armies is moving."

Cassius didn't look up from the card game and ignored the squealing pig that ran past them. "Really? How droll."

The emperor shook his head. "Don't tell me you're doing this just for my entertainment."

"Of course, dear cousin," Cassius said, and waved his hand. "Everything I do is for your entertainment."

"The one near Demf, that's one of your unproven armies, yes?"

"Yes, that's right... Oh look you've won again."

"Well, I guess I have." The gaudily dressed emperor leaned over the card table. "Well, that's that... I can't wait to see this spectacular display of power, Cassius. I really can't. Although then again, I may be busy that day."

"How disappointing."

"Yes, well, I might be taking Cambiga that day."

"How lovely." Cassius shuffled the cards. "Planning on cultivating the land, are we?"

"I know they don't have anything worth taking but it gives me something to do, and maybe there'll be some pretty girls to be had." Emperor Raven's mouth curled into a thin smile. "I'm sick of all mine."

"Even Xzelleminiya?" Cassius asked, still not looking up from the cards.

"Who?"

"Your consort. You call her 'Mina'."

"Well, I never really tire of her. She *is* the most beautiful woman in the realm... Will someone get that swine out of my courtyard?!" The emperor's voice changed from its normal tone to a shriek as the hog ran past them for the third or fourth time with the young swineherd chasing after it. As the boy ran past yet again, the emperor lunged and gutted the child with a jeweled dagger after which he struck the pig down with a pillar of flame. It would have killed any plants around it but the courtyard was already a barren waste. "Hungry?" he asked Cassius.

"No, thank you," Cassius said. "I just had some exquisite flambé alligator from the moat that should keep me for a while."

Raven sat down again and sighed. "I've had little patience since that whole situation with that crazy sorceress woman."

"Really?" Cassius looked up from his cards. "You've always been so patient; it's quite difficult to believe."

"Oh yes, it seems that I got her a child and now she's swearing I stole it. I told her it wasn't bloody likely since I already have enough children after my head, but she doesn't listen. She told me he would come here to kill me."

"I certainly doubt that. It would take a very skilled seeker to infiltrate and defeat you, dear cousin, and I assure you the graduates Kegero has been producing are lacking. Hopefully with recent improvements that will change."

Raven looked at Cassius with his usual dull expression, the one he often made when trying to understand.

Cassius refrained from rolling his eyes. "I suppose you had to kill her?"

"Oh yes, after a good-bye tumble."

"Of course."

A servant placed wine in front of them both. Cassius just looked at his.

Emperor Raven continued, "so tell me about this adventure your army is about to go on."

"Oh, I just thought I should turn them loose on the countryside as you do, it works so well for you I thought I might try such a brilliant plan."

Raven was tickled with his own form of joy. "Doesn't it feel wonderful having the masses shrieking before you? Laying waste to everything in sight? Save the pretty young things for me, eh?"

"Of course, of course. But for that reason I must depart sooner than expected."

"I understand." Raven smiled. "You should find a girl for yourself, you know. I liked that Vellura woman, or even that other woman, what was her name? I don't know how you remember all their names."

Cassius smiled. "Certainly after you've showered so many with your attentions…"

As if hailed, Mina, Raven's consort, passed through. She'd always been a beauty. Her hair was nearly floor length and it was braided and arranged, every hair chain and jeweled pin perfectly placed. Her gown was the appropriate style for the time of day, and was expertly fitted and sewn. Living in this place, she must have miracles available to pull off such refinement. "Good day, majesty," Cassius greeted.

Mina gave him a smile. "Only you could make such a title sound vile."

He returned a smile as bright as the summer sun. "Ah, but that responsibility lies with someone else, and your strange sensibilities." He kept an eye on Raven who gave himself a headache from thinking so much about his next play. "Your majesty must be quite skilled at curing diseases now, I suspect?"

She shook her head and sighed a little. "I still haven't been able to cure the biggest disease Xzepheniixenze has ever seen."

He cocked his head. "Apparently not. But as I've told you before, you should aid me in doing so for I do believe I have a better chance at it." He recognized her fantastic restraint as she fumed. "You know, Xzelleminiya, it wasn't that long ago I was bird watching and you wouldn't believe what I saw."

"I can only imagine."

"A curious chick. What he was I do not know, at first I thought perhaps he will become a swan, or a bird of a more fiery nature, but then I decided a dodo or cuckoo might be closer to his mature state for he lacked the grace of a swan and the supremacy of the latter."

Raven was confused and angry. "Will you two stop talking about healing magic and bird watching? Mina, we have more important things to do besides listen to you," the emperor growled. "Healers."

Mina curtsied and turned on her heel. Cassius spoke. "A pleasure as always, your majesty."

Once Mina was gone from sight Raven spoke again. "So let me tell you about this new plot I have..."

***

"We're making better time than the Lorkeign army," Dallen said.

"Good," Gellia replied. Amarynth easily kept the lead of the group, the others struggled to keep up despite also being bond horses.

"We should be on the outskirts of Alasdaira within a day at this pace," Dallen continued.

"I don't think I've been on an outing in decades," Vellura said. The courtesan had invited herself along. When Gellia asked her how the "armor" she wore was supposed to protect her, Vellura laughed and told her she didn't plan to fight, just to watch. It was probably just an excuse to show flesh.

"The Lorkiegns will ignore us if the seekers have done their jobs," Dallen told them.

"I don't doubt anyone who his lordship hired," Gellia called. "Do you?" She didn't. Since she mentioned Idris to one of the seekers they all were happy to tell her his every move, joining her gallop briefly to give her news or Idris' growing boldness as he tried to gain more loyalty in Tintagel. Sian seemed to be the only one interested out of the mages, and Gellia knew that to be a sham.

Dallen smiled. "No."

What *would* Cassius say when he found out about this? But it was no time to be indecisive. She listened to how the horses' breathing matched the rhythm of their galloping. One of them sounded ragged. "How are your horses holding up?" she asked.

"I don't know if mine can keep it up," Vellura said.

"You may have to go on by yourself," Dallen told her. "We can always catch up."

By herself? *I know exactly where the army is*, Amarynth told her. *I also know a short cut and these people won't be able to keep up.*

"I'm going ahead," Gellia said. "I'll meet you there." Amarynth jolted under her in another burst of speed.

"I hope she knows what she's doing," Vellura said.

"Listen to you, all concerned," Dallen snorted.

"I don't want to be taken down with her when he comes back as well as I would like to be a recipient of the reward when she makes this work."

"Where *did* she come from?"

"Haven't the slightest. He tells me what to do, not about what he's doing," Vellura said.

Dallen rolled his eyes. "I guess it's the old rule, the fewer who know what's going on the better."

"Yes, and I see you haven't volunteered the information about the armies moving in Zephronia, either," Vellura said.

He shook his head. "She's not the baron. I wouldn't want her launching an attack like that, not on my watch. No matter who wins in this conflict it is nothing but a tavern brawl compared to a war with Zephronia."

Vellura laughed. "And she might have too much on her plate as it is."

***

"General! General! A rider approaches!"

The general strode from his new tent, and the soldiers practicing stopped to see who it was. They were expecting someone from Tintagel, one their seeker told them was 'directly under the baron' in rank, whatever that meant. "Lieutenant! Our envoy is arriving!" he called.

The lieutenant cantered his mare to the general while she whinnied a greeting to the incoming envoy.

…What Gellia first saw through the mist was a massive, bright chestnut horse with a knight, and next to them a rather large man. Would they listen to her? Amarynth slid to a stop near them and nickered to the other horse. Its rider was about Gellia's age, and *quite* handsome. "I'm Gellia," she said, "from Tintagel." A herald would serve her well, she realized after introducing herself so plainly. She slid from Amarynth's back and tried not to show how much her legs shook from the ride.

"Then we have matters to discuss, milady," the general said. "I'm General Telvyc and this is my right arm, we call him Griffin." He chuckled at some private joke. This man reminded

Gellia of an ox. However he seemed quite friendly, especially for one with Xzepheniixenze blood.

Griffin smiled at her and saluted.

She nodded. "Wonderful, well, shall we talk?" They led her to the general's pavilion in the center of camp. It was strange to see weathered tents, weaponry all around, and many rough men amidst such a stunning landscape—but somehow they fit into it as well. There was nothing ugly to be seen in Xzepheniixenze, only to be heard or felt. Some of the men watched her as she passed, some followed, many stared.

After some discussion of her desires, the general revealed what his army's role would be to bring the fruition. He respected her intelligence, but kept his explanation simple and without military jargon. Gellia began to understand the man she had read about. She smiled. "I know you will do your best to accomplish this and I am sure you are every bit as talented as I've heard."

"Thank you, milady. The men are anxious to prove their worth," the general told her. "If there is nothing else I have to check on a few things, excuse me milady."

Gellia nodded and the old general left her and Griffin alone in the tent. He sat across from her, polished an elegant two-handed sword. "That's a fine sword you have," she said.

"It is indeed. Do you know how to use one?" He smiled at her, a genuine smile.

There was something about him that drew her in. "Well, a longsword, yes. Not as well as most, I'm sure."

"I have a longsword as well, I usually carry it around with me and this stays with my horse, but one must keep a blade in good condition, especially with battle near."

There was something a little odd about his look. His hair was black, and he was very handsome as most Xzepheniixenze, but... "You have very nice eyes, Griffin, are you a half breed?" Gellia said, noticing they were amber, not violet.

Griffin frowned and polished the sword more vigorously. "I suppose I am."

Gellia smiled. "So am I." Her powers nearly reached out on their own to find him, and found the walls surrounding his mind were woven so perfectly, so meticulously, there wasn't a chance of her taking a look. But it was not of his doing. It was his bond horse, a truly ingenious animal. She backed away from his mind and even apologized to his mare, who she felt smile at her.

"Then we two half breeds should stick together. We certainly don't have anyone else we can trust," he said.

"I'd like that." There was something genuine about him. A trait that seemed to be rare in Xzepheniixenze. This was a man of honor, she was sure of it.

"That's very nice armor you have. It's rare you see scale mail so beautifully done."

Gellia smiled. "Hand-me-down. My sword as well. Would you like to see it?"

They discussed swords and horses—their two horses were very different in personality but both brilliant. In time they laughed and seemed to have a rapport. She might have even had a pleasant flush to her face for the first time in a long time.

***

"None of my people are mages, they're all warriors and a few healers," Telvyc said. "Did you bring any mages with you?"

Dallen sighed. What *was* their mysterious lady planning? "No," he quickly added, "his lordship left our lady in charge so we must believe that he knew what he was doing."

Telvyc frowned. "What a mess. I wouldn't have moved if I'd known she was so green. Too late to turn back now, I suppose, and ours is not to question why. His taste in mistresses has changed, but I suppose every man needs a change now and then. What think you of she-who-is-directly-under-the-baron, lieutenant?" He ignored Vellura's laugh.

Griffin chuckled. "I think we should give her a chance," the young man said. "I think she'll surprise us." Furthermore, his mare liked her and agreed with him, and she'd never steered him wrong before.

"You let a boy advise you?" Vellura asked. "And she is *not* his mistress. Of that I can assure you."

Telvyc scowled. "I'll thank you for not undermining my authority before my men. He's like a son to me, not to mention a natural at this sort of thing. He's quite gifted."

Vellura shrugged, eyed Griffin. Gellia walked through the flaps of the great pavilion and the group of them went to the table where a map was laid out. There was extensive discussion on how the battle would play out.

"What about Ziyad?" Telvyc persisted. "I don't want my men dead before they even have the chance to cross swords with the enemy. I hope you brought a comparable mage with you."

Gellia spoke. "He's in the castle from what I hear, but would a mage come out for the puny army that's beating on their door right now? Not if he's worth anything." She would be in a real mage fight. Hopefully Cassius hadn't lied to her about her half-trained power. Her stomach flip-flopped and she took another sip of ale. It tasted horrible.

Telvyc had to admit what truly surprised him was how— over time—he started to feel at ease with this woman. She was not just someone's mistress. Someone of her quality would be wasted as a courtesan. Perhaps she didn't understand all the finer details of war, but she seemed to follow what he explained and didn't usurp his command. He also reminded himself the baron left her in charge for a reason. He liked to think it was because she was qualified and that he wouldn't lose hundreds of men. Nevertheless, there was little more to be done about it. "Well, let's get ready for tomorrow. Come lieutenant," Telvyc said, rising.

"I hope you know what you're doing, Lady Gellia," Vellura said for Dallen. She knew he was too respectful to say it to a superior but Vellura had no such qualms.

"Go find some employment, Vellura," Gellia said. She knew she could say nothing to make them to believe her, but she felt in her heart that this was the correct course of action. It felt right, like someone unseen was telling her to go ahead— someone far wiser than she. She had to trust in herself. She thought of the mountains, and who she met in the dream.

7

"They're on their way, milady," Dallen said as he rode to Gellia through the early morning haze. "They're moving quickly—most have bond horses." His horse gnawed on his bit and ground his teeth as they waited.

"How much time?" Gellia asked and shifted in her saddle. She was still stiff from sleeping so many nights on a cot in a tent. She could feel the battle in the air—she wondered if it was how Cassius did when Fuarmaania was under attack. It seemed so quiet.

"Not long, as you suspected," Dallen told her. Who was this woman? "You still won't tell me who you are." She seemed to have the uncanny knowledge of terrain and distance.

"I'm no one of consequence." it pleased Gellia that she could be a mystery.

He smiled and shook his head. They would all have to wait to see her final plan.

The sound of the army excited Gellia more than she ever imagined. Jingling tack, the thump of hooves, the rattle of armor, and the murmur of so many voices. All the horses seemed to feel the tension building in the air as they were armored and tacked. Some of the soldiers were nervous, others energized. How was it she came to this day? Never would she have thought she would be here, now, leading a great army and testing her mystical strength. One person apparently knew. He knew all along she had this in her.

***

"I don't sense any mages yet," Vellura said. "Ziyad likes a showy entrance." The courtesan seemed excited and amused. She'd dressed with flare and her barely there armor and was quite striking. Luckily the soldiers were focused enough to ignore her. Telvyc had questioned her, of course, and her reply was thus: "It matters little to me who fills my bed and lines my pocket. If you all die, there are plenty here who will oblige me."

Gellia would remain uneasy until the mage appeared. She tried to be reassured by the pendant under her armor—it would be the first time she used it in earnest, and already it warmed against her skin. In the distance they could see the city, the castle with its twin spires, and their other army at the gate, and the Lorkiegn reinforcements swiftly approached from the north. She continued to assure herself she made the right choice. Tunnaig said little of his misgivings, but she knew how upset he was. Perhaps he was there to get himself killed. "A few more minutes," Gellia said.

Gellia and her retainers rode around the final strip of forest before seeing the enemy army setting into their allies. They were close enough to count horse legs. "This is it." Gellia whispered, trying to keep her composure. There were so many people. Telvyc shouted commands.

The air was filled with arrows from both sides as the Tintagel archers took down people on the walls. Soldiers poured hot oil over the wall, ballista bolts flew, trebuchet hurled boulders, stones scattered over the fighting. Lesser mages cast their magic.

"We're getting closer," Gellia told them and moved Amarynth on. The smell of blood was strong, almost overpowering. Gellia focused on keeping her breath steady, her mind focused.

Tunnaig was uneasy. "I have a bad feeling about this. We'll be lucky if they kill us, if his lordship gets a hold of us after this it'll never end."

Gellia didn't reply.

It was indeed a fiercer battle than she saw at the old castle, but she was impressed with her own calm. She couldn't worry about Cassius' reaction, it was no time to think about that. If it angered him she would take full responsibility and make it clear the others were only obeying orders. Deep down she knew he would be pleased. It was only the others who thought he'd be angry. ...Although she'd been wrong about him before...

"There he is." Vellura said. "Up on the wall. A handsome fellow, indeed."

Gellia jumped in her saddle as a wave of fire blasted through the battle, clearing a wide path through the men and horses. Her nose burned with the smell of scorched flesh. A man stood on the city wall and shouted a threat.

"He's as talented as I'd heard," Vellura said as she leered.

"Now what?" Tunnaig spat at Gellia, who turned to look at him. "Don't think I'll stay for the end," he said.

Gellia could feel Ziyad drawing energy. She closed her eyes. In her reading it was a common thought that if you awed them, the battle was half won. This was it, a test of her magic. Now, before there were more casualties felled by Ziyad. Now, she'd built enough courage and before she lost her nerve. The noise around her seemed to die away.

The power coursed through her as Gellia drew it around her in a volume she had never attempted before. The pendant warmed even more against her skin. Winds blew, around them, the sky darkened. She found her voice. "You were foolish to attack my people," she called.

There was only she and Ziyad. He saw her mystically, and she felt that for a split second they stared at each other. Then she lashed out with her power.

Her magic destroyed his barrier before he was done building it. Stone and dust filled the air. There were screams. The gate and much of the wall no longer stood. Any mage or seasoned knight undoubtedly could tell of her unfinished training. Her attack was sloppy and wild, and definitely overkill for one mage, however, they could also fathom the extent of her power. Ziyad could have never expected such an attack and paid with his life. Both armies were stunned.

Perhaps it was the excitement of the moment or the victory she felt in her heart, but Gellia was anxious to make another move. Without a look at her companions, Gellia and Amarynth lunged through the path created by the fear of her magic. Amarynth navigated through the dead and dying with astounding grace. Gellia finished some with her sword, others with bolts of her magic that crackled like lightning. And no, she had no idea what she was really doing, other than moving forward.

Her army climbed over the rubble that had been the wall. The air still pulsed with residual magic. Amarynth bounded over the rocks until they reached a clear road. She remembered her teacher's words. Show them what you can do, then show them a glamour to chase away those shaken. Gellia wove her energies into a visual form, crackling streams of light; brought the winds to flutter her cloak and ruffle her hair. Indeed many ran. Gellia was starting to enjoy this.

A few braver people charged her; these she promptly struck down, hitting them with magically moved chunks of debris. Amarynth spoke, *Ally approaches, behind.*

It was Griffin. "We stick together, remember?" he said as he caught up. "To the castle?" He was covered in blood, streaks of it across his face, but his eyes were bright.

She smiled. "To the castle." She started to feel comfort in her magic as well as an intense rush. She was far more powerful than she imagined and she knew there was more. Oh what she would have done to Old King Hugh, and to her slimy near-husband. Cassius had been right.

"You're just going to walk right up to the castle door?"

She raised her head to look at their goal. "Why, do you have a better plan?"

He shook his head and smiled, his horse danced under him. She noticed the two-hander still hung from his saddle, longsword was in his hand.

"Let's go then."

Amarynth and the mare thundered forward, their hoof beats echoed on the cobblestones of the empty streets. With such horses much of the city was quickly behind them, Griffin's mare was the first able to keep up with Amarynth. They left their army behind. As they neared the castle they were charged by an increasing number of soldiers. Gellia started to sweep them away with her magic; Griffin cut them down with his sword. "Where do you think is a likely place for a lord to hide?" she asked him. While her army proved its superiority over the enemy, she would do the same to the lord behind it all. The high from her magic was still coursing through her veins.

"The throne room waiting to hear of his victory?" He cut through several more soldiers.

"So we're going to join them at court?"

"It sounds like fun, doesn't it? It will catch him before he's able to flee."

Gellia laughed. "You're as reckless as I am."

"I'm not the one who's decided to take the castle by myself. But a little recklessness can get you places. This will certainly be a surprise for them."

"Very well then. There's the door." Gellia rode to the stairs onto the top step before she slid from Amarynth's back. "And there's the castle guard."

"Right." Griffin leapt from his horse and took up his two-hander.

"I can just—"

He didn't wait for her to continue. With just a few flashes of steel he'd obliterated four men. It was the first time she'd really watched him.

"Well," Gellia exclaimed. There was something almost primal about him, as if he were a tiger. His reflexes, his speed were astounding. And he used all his sword, blade, pommel, whatever was handy.

Griffin bounded over the dead bodies and smiled at her. "Shall we, milady?"

Gellia gathered the energies again and projected them at the great wooden door, smashing it to splinters before wondering what could be on the other side. Luckily for them when the dust cleared only startled guards stood before them, and they were already injured from the blast. Head held high, Gellia marched through the door and promptly used her magic to crush them. The cracking echoed through the long corridor. "I should have asked them where the throne room is," Gellia said.

"Hind sight is perfect?" Griffin said. "There'll be more. Let's keep alert, hmm? You're too beautiful to get killed."

"Aren't you the poet? You don't have to come with me."

"Who's going to watch your back?"

"True," Gellia said. "Let's make this as quick as possible while we still have the advantage." They marched down the corridors searching for what might be the right place, easily cut down enemies. Although as time passed, there would be swarms of soldiers, they needed to act quickly or be proven fools. Or dead.

After slaying many more men, they finally came to another door that might be the door to the throne room. It was as large as the first, but much more ornate with gold leaves pressed into the wood, a gold griffin in the center. "What do you think?" Gellia asked.

"It looks good to me." Griffin said. "There are definitely people talking in there, maybe ten, maybe more."

They heard shouts down the corridor. "Well it's now or never," Gellia said. They pushed the door open. "Well, you were right about what room it is," Gellia said and took a deep breath. Who could only be a lord was there. And more people than expected.

"I guess I was wrong," Griffin said, holding out his sword.

Gellia snorted. "A little."

"Who are you?" The Lord Lorkiegn. He was a purebred, there was no doubt about that—and he wasn't going to give up easily. From physical appearance he was not of the same caliber as her liege, not even close.

She drew herself up, sword still in hand. "If you surrender now we will spare your lives." She knew he fancied himself a king, but he certainly wasn't that.

"How comical. Two children. Kill them both," the lord said.

As guards ran towards them, Griffin leapt into action. Lord Lorkiegn was making his way to his seat—perhaps to watch the amusing battle in his court. Gellia felt for any magic in the room—there was none other than she. Her magic swept around the lord, lifted him into the air. He yelped to his men.

"Drop your weapons," Gellia said, "or he dies."

Griffin shoved an attacker away. Swords clanged against the floor and echoed through the room, Gellia moved towards the hanging lord. "You must surrender."

"Who are you, cretin?" the lord spat.

An anger, a power, she had never quite known was there welled up within her and Gellia used that power to speak. "You need to look out your window to the banner we carry. Did you think there would be no repercussions for attacking my people?" The pressure around his body increased, a few bones made crunching noises.

She heard a noise. A bow being drawn.

Griffin shoved her and the two of them fell to the ground.

From her back with the young warrior on top of her Gellia could see the archer on the stairs and magically ended his life quicker than another arrow was knocked.

Griffin choked on a laugh as he propped himself up on one arm. "One more thing to do," he said and rolled over, taking her with him. His muscles tensed and flexed under her. She had no idea what he was doing, but kept her head low.

The tension in his arm changed and his body shifted. The lord collapsed next to them, the two-hander through his chest. "That worked better than I expected," Griffin said. "All that practice paid off."

She let out her breath and rested her forehead on her compatriot's breastplate. Her hand found something damp and warm on his armor. "You're wounded!"

"It isn't the first time, it won't be the last," he said.

In anger, Gellia summoned her magic to swirl through the castle; it shook the structure to its foundations. They heard glass shatter, the people around ran away. It was her hope that her taking the chance here would end the battle quickly, save the lives of her men. But Griffin...

The arrow that was meant for her had hit Griffin. "My word," she said and pulled at his chain mail and the buckles that held it in place. When she looked up Gellia saw their men running into the room, securing the castle. "This is too serious," she said. "I don't trust my ability to fix this..." She looked up and called for a healer.

Griffin chuckled. "I'm not..."

She leaned over him. "Don't worry about that right now. Let's get you healed. I'm not going to let you die after saving my life... and you're quite becoming yourself."

"Ah, a complement from a royal. My luck has changed."
She smiled. "Maybe not at lucky as you think."

"My luck can't be any worse, but it has nothing to do with you."

***

Dallen had just given the numbers of dead and wounded. They'd lost Telvyc, but the numbers of dead were acceptable.

The army would remain there, cleaning up and keeping things orderly. It was against Tintagel policy to pillage a conquered land, so the residents were safe and free to go about their business. It was weeks before everything was sorted out enough where Gellia felt she could leave. The only thing she didn't do was assign a noble to the city. That she'd leave up to Cassius. For the time being the military would keep an eye on things.

Tunnaig laughed. "Why wait? You've done so much on your own already. We're all going to die when we get back, especially with you always calling them your people."

"Will you stop?" Gellia was tired of his complaints. "I thought it went rather well."

"I have to agree," Dallen said, eyeing Tunnaig. "...All things considered."

Gellia collected her thoughts. "We should pack and head back to Tintagel." She shuffled some paperwork on the table before her. Dallen sat there and looked at her. "How is Sir Griffin doing?" she asked.

"He'll be fine. He's a brilliant young knight... Telvyc is a sad loss."

"He was a commendable leader from what I could tell," she said. Dallen nodded.

"Yes. To have an army like that and take Candiem..."

There was silence between them while Dallen watched Gellia read paperwork.

"So we know now you're undeniably a mage," Dallen said. "But we know nothing else. I certainly don't have enough money to buy secrets from the mages."

"I'll tell you only if you promise not to tell anyone else," she knew it probably wouldn't stay a secret.

He chuckled. "You have my word of honor."

"My father is Decius Iolair." Someone she'd never seen in person or portrait, nor met.

"That goat doesn't have any children... and he's not a mystical person."

"He does—me. And my magic comes from my mother's side."

"Wait a moment, I think I've heard about this. You're the one he went after in the Outlands... but you're too clever and beautiful to be half human. This doesn't make any sense." He shook his head.

"You flatter me." Gellia smiled. She had never really looked at him before, her mind being otherwise occupied. Dallen was handsome as any Xzepheniixenze with the well-defined features and the over-all striking appearance. But what was it that he wanted? What else did he want from her, was there something to gain from such flattery? An object? A tryst? She *was* attracted to him (maybe it was the manners). It had been lonely. Not like she was in Fuarmaania—different. Now Gellia had plenty of people to talk to and many willing to be her friends even if for the wrong reasons. Tintagel was a lonely place and she wondered if Cassius ever felt the same. *Cassius.*

"Where did you go?"

"What?"

"Where did you go just then?" Dallen asked.

Gellia shook her head. She had to remember to keep up her guard. Xzepheniixenze always looked for an opportunity and she was lucky Dallen was on her side. It might have been different with Sian or one of the other mages.

"I have to say that I'm impressed," he said and leaned back in his chair. "Most youngsters in command go in and try to become field commanders but not you, you let your general do his job and left your ego out of it. I thought it was a bit rash of you to charge the castle by yourself but I quickly realized that you are far more powerful than anyone suspected... I wonder how it is that your human mother gave you magic."

She smiled. "I wonder that myself. You'd have to ask the baron because I'm sure he's the only one who knows."

"Well, you're quite the woman," Dallen said. "If you're ever bored, you know where to find me. I would be happy to assist you in any endeavor."

It took Gellia several days to come to the proper realization of what he said.

***

The echo of her victory quickly spread across the region, but even though Gellia had the respect of farmers, merchants, and many knights, the courtiers of Tintagel did not seem as impressed. Certainly not the court mages who sneered at her and told her of her impending doom. She did her best to ignore them. Holding her head high she went about sorting through the mountains of gifts that accumulated in her absence.

She was sitting in the office when the mages filed in, looked as smug as ever. "Yes?" she asked.

"You *are* a mage," Mephibosheth said. "A gifted one at that." He knew it before, so she wasn't sure why he said it.

"So I am," Gellia answered. "I know it's been bothering you."

"You shouldn't be so impertinent," Una said.

"Perhaps you should listen to your own advice," Gellia told her.

"I say whatever I want to a corpse," Una replied.

Meliot spoke. "Now, now, let's not jump to conclusions. He might let her live for a while."

Gellia glared up at them. "Those are quite the statements from people whose life expectancies are less than a year. It's obvious the only use for you *is* to siphon energy. Why don't you go enjoy the short time you have remaining?"

Sian smiled and mind spoke to her. *Idris doesn't think you know about him. Since his alliance turned out to be useless he has decided to stay here and continue on with his life.*

Gellia gave him a mental nod. *We'll see what his lordship wants done with him...when the baron returns you and I have to set dates to practice.*

The mages left. Each eyed her as they walked out the door. Mephibosheth remained a few moments longer, searched her, and he didn't care that she knew it. She rose to her feet and looked at him. "Is there something I can help you with?" she asked.

He shook his head, his white braids swung gently across his shoulders. "I know now, your magic is unmistakable. Who am I to question Zapheny?" He turned and left, softly closed the door behind him.

She sat back down and buried her head in her hands. Was there nothing she could do to gain their respect? If only to keep them from stepping on her would be enough. What about Mephibosheth? What was this last exchange all about?

How long had their lord been gone now? Six months? More? Time was a blur. Gellia wasn't even sure how old she was; the seasons were different here. It always seemed like spring or summer.

…Gellia dragged herself to bed and looked forward to its familiarity. It was dusk; it wasn't too out of the ordinary for one to sleep. After all, it had been difficult sleeping in tents with all sorts of bawdy racket and carnal noises coming from all around. Tintagel was so peaceful. Sleep was good. The servants slipped her out of layers of waking clothes and into a nightgown. The feather mattress was so wonderful and the blankets so cozy. "Let some fresh air in, will you?" Gellia asked from her burrow.

After the servants retired she watched the night through the glass doors, listened to her wind chime. The stars were out by the thousand, pinning up the blanket of the night. She thought she heard waves against the base of the castle…

"Milady, milady,"
"Hhmphf,"
"Milady must rise."
Gellia rolled over. "I don' want."
"Milady—"
"Is it morning yet?" Gellia asked. "It's still dark out."
"It's very late, milady. Here's ladyship's robe, hurry, milady" The woman helped Gellia shrug on the satin robe and tie the belt. Gellia ignored the servant with her slippers.

"Are we under attack?" Gellia asked and rubbed her eyes. "I'm too tired to deal with an attack. Who is it, the Grians? Their young mistress is angry with the baron for some reason...Let them beat on the walls from their boats. I'll destroy them in the morning."

"No milady, come with me please."

"Oh for pity's sake," Gellia followed the maid through the corridors, too asleep to care she was in her nightclothes. For all she knew the purple robe dragging behind her was the train of a dress. "Where are we going?" The stone of the floors were cool under her bare feet.

"Follow me milady, hurry."

Only when she saw the dozen looming court mages did Gellia wake completely. What were they up to? A rebellion? They smiled at her as she followed her servant between them. The woman guided her through a door, but Gellia still watched them until the servant closed the door between them. *Where* was she? Gellia turned around expecting to see some ogre or something but instead she saw a dragon. It was the office—and at the other end was Cassius with his back to her.

Gellia shivered, but then stood tall, unafraid. He just stood there, the moonlight cascading over him, his hands behind his back as he looked at the moon. A few candles were lit on the walls. She couldn't tell if he was angry or not, he seemed so serene. She didn't realize how much she missed him. She held her breath and waited for eons for whatever fate he would bestow upon her. When he took a breath to speak she tried not to cringe.

"You took it upon yourself to attack the Lorkiegns," he rumbled.

"They were..."

He raised a hand. "You moved three armies, one had seen little battle, and attacked an army of seasoned men. Did Tunnaig put you up to this?"

"No."

"Nor Vellura?"

"No."

"And Dallen?"

"No."

"The mages?"

"No. It was my idea," she said with conviction but not pride.

"Really."

Gellia swallowed and waited to be spoken to.

"Did I tell you to move my armies?"

"No," but wouldn't he have done the same as she? She tucked her hands in her sleeves.

"But you did."

"Yes."

"Do you have something to say?"

"I did it for the people."

"To please me even though I didn't give you approval to assault Candiem?"

Gellia braced herself where she stood. She would not back down. "No, not to necessarily please you. They were destroying your villages, turning your people against you since you weren't protecting them…They warned me—Dallen and especially Tunnaig—more so Tunnaig—but I thought it was in the best interests of this establishment…" She watched the back of his head for a moment, and he waited for her to continue. Didn't she hear Dallen say they had to have confidence in Cassius' judgment about who to leave in charge? "…It was your fault, really," she added.

He looked at her over his shoulder. "*My* fault?"

"Well you left me in command. You must have known how I would react in each situation before you set me up in—" She squealed as he appeared directly in front of her from his pillar of green light. "—this place," she finished.

"You're blaming *me* for *your* actions?" he demanded.

"I think you *wanted* me to do what I did. You had to have known I would." Her speech quickened. "You knew that I wouldn't stand by and let the place fall apart. You knew I would have to do it all by myself because no one here would help me, and most would oppose me. You *knew* somehow I'd be the only one to deal with the problem and not tuck my tail and run. No one else in this place would bother, not seeing the big picture, not looking towards what the future may hold. You knew I would see that this situation would escalate unless it was stopped now when it wasn't completely out of control. If left alone it would have been much more of a loss—I wouldn't let them do that to our people. In fact, after what you said when I first came to Xzepheniixenze, I wouldn't be surprised if you used me to flush Candiem out, they would be much bolder with a child like me left in charge. But they didn't bargain that I might be more than just a pretty face. Oh no, that they didn't."

He smirked. "Breathe, princess."

"What?"

"You're turning blue."

Gellia puffed. "What are *you* so happy about?"

"Anything else you need to tell me?"

"Look in your desk, there's evidence of a traitor in Tintagel, Lord Idris conspired with the Lorkiegns... and, and I believe I've made a little name for myself so I'm no longer just your pet. It's a beginning, at least."

He still smiled. "I've seen the papers... you don't know how big a name you made for yourself. Send Una in and wait outside."

Gellia exhaled and left, her energy spent in keeping herself alert in the middle of the night. The door closed behind her. "Una, he wants to see you."

Una tossed her hair and strode inside the room. Gellia made herself comfortable, leaned against the railing of the landing and took a peek over the edge to the hall below.

"What did he say to you?" one of the mages asked. They all loomed around her like great dark trees but for Sian who smiled at her from behind the others.

She smiled. "I think you lot are in worse trouble than I." Gellia realized she must have looked a fright; her hair disheveled, wearing her nightgown, robe, with no slippers. Of course they were all neatly dressed and prepared to look their best for their lord. Dogs, Gellia thought. They were merely his dogs, wearing fancy collars would not make them more forgivable.

"Just because he hasn't killed you yet doesn't mean he won't," Meliot said. "You've learned so little."

Gellia chuckled. "That is what separates you and me. You cannot see past your own arrogance to realize all your inane plots against each other will never win favor with anyone, nor will it advance your stations." They no longer seemed as intimidating as she once thought. "I have confidence in my position here, unlike you mages who live in continuous fear of the baron's disposition." She would have said more but the door opened and Una stumbled out—she looked quite distraught. None of the others rushed to her aid, but stared at her. All of them looked distressed, most likely about their own fates.

Cassius stepped from the office, the mages looked at him. "I expect to see you tomorrow for court," he said. The mages scattered. Gellia chuckled. "Aren't you full of yourself," he said.

She was nearly drunk with sleep deprivation. "You like to see them scramble as much as I do."

He smiled. "...You look a mess. Haven't you been eating? There's something different about you."

"Oh, well I've been so busy and the food where I've been hasn't been wonderful."

"Are you telling me my armies aren't fed well?"

"It's not that, the type of food *they* like *I* find intolerable."

"Well then, spoiled by Tintagel. You can tell me all about it while we gorge ourselves on the best diet anyone can have."

"Right now? It's in the middle of the night. I should be sleeping."

"Are you rejecting my offer?"

Gellia exhaled. "No. Can I dress first?"

"Oh please. You've nothing I haven't seen a thousand times before."

She was too tired to argue. "I'm starved."

***

"...and that's how it all happened. The village in the mountains is still in a bad way though. I didn't know what else to do for them... this food is incredible." Gellia delicately dismantled a roll. "I've spent a lot of your money, but it's all accounted for through the treasurer—he's not at all pleased with me. Some of the seekers whose loyalty we bought were expensive, certainly more expensive than the supplies for the village."

"Yes, I've seen the reports of your spending. Money is insignificant," he said. He looked over a letter and pushed his food around his plate. His attention snapped back to her, though. "There is something vastly different about you."

"After all I've been through…"

"No, not that." He nodded as he thought. "It will come to me in time."

It was very quiet in the grand dining hall for they were the only two there, and probably the first to use it in years. The hall could easily host one hundred, but never did, everyone being too busy to sit—she now understood why. A servant brought in another decanter of wine. It, like the place settings before them, was a work of art. She picked up the crystal goblet and sipped some wine. It was so wonderful. She let herself sink into rapture.

"Where is my steward?" Cassius called down the servants' passage. "Send him in… We'll go to that village and see what can be done."

"I had a strange dream when I was there."

"Oh yes?"

"I dreamed that Connylia spoke to an apparition."

"If you were anyone else I'd think nothing of it."

"I lost time. I didn't remember arriving at the village or the final days of travelling. Everyone else seemed, to, though."

"Did you go through the mountain, or around?"

"Through, I believe. On the way back we took the pass."

"It is a strange place with strange occurrences. Unfortunately none of it has happened to me, but there are many superstitions—I'm sure your peasant friend was thrilled." He smirked. "You needn't worry, we'll use magic to go there." He tossed the letter behind him where another paper appeared with gold writing on it, folded and sealed itself.

She clenched her napkin in her hand, which was still sore from all the writing she did. "You write like *that*?"

"Yes, how do *you* do it?"

"By hand."

"No wonder you were so far behind. No matter. Perhaps some time I'll teach you the trick... Where is that man?"

"Probably with some serving woman. Why do you need him?"

"I have work for him. He and his wenching..." He waved a hand.

"I know. I don't understand that," Gellia said.

"Either do I." Cassius rolled his eyes. "*That* much time spent doing *that* is a waste when he could be taking care of household matters..."

"Maybe he *is* taking care of household matters."

He chuckled. "You *are* a clever one. Did you make an allusion to something naughty and you haven't been burnt to a cinder? I don't see the servants scurrying away giggling."

"If that turned people to cinders you wouldn't have an army left."

This made him laugh. "How dreadful for you to live in a camp."

"I survived." It was the first time she'd heard him laugh with true cheer. She could be addicted to the sound. Cassius looked at her with the expression she was so accustomed to—but she realized it seemed to be an expression he reserved for only her. "How was Ravengate?" she asked.

"I was so bored I calculated my age for you."

"And?"

"I was born in year one thousand seven hundred forty nine of the reign of Razhiede Zapheny, therefore I am one thousand six hundred sixty three."

Gellia choked. "You can't be serious."

"Of course I am. I'm older than many of the trees around here."

"You don't *look* that old."

"Either does Connylia and she is *least* a few more centuries older than I am. And Gallylya is older still."

"Excuse me if my mind has a difficult time grasping the idea." She knew Connylia was quite old, but she never thought to assign a number to her years. A figure for an age no longer seemed important.

"It is difficult for mortals to understand." He said. "Although once they realize that they will witness all the people they knew dying around them, mortals tend to *like* being mortal—or so I've read."

"You've been through that then, I mean, losing your friends."

"All my younger-year associates were immortal. One was killed by Gallylya, one killed by my own hand and the other sits on the throne, and I haven't ever called him ally, certainly not friend."

Gellia nodded and didn't say much more but stared at her plate and took another sip of wine. It was true; immortality must have been difficult to deal with. Over time everything changes, and what if one didn't like the change? What was a day in the life of an immortal like? Does it flash by? Does life get boring?

"...I don't remember many mortals I have known in my life." Cassius said, guessing her thoughts. "Days are the same length for everyone, but the little things in the past can fade away if they weren't significant enough. People like Sir Dallen and Sir Telvyc I will forget soon after their deaths if they don't leave outstanding impressions on me... the same goes for mistresses—and mages. I can tell you the names of people in the last few centuries but beyond that I only remember significant people. But while they're here before me I certainly watch them for any noteworthy movement, and be assured if I need information about some lord or servant from six hundred years ago I can find it out."

"Will you remember *me* after I die?" Gellia asked.

"I don't have a choice."

"What do you mean?"

"You called for me, milord?" The steward, Kiore, entered looking tidy and ready to serve.

"What in the world took you so long? It wasn't Hillina again was it?" Cassius said.

Kiore bowed. "I'm terribly sorry milord, please forgive me."

"At least I don't have to see your face for a while."

"Milord?"

"I'm sending you and two hundred of your servants to Shahyrahara to freshen it up. We're going to have a ball there now that it's finally restored."

"Sha-ha-h, milord?"

"Yes, Shahyrahara. I'll send a guide with you. You leave immediately." Cassius waved at the dumbfounded man.

Kiore hazarded another question. "Where is it?"

"Details. Don't pester me with details."

"Yes milord, I'll leave immediately." The steward bowed several times before backing from the room.

"You're throwing a party?" Gellia asked. "That doesn't seem like something you'd do."

"It isn't." He rose from the table. "Let's be going."

"Where?" Gellia hefted herself from the chair and arranged her robe.

"To your village."

"It's barely dawn."

"I know. What a lovely thing for them to wake up to."

"Will you allow me to dress?"

"No time, and they don't care."

A portal blinked into existence through one of the archways. It was just registering in Gellia's mind what was happening when Cassius took her sleeve and tugged her through the vortex and into the dirt street of the village. "I don't know if I like this way of travel," Gellia said, steadying her head.

"You'll grow accustomed to it. It's very convenient if you have the ability and the strength… Indeed, the magic here is quite unstable. Luckily I'm able to adjust for such situations."

Gellia watched Cassius as he surveyed the village. The sky was still dim, the first light was just arriving over the mountain and no one was out yet. He looked very out of place amongst the browns and greys of the landscape in his rich greens and black, jewels sparkling in the pale light. A dust devil traveled by. Cassius stepped into the road and looked up and down at the houses while Gellia stayed put. Dust started to collect on the back of Cassius' cloak. Why she noticed this Gellia had no idea. A tiny girl tugged at her robe. "Hello," Gellia said.

Someone spoke. "Have you come to save us?" the girl's spindly mother asked as she approached.

Gellia didn't answer, instead looked for Cassius. He wasn't where she saw him last. Gellia walked out onto the main road.

"Is that who you're looking for?" the woman asked, pointing the opposite way. She pulled her children in close to her as they stared up the street. "He's his lordship himself, isn't he? He came all the way here? He..." her voice trailed away as her apparent wonderment took hold of her senses.

Cassius stood over a slumped figure in the gutter. Gellia walked towards him; the child still clung to her robe. She came to stand next to her liege, her clinger scurried away. "They're scared of you," Gellia whispered, "or in awe."

"Wouldn't you be if you were them staring at a spectacular a person as myself? Well, they're lucky I'm here—I don't know who else could repair this mess." He walked towards the center of the village. "Look at this, there is not a hint of equilibrium to be found anywhere; all the land is scarred or devoid of energies..." Gellia tried to look but her inexperience made it difficult for her to decipher mystic anomalies as easily as he could. All she knew was it was a mess. Cassius continued. "...of course nothing can grow in these conditions. If those mages were fighting over land they did a lovely job of making it worthless to either of them. Must have been foolish youngsters to use their magic in such a way..." Gellia could barely hear him as he muttered about it, and then went silent as he was so irritated he couldn't speak. She smiled.

Other villagers were beginning to stir. Many stopped in their doorways to stare at their visitors. Gellia's former hosts appeared. "Who is he?" the woman asked. Gellia didn't answer, just watched him stop in the village square. He was very still, and so became the village too. The little breeze died down to nothing. It was so quiet it unsettled her. Then Gellia could feel the energies rising around them, it gave her a chill. It wasn't the gut wrenching magic of others she'd experienced. No, this magic was soothing and familiar. She felt its workings all around her, in the ground, in the air, all throughout the surrounding lands. It was subtle at first, and grew stronger at a gentle pace just as the sunrise. She could smell the moisture in the air, and the villagers started to point at clouds forming above them. They didn't, however, see the ground already showing signs of dampness as water rose from below. The clouds started to mist and the villagers clamored. Gellia watched her liege. He was still deep in his concentration, his power swept carefully around them.

She approached him with great care, but didn't interrupt, just stood a few paces behind him. The hills surrounding the village started to turn green with new growth, and it came closer to the village until there were sprouts all around. Then she heard him speak. "And for the final touch."

The villagers started shouting about a rainbow. Gellia smiled and looked for it. The villagers' elation was almost catching.

Perhaps that is why she chose to stay with him. Perhaps that is why deep in her heart she knew…

The cavern temple. She remembered what was said to her, what she felt. Her magic responded and rose up around her, she closed her eyes. This was the way to save Xzepheniixenze; she would need Cassius' help. He was her means. She heard a whisper in the back of her mind, she was sure it was Razhiede. But could she ever discuss it with her liege?

The land was at peace, she opened her eyes. "They do like a show," he said to her, startling her with his proximity.

She resisted gushing about everything, but she really wanted to. *So you finally showed me something you can do with your magic,* she mind-spoke.

One of the many, he said, looking rather modest for him. *I've never heard of anyone else with the ability other than my mother's family line. I think some would make it worse, too. You have to make the ground water rise, not just dump rain on them, for the rain would just run off. And you can't put too much water in the ground because then you have landslides. Get the plant life growing and it helps with all of that. A few days of gentle rain and some sun will get them growing well. I've also given the land a bit of a mystical boost to help things move along a touch faster, and I've given the locals some care so they feel better and can get back to work.*

Gellia smiled. His speech was that of a gardener who just finished a landscaping project. Rather humble and matter of fact.

People gathered all around him, asking if they could touch him to see if he was real. One of the knights she left behind finally made an appearance and looked quite shocked when he saw his master and mistress. "You're not the one in command," Cassius said.

He bowed. "No, milord, he went for supplies," he said. "I was out looking for game."

"It wasn't a question," Cassius said. "Nevertheless I'll be sending assistance to help with crops and what not. I'll be expecting your reports." *Shall we?* He asked Gellia. Some of the people kneeled before him.

Yes, before they start groveling too much. Gellia lifted the hems of her wet clothes. If she fell on her face in front of the knight the whole empire would surely hear about it.

The people parted so she could join him. Cassius took her hand and led her through the throng. *What do you say we give them a grand exit?* He asked.

I just want to go back to bed. His hand was warmer than she expected.

A huge circle of green energy swirled up around them, lightning crackled. And they were in Tintagel again.

"To do something like that would take all my strength, wouldn't it?" Gellia asked, wondering why he set them down in a corridor.

"It would take all your concentration and would take much longer for you to accomplish, but it wouldn't tire you mystically. Now, most *other* mages out there would probably be exhausted. Actually, considering the times, most mages can't teleport over that long a distance," Cassius he moved a black curl out of her eyes. "And learning to build a *portal* can be a trick."

She smiled at him; happy to have him home and astounded he treated her so familiarly. She decided it was because they worked so closely together for so long. "Wait a minute," Gellia said. "This is the corridor to the garden."

"What?"

"The courtyard garden." Gellia walked past him to the door of the sunlit garden and motioned for him to follow. "It's the rose garden, see?" She stepped into the sunlight amongst the fragrant blossoms and turned to him.

Cassius followed, but stopped on the edge of the plot to watch the roses unfurl their petals in her presence. Their beauty had never been as perfect. You truly are Zapheny, aren't you, he thought. "...You should learn to use your magic to help yourself."

"What do you mean?" She asked as she strolled.

Cassius shook his head and snapped his fingers. There was only a moment for Gellia to recognize magic flowing before a warm breeze blew over her and her wet clothes were gone, her hair was dry and she was wearing a flowing dress of violet, rose-brocade satin. It reminded her of a dream. "Thank you." She smiled. "This place is so unlike Tintagel."

"Why do you say that? Because you don't expect to see rose gardens in fortresses?" He watched her closely. "These were gifts to my mother from a place far away from here."

Gellia bent to smell a shimmery white rose, held her hair back so no part of her touched it, out of respect. "It isn't very usual, is it? The old castle never had anything like it." She watched a few butterflies flit over the bushes. Cassius was going to say something, she could feel it, and so she looked at him. His magic was calling for something, but in a very delicate, welcoming way.

"You can come out, she won't bother you."

With him and the dark walls as a contrasting backdrop, tiny white lights floated from the plants around her. "What are they?" Gellia held out her hand to try to touch one. "Fairies?" They reminded her of the light she saw in the laboratory.

"No. I don't like fairies. They're whispers. They won't be in any book you might have seen in Fuarmaania," he said. One landed in Gellia's hands. "They can take two forms, this during the day and a more person looking form at night. If you're kind to them they tell you secrets."

"Hence the name," Gellia said, holding one up to her ear from where it promptly floated.

"You have to gain their confidence first. For you it shouldn't take long."

"They look like the things I see flying around outside at night," Gellia said.

"Those would be fairies. Fairy lights can be colored as well as white but only have the one form. If you catch a fairy you're destined for trouble. Whispers are harmless but for their information... you like this place."

"I found it when I first arrived and I met the old woman who tends it. It's so peaceful. It's like a sanctuary. I could stay here forever."

"That woman has been tending this garden for a very long time."

Gellia walked to the far end of the garden where she could hardly see her liege as he stood under the loggia. "Is this where you got the rose you gave to me back in Fuarmaania?"

"That one was an illusion to inspire you."

She gazed at the sky, tired but feeling alive. "Yes, I like this place." She turned to look for him, expecting that he moved but still Cassius stood in the same place as if frozen.

"Come here as often as you wish. You'll be allowed to take the roses if you like."

"Thank you," Gellia said, surprised and wanting to say more, but she knew just that was good enough, and a drawn out 'how wonderful you are Cassius' speech would irritate him. She sniffed one of the pink roses. A whisper flittered by. "I suppose we're wasting precious time."

He smirked. "Yes, but everyone's too frightened to question." Gellia looked at him. He continued, "I knew I would have to listen to the mages tattle on you for days. Indeed princess, the only thing not part of the plan was your village." He waved his hand in disgust. "Now I have to go hold the audience."

"You're already late," Gellia said. She was so happy it was no longer her responsibility.

"It's impossible for *me* to be late." He straightened himself and the magic gave him a complete change of wardrobe. "You can stay here if you like."

She joined him once more and said, "no, I think I'll come with you."

"Suit yourself."

8

Yes, that Zephron girl of the Countess arrived shortly after you left. I never saw her, though, Gellia said. *I didn't have the time to seek her out.*

"...and they wished to offer you this, for your generosity." the man said, waved to some servants to carry in a huge case.

My mages haven't said anything so who knows where she went, Cassius replied. *I'm certainly not ready to put out the effort to find her. If she's smart she'll find employment as a servant.*

Gellia stood amongst the courtiers, watched all the visitors as they came in, and finished her reports to their baron. She could see the white haired Mephibosheth on the other side of the room and Sian by Lord Idris. It was difficult for her to visually find the others since they blended in so well unless she used her magic—her magic could find them instantly. *Have you looked at the other papers I left in your desk?*

Yes. Well done. Sian was of some service then?

Yes, he really did most of the work. Do you want to hear the whole story?

No, I can already imagine what happened. What does he want from me?

Nothing. He just wants to practice magic with me, that's all.

Really. Well I can see what he's up to now.

What's that?

He's been vying for Mephibosheth's position for some time now. It seems he wants to learn his magic well enough to do the job himself.

Are you going to stop him?

I let these things work out naturally.

What's to be done with Idris?

You should have had him publicly executed while I was away but one can't ask for everything, hmmm? We'll deal with him, or you will, soon enough.

She had a sinking feeling in her stomach. How would this work out? Would she have to kill him there on the spot with her magic? She wasn't sure if she was up to such a thing. A big battle was different than this. What it would have to be was Cassius would give her a cue and she would have to do as he said if she wanted to keep this new structure intact. She, too needed to prove she would find out and deal with such people.

So what do you think? Cassius' voice rumbled into her mind again.

She was happy about the change of subject. *This one would like you to kill his friend who stole his mistress? A waste of our time,* Gellia said, hearing the speaker's thoughts. *He finds you extremely intimidating and he is having a very difficult time looking at you.*

"...and wonderful..." He was using all sorts of flattery to impress their baron, looking to the courtiers like he was addressing them as well.

Yes, I was noticing that. I rather like my audience room...Does he know we're listening to his thoughts? Cassius asked. He never took his eyes of the visitor, never changed expression.

No, I don't think so… That's right, she thought. Scaring people was his favorite pastime.

The corrupt ones squirm the best. They start to doubt all they've done, worry about where they could of slipped up in their scheme then they start to panic and run through all they know in their mind, fret about every last person who might have discovered them and reveal everything to me, everyone who's involved. Then they make their escape plans—how they're going to try to run away from me… You'd never make a Zephron struggle like this. What do you think we should do with him?

She thought before she spoke. *He's amazingly arrogant. He thinks he can win your alliance without difficulty. He thinks he's quite the aristocrat but he's only the mayor of a small village that he believes isn't particularly prosperous. I'm sensing that if he won an alliance with you he would endeavor to take whatever he could then turn against you; his true loyalties lie with the Claidheams for he allows them to stay in his village as long as they like and do as they please. Anything they please. I'm finding some very disturbing images, ones he's already forgotten. He and his guests are very cruel and his people hate him but it makes him feel...alive. I can't find a redeeming quality in him, not one.* She felt her mysticism sigh as her magic swirled up around her, but no one could see it. Her world was filled with color and light, everything seemed to be obvious for a moment. And she even looked around at all the others in the room and felt pity for them, did not fear them.

Impressive, princess.

I think we should dismiss him. She no longer felt small, no, she was vast as the sky. Her mind voice changed on its own, to a tone that matched her liege; spoke in elegant images and swirling light. *It's in his mind that his brother would be a fair mayor. His brother has great ambitions and will do whatever he has to accomplish them—will use his head to do it. His brother is also a talented warrior who takes pride in training his men who are some of the finest in their region; he's also a good field commander and is well read, I'm seeing. He also respects you greatly.* Although Cassius never turned his gaze, she could feel that all his attention was on her. But fate spoke to her. This change in the aristocracy needed to be made. *Which is enough, I believe, to put him in power.*

I know his brother quite well...you realize you read that from his brother's mind, not his, and his brother is very, very far away from here. That *is no small feat.*

Gellia was sure she could see a smile touch Cassius' face as he tapped his fingers on the arm of his chair. His gaze shifted over to the castle guards who promptly walked out to take the mayor, who didn't understand why anyone would want to punish him. No one was impressed and Gellia saw Sian yawn. They'd seen actors before.

Alright. I've had enough of this, Cassius said into her mind. He rose. Everyone in the court bowed as he walked down the steps and strode from the hall. *You are quite the distraction, princess. Meet me in the library.*

***

Emperor Gallylya watched at his sister for a moment. She'd just asked him for another escort to visit the countess. He hoped that's exactly where she was going and didn't let himself believe otherwise. He didn't want to think of the possibilities. "Very well," he said. It was convenient. She wouldn't like what he was planning if she ever found out, and even though she spent much of her time in her rooms she seemed to always know comings and goings.

"Thank you. I'll pack my things." Connylia smiled again and left her brother to his thoughts.

His spies always traveled with her, confirmed her continued presence with the countess, but that didn't promise truth. These were worries he had no time for, not when Xzepheniixenze was once again proving to be a threat. Yes, Raven was on the throne of Xzepheniixenze, but he would not try to attack Zephronia while Gallylya was there. Raven *knew* better despite his lack of intelligence. But Cassius... Cassius was another story. Gallylya rubbed his forehead. That boy had been an annoyance in his youth. Perhaps those centuries ago Cassius didn't have much knowledge over his magic, but now... wild talents were supposed to burn themselves out; it was the way of nature. No schools would have taken him; his power was too dangerous for them. Could he have been self-taught? How ridiculous. Was it? His mother was a shrewd, vicious individual; his father was magicless, but a skilled and intelligent leader. Cassius no doubt was every bit as intelligent as they. With enough study it might be possible to be self-taught.

It could bring a whole other angle on the situation. A thousand years of practice would make Cassius a brilliant mage—and no one could know the true extent of his magic. Gallylya rubbed his eyes. Was he trying to keep his whereabouts a secret? Was it Cassius who taught Gellia her magic? With her bloodlines it was possible her potential was as limitless as his, maybe even more. No one ever could measure Razhiede's magic, it was possible Gellia was the same, and with Connylia's heritage it was a possibility she had the forbidden magic.

But rumors about Razhiede's knowledge of the mystic—
if the rumors of old were true—and that magical potential was
passed down through the generations as humans… What if he
was trying to harness the wild magic? That terrifying, barely
definable monstrosity that all mages feared. If he thought Gellia
had access to it…"I'm too old for this." There was something on
the horizon; he could feel it. His warring years were not over yet.
His only comfort was the knowledge that the other Vega Knights
were moving.

***

"Let's see. We'll need this one, this one. That blue one
over there." Cassius pointed out the ancient books, Gellia
plucked them from the shelf.

"What are we doing?" She asked. He seemed quite
driven, more so than usual.

"We're going to make large explosions." He opened a
tome and started to leaf through it.

"Sounds delightful," Gellia yawned. "Why do we need
these?"

He didn't look away from the book. "Oh, some old
recipes… You said you had a dream of Razhiede in the
mountains."

"Yes?"

"Do you remember what words were exchanged?"

She'd always had strange dreams, she wondered why he
was concerned about this one. "Some. He spoke with Connylia in
a different language. He said that hope was not lost and that
things change and told her not to regret the past and something
about balance in the future. Then he looked at me." She
remembered what that felt like and felt it renewed. It was… it
was like he loved her. She'd never felt that from someone before.

He paused to watch her. "Go on."

She had never seen Cassius so enthralled before. "He
knew who I was. He called me the newest Zapheny…he said
Connylia had to do a dragon a favor and said his magic would
live again. Then I woke up in the village. Apparently I fell asleep
and was very tired, then I knew it was a dream because no one

else knew about it and they were all there. Thinking back I do vaguely remember arriving at the village..."

"Did you ask Connylia?"

"No, there was no time, and I thought it was a dream."

He nodded. "In *you*."

"What do you mean?"

"His magic will live again through *you*. *That's* what I've been sensing in you. You are linked to him through your lineage. *That's* why you seem older, different to me. It's your magic. I knew there was something. It was no dream—Razhiede awakened in you the true depth of your power, unlocked your full potential all the way back to him. Let's be off."

Her mind wouldn't work out what he was saying. "I'm concerned about Lord Idris, shouldn't we deal with him soon?"

"Idris is nothing. He's already been revealed as a traitor. He is nothing compared to what Razhiede has unearthed in you." He read through one of the books on their way.

"It was a dream," she said.

He shook his head. "No, I doubt that. I'd bet Connylia used her magic to orchestrate your travels after the village, and Justin probably helped her. She's a bloody brilliant mage but no one gives her any credit, and she won't admit that she is."

"How could she accomplish such a thing?"

"She has magic that no one else in this lifetime has, and may not ever have again. You're the only one who questions because only your power could try to resist it."

It was a lot to think of for a tired mind, and it was easier to think on the village. "That village," she said. "Was it part of your lands?" It was very far away from Tintagel.

"Yes."

It may have boggled her mind. The borders of territories weren't very clearly drawn. "It was close to or in the Enki territory," she said.

He nodded, his nose still in the book.

"How much of the lands do you control?"

Cassius took a quick turn and within a few corridors they were at the map room. Dallen wasn't there. Cassius closed the book and looked at the great map for a few moments, thinking. She knew he couldn't be thinking of what his lands were. No, she had the feeling he was deciding if he would tell her. Meanwhile the books she carried were starting to tire her arms. "Some territories are controlled by a king or queen, some are controlled by a lesser noble in a great city. Royalty is only recognized as such if the emperor commands it, as you may already know. Some lords think themselves kings, but they haven't been recognized. That is our time. Raven only recognizes kings and queens whose families have been in place, not upstarts, so some territories are kingless. It's all things that need to be changed at some point." He motioned to parts of the map. "I have strong influence over the Kaymarian kingdom, and the Enki Territory. I control Myste, the Shadowlands, the ancient Serenity Territory, Qenai, a good swath of Azimuth and the Sanguine Plains, and of course, Caddyan."

Gellia was slow to digest the information. It was treasure. "That's nearly half the empire," she said softly.

He gave a dismissive shrug, and spoke thoughtfully. "It's taken a long time to control so much without open war." Gellia continued to gaze at the map. "Surprisingly, Raven has many supporters." He motioned to other territories but for one.

"What about that one?" she said, pointing at the one called Dragonlands.

He shook his head. She couldn't tell if he was very serious or just thoughtful. "There is a great city there, before the wilds of the giant trees and jungle. Their lord thinks he controls those lands. But I tell you, princess, even though he has not been seen in many centuries, Zaphaniah still rules. Most have forgotten him now, but I have not. Not I. If he opposes me, he will assist Raven, and that is a greater threat than Raven himself. He'll show himself one of these days, because at some point, many years from now, I'll flush him out. I haven't decided exactly how yet. Unfortunately it will be a long time, and I don't think you'll be here to see it." He changed postures. "Now, back to what we were doing." He swept from the room, Gellia on his heels.

Gellia thought on his words as they traveled to the most secretive parts of the castle. Cassius' private laboratory. She heard it was real, but had no idea where to find it.

The public one was a huge coliseum type of place, empty and magically sealed so no magic could escape. But as they entered it was nothing like it. This was smaller and not as gloomy. It had three huge arched windows that overlooked the lake, and a lovely etched design on the floor around a recessed circle in the floor. He was still reading as she stood dumbly near. Finally she said, "Where do you want these?" The books weren't any lighter than when she first carried them.

"Over there in the corner."

She felt his magic rise, and a massive sphere of red crystal materialized in the center of the room. He finally set down the book. After tossing off hat, cloak and doublet Cassius took a lap around the room with his fingertips brushing against the walls.

Gellia watched this ritual with curiosity. "Why are you doing that?"

"I'm looking for weak spots. See, here's one." A green flash spread up the wall, resealing the magical barrier. "Make yourself comfortable, we're going to be here for quite some time."

She sighed and flipped through one of the books. It was a book about studying uncontrollable magic. As she read, what was written made little sense—it wasn't that she couldn't understand the concept, but they were going about it all wrong. Cassius stood by the orb, his eyes closed in concentration. When his ability engaged it felt like a torrent. She had no idea it was possible to pull that much energy so quickly. "Come here," he said. Gellia regained her senses and did as he bade. "This is another reason why I brought you to Xzepheniixenze—I had hopes this would be true. Razhiede's magic courses through your soul and he has brought back its memory. I need that memory. Razhiede has opened the door." He held out his bare hand. "He was speaking to us from the Beyond."

Gellia looked at it for a moment and then put her hand in his—it was always a strange feeling being so familiar with him. The red sphere glowed an angry red; she watched it with curiosity, feeling the energies growing around them still. This was correct. Cassius had figured out some of it on his own for the book was wrong. She didn't know how she knew, but she did.

A green bolt struck nearby, sparks sprayed over the stone floor. Gellia jumped. Another. The winds blew around them and a shower of the bolts rose and fell throughout the entire room. Gellia moved closer to her teacher in hopes he would protect her from the unknown, but then realized he could not protect her from this—she had to protect *him*. She didn't think of her magic, didn't draw it through herself as she always did, she just concentrated on the screaming energy around her. She felt she could control it without using herself...

The bolts turned to solid beams of green light that slowly angled towards the sphere until they all joined at the sphere's center. Gusts of a powerful invisible storm beat at their clothes; Gellia couldn't see through her own disheveled hair. Part of her was in this mess. Her magic started to do something, Cassius led it—she could feel him all around her, drawing out her magic, speaking to it with his own. It felt so strange. Blackness and beams of light were all around them. A few streams of purple were joining the green. The sphere grew. Gellia felt she was vibrating with energy, so much she thought she was going blind. The floor didn't seem to be there anymore, nor the ceiling. The only sense of the physical world she still had was the arm she clung to. There was a wailing, a primal howling that rang in her ears. Something was out there. Twisted faces appeared in the dark. The beams of green and purple light arched up until they were one pillar falling from the sky into the sphere that swirled with energy. Gellia peeked from under Cassius' arm to watch the foreign powers swirl where the circle should be. It started to rain.

She heard Razhiede's voice through the deluge but couldn't understand what he said. This was dangerous, far too dangerous for Cassius despite his god-like power. She shoved her will into the mess to wrap his magic in hers.

Where was she? There was no pain but a feeling of pressure. A flash. A handsome young man—a half-breed. Glimmering dragons. Children play fighting. A beautiful Xzepheniixenze woman. Fuarmaania. Mother. Apocalypse. Blue. Ice blue. A woman. Abandoned child. Black, feathered wings. Razhiede. Zenobia. Wisdom. Fate. A silver-dappled unicorn. The ocean waves crashed on the rocks. Zenobia. She could see the past in flashes; felt it was the past like part of her lived through it. She wasn't sure what was real, what was hers and what belonged to him. Great magics dying, the world cracking, and destruction. Gods fell from the sky. She reeled out of control. There was an entity standing near, no, more than one. One she recognized as her teacher the other she realized was Razhiede. Razhiede looked at Cassius and smiled. Razhiede spoke to her with his soul. He led her from the mess of swirling energies into a place of brilliance. "You are starting to understand," he said. "But you are still new. Death is but a doorway, do not fear it, for in this time it is a doorway you can pass through from either direction." Gellia was comforted by his presence. Her great grandfather would not lead her astray.

The rays of light split again, rotating downwards like a breath, drawing the howling thing up into the sphere. The darkness cleared. The light dimmed. Water had pooled all around them. Gellia was back in herself. The sphere glowed, swirled with angry mottled magic. The sky outside was dark.

Gellia raked her soaked hair out of her face with her fingers, tried to catch her breath and looked around at all the water. "Look at all the—"

"Stranger things have happened," Cassius said. He didn't seem to care that they were both soaked to the bone or that Gellia still hung off his arm.

"What is it?" Did he understand how dangerous it was?

"Normally any mage who comes in contact with it is immediately destroyed. It runs rampant in the empires, grows in power and size. It isn't something that can be controlled. Until now," he said. "Thank you, Gellia."

"I don't know if I really did much." He said her name. He thanked her.

"You did plenty. I'm genuinely pleased you were born."

"Yes, and I'm *very* tired now." He hadn't called her princess like it was an insult.

Cassius threw back his head and laughed wildly. "You cannot appreciate your own magic." He put his hand on her shoulder. "You cannot sleep yet."

Gellia felt renewed strength from his touch. "Thank you."

The smile remained on his face, forgotten. He turned to the sphere then and with a final light display the wild magic dispersed into thousands of red sparks.

"Perhaps you're right," Gellia said. "It's very dangerous, you realize."

"Well, now that we have it I can study it." The water around them evaporated as the laboratory restored itself to equilibrium. Cassius waved a book towards them; the pages flipped open as it floated over. Being enchanted as all the books in Tintagel were, it was perfectly dry. It rested on the floor as Cassius did likewise, muttering to himself as the pages opened to a blank space. Words appeared on the paper as he thought. "...wrong, wrong, this is wrong…"

Gellia sat next to him, looked over his shoulder at the words that burned into the page. As he ruminated Cassius jumped up and wandered around the room tapping his chin. Eventually he sat in front of the book again. She rested quietly for a while until she saw something worth mentioning. "It wasn't like that," she said and pointed out something he had down. "It was more like, uh," she summoned her magic and tried to illustrate it. She was confident he wouldn't bark at her, this was his research and he wouldn't want a mistake in his notes. This was part of her ancestor's life's work.

"I see," he said, and changed his wording. "Nicely done… You see, the world is damaged, its energies are damaged and it creates what's known as wild magic. Before the war it was minimal, but it grows stronger with each passing decade. Once we understand it, we can work to repair the damage to the world."

"And if the damage isn't repaired?" she asked. He had a lot to contend with. Good thing he was immortal.

"The end." He concentrated on his notes for a moment. "Without repair the world will tear itself apart in time. The more powerful the mage, the more it hastens the destruction."

"Hence the weather changes with magic."

"Yes."

"It seems what you're telling me is only the surface. We have a lot to do."

He exhaled. "We do."

She wasn't sure how long they sat there, Cassius noting all his thoughts in the book. However long it had been, it had been long enough for their clothes and hair to dry. Gellia knew she could probably find something more productive to do besides sit and look over Cassius' shoulder, but this was interesting enough to her. She was far more comfortable in his company than she was with the others and even was relaxed enough to absentmindedly finger comb his endless black mane. She had forgotten the rules about Xzepheniixenze territorial behaviors and their midnight tresses, and Cassius didn't notice or didn't care.

This magic—this was something he craved for a long time, to find and study it. In theory, to gain control over the wild magic would also give him great power over others. He could use it against the emperor and against others like Gallylya. No one would know he had it if he controlled it; he could create destruction beyond her wildest dreams. But he would not achieve this control. This she knew. He could never, even with her help, for his blood was not correct. Only *she* had the power, but he did not know this yet. Only the Zapheny were entrusted with its power, with all magic. Suddenly she realized how Quenelzythe felt. …Yet Cassius had the ability more than anyone else to help restore the world.

But what of the rest of what she saw? When he found her magic's memory it seemed that she was lost within him, swirling around in his mind. It felt strangely intimate. If only Gellia could remember what she saw, then she could make some sense of it. Eyes closed, she concentrated on what she'd seen. What was it? The old magic rushed forth, flooding her senses.

…Through a haze of time, centuries, stood an army, a huge army that extended past the horizon. A dragon towered over them, their friend. Xzepheniixenze with wings? Chaos. Betrayal. The magical energies through the battlefield were immense. Terror but not from fear of fight—from not knowing what was to come. Something horrible....

"You don't want to do that."

Cassius' voice snapped her back into reality. Gellia looked at him, not knowing what to say and not sure how he was going to react. Her magic had allowed her to trespass, and in a very dire way.

"Remembering my memories. It's not something you want to do. My life is not a fairy tale."

"What was it?"

"The Holy War. Look it up, I'm not going to tell you."

"You know everything about *me*."

"Not everything."

Her voice quavered. "That's a lie."

He sneered at her. "With such a short life it's easy enough to know it all." He slammed the book closed.

She nodded. "Oh? How long did you watch me?"

"I've watched your line for centuries for someone worth the effort."

Was that a compliment? He who didn't sleep because he was too busy plotting against the throne, who came to a tiny outlandish country to convince a girl to come back with him. How long had it taken him?

"Three years, wasn't it?" Cassius said.

"I must be special."

"Maybe not as special as you think."

Gellia teetered on whether to be angry or hurt. After failing to make herself angry she settled on hurt. She was such a fool. They both rose to their feet—he looked ready for a fight. She didn't say a word, only tried to keep her composure, turned on her heel and left the room. After emerging in the solace of the empty hall Gellia scolded herself. Xzepheniixenze were pitiful… Now if she could only find her way back.

A few paces down the corridor she was almost deafened by the racket of shattering glass. Gellia whirled and saw the door of the laboratory blasted off its hinges. She froze. Cassius marched from the room and towards her for a short distance; she had never seen him so angry, but Gellia stood her ground. He stopped a few feet away from her, and she quickly wove her barriers around herself and braced herself for the attack. She didn't have the strength to be angry back at him. Cassius suddenly recoiled, not because of her reaction but of some thought. He spun around and strode back into the laboratory muttering: "damn it all."

Gellia continued on her way. The door behind her lifted off the ground and slammed into the doorway.

***

Amarynth munched the hay and eyed Gellia watching him over the ornate stall door. The door was truly more for privacy rather than to keep them in, there were no latches. "Do you already know everything?" she asked after a while. The sun was new in the sky; she was up early from a restless night. What kept her from sleep even further were the lights in the sky, the layers of magic that ground together. They were far in the distance; she even felt them more that saw them. The area around Tintagel was very stable. Now that she understood them better they were even scarier.

The stable boys filled grain buckets for the horses; the stalls were already filled with fresh straw that glittered gold in the early light. All the walls were cleaned, all the silver trim polished, and all horses, domestic and bond were thoroughly groomed—although bond horses were often groomed three times a day.

What do you think? Amarynth rumbled.

"You probably know all about what I feel." He just looked at her. "I thought so." There was no use wishing for a chattier bond horse.

If it bothers you so much you might want to speak to Julian? It's about time you met him, anyway.

"Who's that? Wait, I think Currain mentioned him once..."

Someone who can talk to you in a way you can understand. I'll tell him you're on your way, he'll be anxious to see you. Go through that corridor over there and follow it, go through the iron gate.

Gellia turned towards the dark entrance of the tunnel. She crossed the onyx cobbled stable yard and headed down the corridor to meet this Julian fellow. After walking for some distance in the dark and ornate corridor, the gate Amarynth said would be there appeared. It was very lovely, the bars scrolling this way and that with platinum plated spikes. Beyond the gate was an enormous grassy courtyard. Gellia opened the gate and walked through, looked around at some of the beautiful flowering trees and the stone dragon fountain in the center. Walls of the castle reached far above the courtyard and formed towers and battlements. As she walked she could see that at the far end of the field-like courtyard was a grand pavilion of green, silver, and black. The pavilion was empty. What a strange place.

He crept into her mind, slipped past her defenses without the least bit of difficulty, almost like a fortress being taken from within. *I suppose I should come to see you. After all, you are a virtuous girl,* said the voice. It sparkled with laughter. *Do you have a silver bridle?* Her mind filled with color and light and music.

A massive black horse approached from the other side of the yard. He was one of the biggest horses she had ever seen, far larger than Amarynth or Currain, about the same size as Connylia's charger. His mane fell on both sides of his cresty neck and nearly reached to his knees, and his thick tail dragged along the ground behind him. With such a long forelock in his face Gellia wondered how he could see—but there was something else. As he drew near it became more apparent that this was not a horse at all. A unicorn. Gellia's heart fluttered as he stopped before her and regarded her with all too knowing eyes. She found her voice. "You're Julian?"

Indeed. And here you are at last, Zapheny.

Gellia kept her hands at her sides as she tried desperately not to touch him. He was not a horse, not something to be *treated* like a horse. He was a real, live unicorn. She felt that she was twelve again and living in a fairy story.

His mind voice was full of laughter and light. *To answer any common questions I know you're wondering—yes, unicorns are white and smaller than I am. Yes, there are others like me, two in fact, my brothers who are right now with Connylia. Yes, I am one of Cassius' bond 'horses' and I have been with him since he was a child... and I can see that the pointy thing coming out of my head is very distracting.* A shimmer in the air and the unicorn shape turned Xzepheniixenze.

"I'm sorry," Gellia said.

Julian smiled, it was the kind of thing that could set hearts a flutter, warm even the coldest corners of the soul. "Don't be. It isn't every day you get to see a unicorn and certainly not one who looks as I do." He was dressed entirely in plain black clothes; his hair long and a bit messy but becoming just the same. If he were a human he would be seventeen. His face was longish and elegant. "Amarynth said you were coming to see me. About time someone sent you to me."

"I don't know why he sent me."

"He's himself, and not very chatty. He tends to support with magic and presence more than anything, and tends to be subtle. Shall we sit some place? Out of the sun perhaps?"

They chose a tree and sat on the grass beneath it, the petals fell all around them. "Ah Gellia, Gellia. It's so good to finally meet you in person." He gave her a broad smile. "You had a quarrel with him." He seemed to ignore the rainbow colored butterfly that landed on his hair. Tiny flowers started to grow around him in the grass.

Gellia looked away. The birds in the tree above them twittered merrily—she tried to distract herself with them. It seemed after a moment they sang just for Julian. She could be happy just spending time with him for the rest of her days.

"That's my favorite song." Julian tilted his head to meet her shy eyes. "I cannot agree with his temper nor do I condone his behavior towards you. Always remember it's his issue, not yours." He beamed. "I know you consider leaving, but this is the best place for you... Yes, the emperor is an idiot but he has a thousand years of experience over you. That alone would seal your doom. I would not wish that fate on you."

"How do you know what I'm thinking before I say it?"

"I have my ways." Julian looked coyly at her. "The fact of the matter is, Gellia, he's never going to apologize to you, you already know that... Not everyone can be like your great ancestor, I suppose. I knew Razhiede, very well in fact. The three of us were his at one time."

"Why don't I just sit here and you tell me what I think." She knew she shouldn't have said it because she needed his wisdom, but it came out just the same and she felt sorry.

He looked at his knuckles. "I'm not going to play those games with you Gellia. That's not how I work."

"Tell me again why I need to be here?"

"Because you weren't born in the empire. You were born in a rustic country and you have no idea how to survive in this place. From the moment you set foot here you have been sheltered. Even though you have led armies, you have never experienced the world with no possessions, no money, no backing, and no home. And who'll take you in and be able to teach you anything about your magic? You may think you know everything there is out there, and perhaps you could keep the ones who would exploit you at bay for a while but they would eventually win. Don't look so stricken... you already knew all that, trust in yourself. You already know all these things, you just refuse to believe them. You need to find peace within yourself, don't expect anyone to give it to you."

Gellia just looked at him for a while and he looked at her. If a Xzepheniixenze's normal facial expression was that of stoicism, Julian's was a smile. It seemed the troubles of the day left her. As she tried to think of them they no longer upset her, like he washed them away. "What should I do?" Maybe he was someone else's but she felt more connected to him than anyone before, including Amarynth.

He smiled again. "By blood we are yours, by royal decree we are his... Trust in your magic, in your blood. Your true potential has been awoken in you now, and some things you'll feel in your heart even if your head doesn't agree, reach from within. Your magic, your spirit, will guide you. Trust in destiny, for it trusts in you." He watched her for a moment and her eyes finally met his, how deep they were, how they sparkled with years. "You feel better now?" he asked.

She nodded.

"Now skedaddle before I get a scolding."

She rose and butterflies chased her from the courtyard. Julian shook his head. "She's nervous and bewildered enough in her own mind without you confusing her further, Kaz."

After finally having some sleep that night, Gellia woke and sat against her pillows. It was like a dream. This was what her life could be like forever. Wealth, power, but what about the simple things like companionship? Was this it? People entering and leaving her life as often as the tides; delicate friendships blooming and wilting quickly? She rolled over and snuggled into her blankets. Something out her window sparkled in the distance, she wasn't sure if she saw it with her eyes or with her magic. She felt something call to her like the time when she first arrived in Xzepheniixenze.

Gellia shook off her thoughts, crawled out of bed and stepped out onto her balcony to look into the night. The tiny lights on the edges of the lake floated around listlessly, it was difficult to decide where the stars began and whispers ended, but this was not one of them. What was it? She would have to ask someone. No. She could go see for herself, couldn't she? She always wanted to try flying with her magic. It wouldn't take long that way, and it was still technically Cassius' lands. No one else would want to go anyway. Maybe it would cheer her up—sort of like a long walk to soothe the soul. She could always call her sword mystically, and she certainly had her magic.

After donning day clothes and her pendant, Gellia walked out into the cool air again to climb onto the rail of her balcony. The streaks of light appeared on the horizon changing colors from blue to yellow to white and combinations of the three. She paused to watch them, heard the strange voice on the wind as it called, then was suddenly silenced.

The beacon called her, she went. Her magic lifted her from the balcony and propelled her through the air. She was unsteady at first, but found her stability. The glimmer on the horizon became wider. She was moving so quickly she surprised herself. When she looked back, Gellia could no longer see Tintagel, the lake or anything else familiar, but she was sure she could find her way home. Ahead, the glimmer had spread into a line of glowing points along the skyline and eventually took shape into a landscape made entirely of crystal. Slowing down, Gellia surveyed the towers of glowing iridescent rock. It all looked something like a crystal forest; the pillars grew from the ground, there were jagged archways and spikes with patches of weeds and grass between. The brightness almost blinded her in places as the moonlight illuminated the landscape.

She spotted a man-made structure, a great ruin of white translucent stone that looked to have covered a vast expanse of land when it was still kept up. Much of it was overgrown by vegetation. Gellia landed on an outer wall, tickled that she found something so wonderful. She tried to remember if she read about such a place, a crystal forest. She was sure she could smell the ocean on the breeze.

The crystal columns on the edges looked very dense and high, like a natural wall. She touched the stone—it almost seemed to tremble. She felt for it with her magic. Something tragic had happened here and it wanted to speak to her. The wind tossed her hair; she steadied herself on the wall. It was so faint, it reached for her, straining to touch her. "Zapheny," it whispered. Was it possible? If she concentrated enough, could she see what this was during a greater time? …There were flames, flames that reached into the sky…

Gellia fell off the wall and landed in a bloody heap. Before it even registered she was hit, someone kicked her onto her back. She found herself staring up a dark form that started shouting at her. "I- I don't understand!" she choked. She wildly tried to build a barrier. She said the word for her ring and assessed her wound. The ground was already covered in blood. She started to scramble backwards to give her space to rise. Winds battered her.

"Identify yourself! What are you doing here? Answer me!"

"Zapheny!" She cried.

"Liar! They're all dead!"

Gellia's new barrier cracked under the power of the third blow. He was so fast she didn't see his movement. He stood over her once more, great dark wings blocking out the moonlight.

9

...the deadliest weapons in the world... the metal itself is poisoned and incurable... one hit... only a bag of gold for one of these lovely... wounds that never heal... straight from the heavens and the steel smiths of the sky city... the best Lunan steel... a marketplace.

"What are you doing?.... we already have weapons..."

"...but if we make ourselves impervious..."

"...out of your mind..."

"...am I really... the war...you see? It has no impact on us anymore..."

There was warmth and dimness, voices and footsteps. Her room. She heard Cassius. Cassius in her room? "If you wanted to see the Crystal Forest of Qenai you should have asked." He sat by her bed and looked at himself in a nearby mirror, straightened his hair.

The memory was blurry at best. What attacked Gellia she wasn't sure. Flashes of a Xzepheniixenze face, but she was certain he had black feathered wings. He struck from out of nowhere. She remembered trying to fight, but he was too quick. She'd been terribly injured, unable to heal herself. Poisoned. If she remembered correctly, he didn't believe her when she said she was Zapheny.

"You?" she croaked.

"No, not I. Amarynth.... I don't know if I could have reasoned with the Guardian or not, and it would be a shame to lose him. He does his duty even after death."

"Where's Amarynth?"

"He's not talking to you right now... no, they won't miss me. I've put an illusion out of myself and locked it in the laboratory."

The servants she saw move through the room where not the ones she remembered. She didn't want to ask where the others were. In her heart she was sure they were killed—punishment for not stopping her. She couldn't think of it. Gellia wondered how it was Amarynth saved her, but knew there would be no answers. She also knew it wasn't Amarynth who kept her from dying. Cassius was impervious to the strange metal of the undead creature's sword. It was his magic, his resistance to the poison that saved her. It wasn't a spell, it was something else. She could feel her strength returning by the moment. She almost felt that his blood, or his life-force, was running through her.

Cassius was looking out the window, distant, but in a different way than usual. He was baffled. Gellia waited for him to speak. "...I myself am unsure of just how such a feat was accomplished and I was the catalyst," he said. "Death, just one more obstacle to overcome."

She had to say something. "I'll help you study wild magic and you help me with death."

He shook his head. "Holding someone to life and making someone immortal are two different things... You are far too reckless, princess. Storming the Lorkiegn castle, taking Candiem was fine, but running off to Qenai by yourself? I understand you want independence but for pity's sake, think before you leap to your death. There are hundreds of stories about the Guardian of Qenai and this is the only one that doesn't end with: 'was never seen again'."

"What was he?"

"A Lunan, a race that is entirely extinct. They were second to none on the battlefield..."

Gellia sensed his sorrow so didn't pursue the topic, no matter how interesting it was. Maybe someday he'd tell her. "Are you going to continue to look out for me?" Gellia asked. Imagine how many would survive if they all looked out for each other instead of trying to kill each other, she thought. But if he babies me, how will I ever survive on my own? "Or is it I who protects you?" she added, but didn't know where the thought came from.

He chuckled. "I think you might be the death of me."

There was something else distracting him. "You need my memory, another powerful and not to mention beautiful ally, entertainment and someone to argue with and—" and the key.

"I like to be entertained." He looked to the vase of flowers from that morning and glared when he saw they were already wilting.

She watched him for a moment. "Connylia warned me about that."

With the slight motion of his fingers the flowers grew young again. "When you've been around for as long as I have you try to find something to do with your time. Perhaps the better question to ask is why you chose to stay? You are no prisoner. Return to Zephronia if you wish. But enough, your illness has passed, you have other things to think about, like this party I'm throwing."

"As long as no one acts boorish."

"I can't promise everyone will behave, the emperor will be there."

"I'll go anyway, I suppose. I'll need a new dress."

"Certainly. I'll have my personal designer to make one for you."

Gellia gazed at him, remembering his age even though he still appeared so young, but she could see it in his eyes when she dared to look. He spoke of taking Xzepheniixenze and she knew it would be her task as well. It was her birthright. Hers. Once she took it she would entrust it to Cassius who she knew would keep it safe to his best ability after she was gone. It was not just his plan that they should meet; it was fate, a power higher than both of them. Quenelzythe knew it, Razhiede knew it—it was only a matter of time—she was positive that all her ancestors felt it, even the ones before Razhiede, Zapheny no one remembered. This was not a new story, she realized, it was countless thousands of years in the making—but it tried to unravel itself. The world was truly dying. He spoke.

"I will avoid open war if at all possible. It's messy, expensive in more ways than one, including the damage it could cause the empires. I like things tidy. It is much more so if a place is taken from within—which is my specialty. If the town, city or country is already listening to the conspirator it is much easier and neater when the time comes to tip the ruler off his throne, especially when the ruler is as powerful as Raven," he said.

Gellia frowned. Fuarmaania...

"Every time you thought you were evading me you were really running to me. The whole situation was in my control down to the moment of your escape."

"You're serious, aren't you?"

He nodded. "Hate me if you wish." He waved his hand at her. "It matters not."

The Gellia that she had been hated him, envied him, but the person she had become only admired him, some part of her understood why fate wanted them to meet. "If you're going to use my new weight with the commoners and the strength of my magic to your benefit then I will rule with you when I am ready."

"Of course." He smiled. "Until that opportunity arises would you settle for being my envoy?"

"What would the position entail?"

"Traveling to places I've acquired to talk to them or beat them into submission—while looking very glamorous."

"Sounds amusing."

"I need someone to slap the nobility to keep their commoners well fed and well trained... You're better now."

She was. She felt like new. When Gellia started to fling off her blankets he averted his eyes as if they would be burned from his head. "Scandal!"

She felt the blood rush to her face. Her nightgown wasn't that revealing. "Get out of my room!" She nearly laughed. Although it seemed that working magic with him was far more intimate than nudity.

Cassius bowed with great drama and left. Gellia laughed to herself as she chose clothing. Whatever he had done to cure her it had done the trick and then some. It almost felt that part of him was still with her, bolstering her, perhaps even giving her a feeling of intoxication.

Gellia suspected she had been bedridden for a few days— at least that's what it felt like. Once she started into one of the main corridors she was greeted by several of the lesser nobles who nodded and bowed at her as she passed. Halfway down another corridor a messenger approached her. "Milady, this came for you," she handed Gellia a wooden box.

She nodded and continued with the box under her arm to find her liege. Her instinct told her he was in his office or the library. She headed to the office first.

The guards at the office door admitted her immediately. In the room stood several of the court mages, their master sat behind his desk and gave orders without looking at them.

Gellia stood erect and confident as she waited for the mages to leave, ignored them as they walked around where she stood in the door. "What do you think *this* is?" she said, seating herself and holding up the box.

"It's not a severed head, it's not the right shape...It came this morning not to Tintagel or the House of Vazepheny but to 'Lady Gellia'. I think you have devotees." He'd barely looked up from his papers.

She lifted the wooden lid to find a wreath of dried flowers tied with ribbon, and a note that read: *Our Beautiful Lady Gellia, Thank you for saving our village. We don't have anything to give but this as a token of our appreciation. -the village.* "How sweet."

"I knew you would think so," Cassius muttered. "You'll have them beating down the doors to pay homage. We'll have to build a temple for you. I have several of my own."

"That isn't a bad thing, is it?"

"Not particularly."

"Are we going to the laboratory today?"

"Are you telling me that you want to?"

"Well...well," she began. "Truthfully I felt like your magic was teaching me." She felt too strange to say it, but her mystical self was driving her to work, to exercise her magic in new ways. It nearly seemed to be urgent.

"Indeed." He leaned into his chair and gazed at her, thinking.

"I can't explain how or why..." But some things he couldn't teach her, this she knew.

He thought for a moment longer. "Well, you'll probably learn more from that than from reading books or your own experimentation."

"Shall we then, when you have a moment?"

"Rather cheeky, don't you think?" Nonetheless Cassius stood up, Gellia rose to her feet, and he opened the door for her with his magic. "Saquime will be here this evening."

"I've missed him, but have barely had time to think of him."

"I know, and I'm sure he'll have all sorts of interesting tidbits to tell you."

...She entered the laboratory and closed the door behind her. Cassius seemed distracted somehow as he checked the seals of the walls. She wondered why he was so preoccupied.

"The enduring mystery of your magic." He walked towards her, arms akimbo. "You *are* an oddity." She had no appreciation of how odd she really was. Since her meeting with Razhiede's spirit in the mountain her magic would permeate everything if it was unchecked. Perhaps only those with magical talents could feel it, only brilliant mages could appreciate it, and no one could really understand it. She was Zapheny. She hid much of her talents as he taught her when they were in Sen Dunea. It was a backwards method—teaching her such an advanced feat so early in her schooling, but now he was certainly glad of it. Her magic was bewitching, frightful to some, like his mages, perhaps because of her seemingly lackadaisicalness towards it. Nonetheless she hid the true extent of her power without even realizing she did so. She also had no idea what her magic awoke in his. For that matter, neither did he. He hoped to find answers, and this seemed like an appropriate juncture to commit to such concentration.

"So are you," she said. He still looked pensive, she wasn't sure why. She worried it would be a sign of a mood change.

He smiled. "These days, yes. But in my childhood I was merely above average. Magic has weakened over the years."

"I had that feeling." Although she had the feeling he was exceptional even then and for some reason was being modest.

"Really?" He raised an eyebrow. "I doubt you can have any appreciation as to just how much magic has changed since the Holy War." He shook his head and looked into the distance for a moment before turning to her again. "So, shall we begin?"

She nodded and still wondered what was going through his mind.

"You're very gifted. This could take all day." But not easily definable gifts, he realized. Most had this and that and the other, but her magic seemed to continuously change its shape. More than likely if she went to apprentice they wouldn't know what do to with her... just how they felt about him. And how did he learn his very first lessons? He almost laughed—his brief and only teacher was nearby, but no longer gave instructions... Perhaps that was the approach to her he needed. Never had he heard of such a feat being accomplished by another. He certainly had the qualifications to perform such a task... Damn the Tarei! Damn the Zephrons taking *that* opportunity from his grasp!

Gellia shifted nervously. What had him so distracted? "What talents do *you* have?"

He chuckled. "Come here." Even though it made her feel unstrung, Gellia did his bidding. She wondered how this would work. "We're trying something new. Remember your awakening; it's going to be something like that. Clear your mind." He wasn't entirely sure what he was getting himself into, but something was telling him he should proceed.

Gellia closed her eyes and tried to think of nothing, but when that failed she decided the next best thing was to think of her teacher and what he was doing. He was concentrating his energies. She could almost see the green magic and hear its brilliance in her head as it swirled around her. His magic was perfection next to hers, all of it evenly pulled and woven into a tapestry of mystical light. She felt she could watch it forever, lost in its gleams and swirls. It was so stable, so comforting.

Their magic made a connection. Gellia blissfully allowed it to delve into the corners of her soul. His magic led hers in a dance, showing her every finite step he knew down to the last glimmer. Her magic rose on its own to match the shape of his as equals. Then her mind was filled with every nuance of signature, who it belonged to, where they were, and how much potential they had. And she could see just how vast his magic was, just how much energy he could pull and why everyone feared him so.

At first she felt dizzy, but enjoyed his magic as it moved through her soul. She felt in her heart that few others could take such a surge of power through their cores but somehow she could withstand it.

He was not normal; he had something about him that wasn't quite Xzepheniixenze, but something else. As she bathed herself in his magic Gellia could hear his life force pulsing through the castle and the surrounding territories as his magic was grounded. He could feel the grass growing on the other side of the empire and see the changes in the air currents in the sky. There were walls to this new world, the walls of Xzepheniixenze that protected it from the ravaged Beyond. His magic held countless miracles yet to be used—power born from the beginning of time, as was hers. They were more alike than she ever consciously realized, their magic created a symphony in her soul. She felt the strength of his passion, his hatred, and his obsession with Xzepheniixenze for he and the realm were one. It was then she realized that her magic now led them both, taking him with her through the passages of time to a place long ago where her blood began.

Gellia drifted back into reality with her new understanding and felt the warmth of the setting sun as well as her arms around him and her lips on his. She had initiated the kiss, this she knew. Their magic had willed it. She quickly pulled away.

Cassius looked as shocked as she felt. He was quick to hold up his hands in defense. "I was a victim of circumstance," said he.

Gellia didn't answer, not wanting to lie about or admit anything.

He looked at her in silence, which frightened her more than anything he could say.

She had no choice but to bolt. As she ran out the door she said, "thank you, I mean, for the—magic."

Alone in the corridor, she took a deep breath. Gellia felt her face; it was still flushed, her heart still pounded, her limbs still shook from the energies. Perhaps the flush was from the kiss. What an embarrassment. But this was not just a kiss, it was far deeper than physical or emotional. There was something enigmatic between them. It was the only reason they could do what they did, but she didn't know what it was or how it came to be.

...Cassius stared at the door for a moment longer. Then he remembered, in the hall outside the rose courtyard. He touched her hair. He didn't even realize it when he'd done it. Had he lost his mind? No one knew protocol better than he, how could this have happened? He picked up a nearby book and flung it. But none of this made sense, the gesture on his part didn't warrant a chaste kiss but something lustier, this was not what interested her. And some part of her was still there, with him, haunting him. He paced the room.

"I know you're not talking to me right now but I don't have anyone else to talk to!"

Amarynth ignored her, slept with his face in the opposite corner of the stall.

Her body felt abused, her magic was tired. "What do I do? *What* do I do, Amarynth?!" She held her hands up to her face. "This was the worst thing I've ever done." She felt Amarynth began to speak, but someone near cut in, a child's voice from behind her.

"What was the worst thing you've ever done?"

She'd never been so happy. "Skip! I'm so happy to see you! I didn't hear you come over!" She hugged him, nearly lifted him from the ground. "How I've missed you!" He looked well, healthier than when she first met him. He was as pretty as she remembered. His black hair was longer and neatly bound, his violet eyes bright as they always were. He seemed older and taller, had it been that long?

"Because you don't have anyone to throw around!" Skip laughed. "You led the army against Candiem, I'm so proud of you."

"Well, yes." Her dear friend, her former page, her companion.

"When I heard that we were being attacked by a renegade woman from Tintagel I knew it had to be you. I have so much to tell you." He looked around at the stable. "You know, Gellia, I didn't think when I first came with you that he was really ...

Cassius… but then I found out that he truly was, truly. I heard about him in Sen Dunea."

"What, that he drinks the blood of the dead and other silly stories?" She smiled.

"No, this isn't funny, Gellia. I fear for your safety." Skip seemed very serious, more serious than a boy his age would ever dream of being, but this was still Xzepheniixenze.

"Well then while we're stuck with him maybe we should take advantage of his hospitality?" Gellia replied. "Let's go find out where you're staying." She took his hand and ushered him towards the castle, nearly skipping.

"Gellia, you aren't listening! Don't be so foolish."

Gellia stopped him. "I don't fear him, Skip."

"You should. What has he done to you?"

"Nothing! Besides, my great grandmother told me if I ever needed I could go stay with her."

"No place is safe from him if you tried to escape," he said.

"I am not a prisoner." Gellia started to lead him away again. "If I felt threatened I could leave and my uncle would protect me." Gallylya was harsh but she did have faith that he would indeed protect her if she needed it. "My uncle is the emperor of Zephronia," she said, almost proudly.

It was Skip's turn to stop them. "*Gallylya Duvray? The Phoenix?* The king of Dragon slayers, the leader of the Vega Knights of legend? Solara's Golden Prince? Is your uncle? Let's leave now." Skip tried to pull her back towards the stable. "I heard Dournzariame is lovely this time of year."

"Skip!"

"Let's leave before it's too late."

"I can't believe you. What have they been teaching you?" She changed course and dragged him into the castle and through the servants' corridors to her chambers. No one seemed to notice their passage.

Upon entering her rooms Skip paused and took a breath, impressed at the surroundings. She had a feeling he wasn't expecting how luxurious it was. There were many things she'd added herself. Artwork, a bookshelf for her private collection, and she'd altered the general decoration to fit her exact liking. Her room had become a plush and beautiful space fit for a royal.

The servants had left tea for them. Gellia poured a cup for him. "I'm not in any danger from him, Skip. I don't know what stories they've told you but I can't leave—not because he won't let me, but because I have a commitment."

"Why? What commitment?" Skip glared at her. He looked every bit like a pureblood Xzepheniixenze.

Gellia heaved a sigh and sat in a nearby chair, sipped her tea. "I have a commitment to Xzepheniixenze." Skip waited for an explanation. "I...I don't know exactly how to explain this, other than I have to stay in Xzepheniixenze. It is my own choice. There are greater... Because of my magic, my soul, I have a responsibility. I can't explain it, Skip. Know that this was a choice I made on my own without any influences besides the empire."

"*He* isn't making you stay and do things you don't want to do?" He sat in the nearest chair to her. He still hadn't tried the tea she'd given him.

"No, I am here of my own free will. We are helping each other, although I have not told him what I have just told you. He may already know, but I can't be sure. We have the same goals, one being to take control of Xzepheniixenze."

"He's better than halfway through all that," Skip drawled. "Word in Candiem is he owns the seeker school, that's why all the mediocre teachers are being replaced by the best."

Gellia smirked. "It's difficult to tell what's truth and what's lies."

He looked at her, the concern apparent in his eyes. "I still don't trust him and neither should you, but if this is the course you've taken then I'll stay by you. I always will. If not to you, who would I be loyal to?"

He spoke with such sincerity, yet part of her was still distrustful, something Tintagel had done to her. However, this was Skip, her friend and companion. She had to trust him, right? "What a gentleman you've become, Skip."

He seemed to be displeased with her reaction. "There has been no expense spared for my schooling," said he, "and I am part human like you, I know how to recognize a true friend as well as those who lie." He smiled but without mirth. "I'll even protect you from *him* if I have to."

She smiled. "You're a seeker, are you sure you won't sell my secrets to the highest bidder?"

Gellia was joking, but her seeker was very serious. He set down his tea, took his dagger from its scabbard and pressed it into the palm of his hand. A small pool of blood started to form. "By my blood, Gellia, I will never betray you; I will serve you and those you deem worthy until my soul has gone to the Beyond."

She took his hand into hers and pushed away the dagger, clasped his wounded hand in hers. Only in books had she ever heard about this, only in the stories. Never had she heard of it actually happening. She healed his skin and spoke. "You cannot know what you say. You're so young, Skip. I release you."

"I know what I say and I give it freely," he said. "I won't take it back. I am yours."

She didn't have a choice but to accept. "I hope I am always worthy of such an honor." It was the only thing a Xzepheniixenze would respect, no matter what their character—a blood bond. She had nothing else to say about it. Gellia didn't know what plans Cassius had for him, but she knew she would care for him like a little brother. "So you'll help me."

He nodded and sheathed his dagger. "In whatever way I can."

Gellia turned just as a servant brought fresh pastries for them, still warm from the oven. They both remembered the day they met in Sen Dunea. It seemed like such a long time ago. "You can have that one, I know you like that kind," Gellia said. "So he never told me why he brought you here."

"I'm here to be your page at the party he's hosting. I get to keep track of the train of your dress and fetch you things." He sipped the tea and watched her look out the window. "This is a nice view, you can see the edge of Qenai from here on a clear night, I bet."

"You know about Qenai?"

"The Guardian of Qenai is one of the most dreaded foes of our time, and no one even knows what it looks like. No one survives, of course."

Gellia chuckled and shook her head. She was such an idiot and so lucky to still be there.

"What is it?" Skip asked.

"A story for another time."

…She was not quite the person he remembered, but she was every bit as familiar to him. It could be magic, but his experience with the magical arts was limited. In certain ways she made him think of his studies, of stories about the grace of the mystic. "You've changed."

"How have I changed?"

"I don't know, you look different, older or something. You're more beautiful than ever," he quickly added. "Even more so now."

"I *have* missed you."

***

"No, I don't like it. Try something else," Cassius said after watching her for a few moments.

Gellia stood on a stool with satin draped over her. She ached from standing still for so long. The team of seamstresses and tailors hurried around the room with measuring ribbons, scissors and other things falling out of pockets, and carrying different dresses while Cassius strode around her admiring a work of art in progress. Gellia tried not to roll her eyes.

"I won't have you going to a party and making a fool of yourself," he said.

"I've been to parties before."

"Yes, and you were an embarrassment by civilized standards."

The seamstresses untangled her from the fabric, leaving her in her chemise. "You know I really hate standing here with you looking at me." She tried to adjust the flimsy garment to cover more.

"How boring, princess. You can't still believe that's what I want from you… It wasn't that long ago you were trying to seduce me."

The tailor tried to hide his smile and Gellia did her best not to blush. She wished she could parry but she knew she would fail. Skip strutted in from a side room. "What do you think?" he asked proudly, showing off his fancy ensemble.

"Too much, you're to compliment her, not upstage her," Cassius said, motioned the designers to take care of it.

Skip frowned, but knew it was best he was close to his mistress to investigate their host. *Did* his lordship treat her well? She didn't seem happy at the moment. Cassius muttered at him, "I'm not going to have her head off, Saquime."

The boy didn't reply, just looked at his liege. Yes, Cassius had looked slightly more common when Skip first met him, but now there was no doubt of his refined breeding. The tales of Cassius' demeanor were true for the most part, so far. The stories, the *legends* the youngster heard wouldn't have bothered him if his friend wasn't with this person. In fact, Skip would be happy to work for such a well-paying employer.

"Curious how stories are passed on from one to the next," Cassius said, reading Skip's mind. "But even the concept of truth can be subjective considering perspective."

"What was that about?" Gellia asked. Bolt after bolt was carried out and sheets of fabric were draped across her to be disapproved by her liege.

"Saquime was thinking and I couldn't help but to hear him. You should learn to protect yourself, especially if you're going to be a seeker. Aren't they teaching anything?"

"Our mages were killed in the battle," Skip said.

Gellia wiggled her toes and immediately stopped when Cassius shot her a glance.

"Such a pity. Then you shall be my second student," Cassius told him.

Skip had mixed emotions about that, too. Skip looked at his mistress and she smiled, gave him a nod.

"No. I don't like it." Cassius disintegrated the newest sample fabric with his magic. Gellia yelped with outrage. Before again addressing the tailor he turned to Gellia. "Princess. Do you think," he put a hand on his hip, "that after a thousand years and hundreds of women that seeing a girl in a chemise is going to put any kind of—" he waved his hand, "thought—in my head?" Gellia blushed all over and Cassius groan in frustration. One of the team brought drawings. Cassius shook his head. "You need to take notes." He tore off page after page. "None of this will do. We are *not* trying to make her look like courtesan. *Someone* needs to figure out what we're doing here."

The designer nodded vigorously, his frazzled hair falling in his face.

Cassius started to give more instructions.

Gellia and Skip looked at each other. "This is going to be something to tell the others at school," the boy whispered. "None of them can say they've been trained by The Dragon himself— it's an opportunity of a lifetime even if I hate him."

"The Dragon?"

"Yes, that's what they call him."

She nodded. "I hope they've taught you etiquette at the school."

"Of course," Skip bowed and the seamstress who worked on him scolded him. "No expense spared, remember?"

"...and I don't want to see any of *this*. Is that understood?" Cassius returned to Gellia and Skip's section of the room. "I'm leaving now," he told Gellia. "Cooperate."

"Yes, my lord," She smiled demurely, fluttering her eyelashes at him. The seamstresses started their work again.

Shrew.

Miscreant.

Cassius smirked at her before he left the room.

"Ow! Watch where you put that pin!" Gellia squealed.

"Are you sure you're alright," Skip asked.

"It was only a prick."

"No, I mean about him."

"Don't worry about me, Skip, I'm fine."

The tailor looked up at her. "Don't worry milady, at the moment he doubts me, but we'll have milady looking like an empress."

***

"Mephibosheth, I want you to take an escort to Zephronia."

The white haired mage looked horrified. "Why, milord?"

"I want you to be the escort for Connylia Duvray," Cassius said, leafing through a book.

Mephibosheth looked around the library to see if anyone was eavesdropping. "Gallylya's sister?"

"Yes, that would be her. Why do you falter? She was here for a visit not long ago," Cassius almost muttered.

"Yes, but…"

The baron looked up at his mage. "Don't tell me you didn't recognize her nor believe the rumors."

"Ah…"

"Go with the escort and bring her to Shahyrahara."

Mephibosheth thought for a moment until his lord looked back up at him. "Are you bringing -ah- Lady Gellia to this?"

"Of course I am. She needs to be formally introduced to the rest of the aristocracy *some* time. Now off with you. I would rather not stand here and repeat myself so your feeble mind can understand…and take Idris with you, make sure he finds himself lost in Zephronia. Perhaps Gallylya can put him on a pole."

Gellia coming out into society would create great upheaval in the empire. Raven would be confused, but even he might know he'd been betrayed… Cassius knew that Raven still squirmed at the memory of Cassius' promise to kill him so many centuries ago. Raven asked him on every visit about that promise, and Cassius always smiled and said it was a long time ago. He left the library and walked back to his chambers.

There would be no more degradation of Xzepheniixenze. Yes, there would always be the brutality and the beauty of the realm but not the genocide and chaos Raven so craved. The emperor couldn't feel the realm dying all around him, nor did he care.

He walked into the first room of his personal chambers. The hiding assassin didn't have a chance to move before Cassius killed him with a mere flick of his magic. It wasn't even a challenge. He would have to write to the school and tell them their seekers were lacking. Saquime—Skip—needed to become an invincible weapon.

He stared out into the night sky and watched the layers grind against each other. She was the only one he knew who could see it, but could she feel it as well? Could she feel the world slowly dying? He poured himself a glass of wine.

…Gallylya would be the biggest threat. Yes, after so many centuries Gallylya was tiring, but he still was who he was—and he with the other Vega Knights was a displeasing thought. Cassius considered taking the Zephron emperor down before *Gallylya* tried to kill *him,* but with a battle that large might damage the key, not to mention Xzepheniixenze wasn't stable enough for such an event. Xzepheniixenze threatened to fall apart any time he tried to use his full potential. But it was said that the realm would be healed… He was certainly doing more than his part to aid in its restoration.

And he couldn't forget about Zaphaniah, the old King of Hadarazade waiting in his high castle in the heart of the Dragonlands. Zaphaniah had been waiting in silence for a millennium, waiting for the right moment. The Traitor. He was partially responsible for the fall of Lunara, the fall of his own kind. But Cassius was patient as well, and his extensive plans were only beginning.

So Gallylya was the current problem. Everything else was working flawlessly. Gallylya would be unlikely to attack Shahyrahara, for it was still protected from outside magic and uninvited guests—it was reassuring—although the magical ward was weakening.

His signature echoed through his head. It was not a common thing. Someone said his name. Or thought about him. Anyone who thought of him as 'Cassius' and not as an entity of supreme power was busy with other things or asleep. Unless the thinker was dreaming. The dreamer was *she*. Perhaps she was a reincarnation of a past relative, she was certainly similar enough. Perhaps the magic just remembered, for there was no other blood as rich with mysticism. In some ways she was still a mystery to him. And it was a conundrum why he had no desire to search her soul for the answers he knew he couldn't attain through regular means. He supposed she was the first person in a long time he respected so much. Strange.

10

"What in the realm of all that's real is that?"

"Connylia's escorts and entourage. She won't bring anyone from Zephronia," Cassius explained.

Gellia counted twelve horses drawing the main dormeuse, which was rather large and ornate for its kind. There were several other less elaborate dormeuses, but they were for attendants and luggage. Another thing of note was much, if not all, of the entourage were enchanted at some level. It was nearly grand to the point of the ridiculous, but hadn't quite come to the point of grandness where it was lacking in function.

"And there are thirty knights, and Mephibosheth to go with her as well as the carriage men and five ladies in waiting." Cassius looked over Gellia's shoulder at the stable yard below.

Leaning out the window Gellia admired the perfect trappings and elaborate apparel of the assemblage. There seemed to be more people gathered than Cassius said there were. "What about all those extra people?"

"Those are for *your* entourage. Are you ready to face your first assignment?"

She hadn't taken him seriously when he offered the liaison position. "I'm to go today?" She thought it would be much more difficult a position to gain than this. He leaned on the windowsill and smugly gazed at her. She continued, "I don't have any training..."

"What a pathetic and illegitimate excuse. Don't tell me you're too frightened to go."

"Are you sending me to my death?"

"Certainly not. This will be easy and you'll be able to see the countryside; Kaymaria is on the other side of

Xzepheniixenze. You don't have to do much but see how they're coming along with their rebuilding, and perhaps on the way you can remember your magic."

"Rebuilding?"

Cassius raised a hand, and on it appeared a stack of papers. "This is the report on their situation. Read it on the way there. By the time you're finished you can just go to Shahyrahara for the ball, it's not far from Kaymaria, just over the mountains. I'll have your things sent there."

Gellia looked at him suspiciously before taking the papers. Obviously he trusted what she would do when she arrived there otherwise he wouldn't send her. But why whisk her away with such haste? They looked at each other silently. It would be in anyone's better judgment *to* distrust him but Gellia was beginning to admit he won hers. "Well then, I'll be going.".

"Stay away from magical ruins."

She glared at him, but with humor. "I will."

* * *

Even with her own lovely dormeuse-and-four she preferred to ride Amarynth, even if he *was* still angry with her. Not that she really knew. At night she slept in the comfortable vehicle and listened to the crickets and other noises in the night and the deep voices of her men. They had several weeks of undisturbed travel through the province of Caddyan, the territory surrounding Tintagel. Gellia enjoyed seeing all Cassius' lands, the rolling hills covered with trees with patches of clearing here and there, shimmering lakes, and slow moving brooks speaking quietly to themselves. They traveled through several bustling villages where locals stopped to stare at the smallish party passing through.

Eventually their road grew steep and rockier as they crossed the Zareh Pass. Set into the rocks of the pass were ancient towers watching the road below, the travelers had to cross through an old, moss covered wall, which must have been a gate at one time. She could see remnants of beautiful stonework, archways and colonnades into the forest. It was as zig-zaggy as one might expect, but the pass was wide and well maintained. In time the winding road sloped back down into the trees. Gellia's neck hurt from looking up for so long.

"Milady," the head seeker said as he cantered towards her on his sleek bond horse. "We'll be entering Myste soon. The road ahead is mostly bridge, but for a few places."

Gellia nodded. The two seekers who stayed on their flanks brought their horses to the group and went on foot into the surroundings. It wasn't long before the road through the forest and fields turned soggy. Camping wouldn't be an option, so they traveled into the night, only stopping now and again to rest the carriage horses.

By morning, when Gellia woke in the dormeuse, the road turned into a wide stone roadway. Great trees rose from a watery plane, there was moss everywhere, and flowers growing from the twisted roots of trees. Little sunlight shone through the boughs, but the vegetation itself seemed to glow with life. The beams of light that did reach the watery bottom were spotlights on one of the eeriest and most beautiful places Gellia had seen yet. Arms of the gnarled trees created a natural vaulted ceiling, the mosses hanging from their limbs in curtains of pale colors. Birds sang above them while frogs croaked their conversations below, the horses' hoof beats echoed on the stone. A dragonfly buzzed past Gellia's head, then past the knights before her.

Amarynth shook his head, dislodging a few bugs, Gellia created a shield around them to prevent that annoyance. She wondered if anyone lived in the area. Gellia found that occasionally there would be something of an island they would cross over before continuing on the bridges, sometimes there were bridges leading off their road. When she asked she was told those roads led to towns set upon the water, some led to colonies built in the tree boughs. Every so often they passed a lone pillar or a mostly collapsed wall, usually anything made of stone was covered with moss and water flowers. Sometimes she was sure she could hear the echo of an ancient cavalry's hoof beats.

The third week through Myste Gellia chose to ride in the dormeuse to study up on her hosts. Even though she didn't really need to use her riding ability to guide Amarynth, it was nice to take a break away from the saddle. Amarynth ambled along behind the wagon unsaddled and unbridled and seemed happy to be left to his own devices.

As Gellia sat on one of the plush seats of the dormeuse she started to read the pile of papers Cassius had given her. Of course, all the events were written out in perfect detail as only he could. Some passages she had to read several times to figure out exactly what happened.

From what she could gather, Cassius heard Kaymaria was attacked, and left Fuarmaania (and her) to inspect it. Gellia remembered when he left. When he arrived at the city it was in ruin, only a young half-breed was there. He had been practicing his swordsmanship in the mountains. The city had been destroyed by a rogue army led by someone named Karn. The boy withheld information, but Cassius wasn't too concerned about it. So the young man set off to join the army to become good enough to avenge his family's slaughter. There was a note made to watch this boy very closely for there was something rather odd about him and he carried a unique sword... Little did he know that many of the residents had fled and later returned to rebuild... Cassius was completely funding their reconstruction.

Gellia was to go to the city and inspect the progress, and decide who was loyal, who wasn't and so forth and decide if they needed more money. She could see why Cassius wanted to keep them strong, the city produced the finest warriors of Xzepheniixenze—and the finest weapons. Not to mention their city was relatively close to Ravengate.

Once more they walked on through the night. There wasn't an island near enough to set up camp. Fairies floated in the distance as Gellia looked out of the dormeuse. The surroundings were blues and silvers as the moons rose over them. Gellia's lantern was the only light around besides moonbeams and fairies. No pureblood Xzepheniixenze would lower himself to travel by lantern for they were able to see in the dark.

Echoing hoof beats changed to soft thuds as the convoy hit dry ground. A seeker appeared—it would have startled her but she felt him arriving.

"We've hit dry land, milady. It'll be this way until we hit the Swamp."

"Lovely. Find a place to camp."

They chose a widening in the road to start a fire and cook a meal. Knights milled around, untacked their horses, some practiced with their weapons as they did any night they camped. The four seekers sat together discussing who would take which watch.

Gellia listened as crickets sang and unknown creatures slithered, crawled and skittered all around them. She told herself not to be afraid. There was no wraith waiting to pounce on her. He magic could tell her otherwise.

Something had plagued her throughout the trip so far: why had Cassius sent her on this mission? He had given her legitimate reasons for sending her, but it didn't feel quite right. She knew him better than to think it was this simple; but she pushed the thought aside once more. There were other topics more worthy of her concentration.

***

The silence of the catacombs had spread throughout Tintagel, a deep silence that was unnatural for the castle. All was quiet besides the opening of the great main door and the footsteps that followed—he was finally there.

Cassius looked through letters in his office, the moon shone through the window. It was a wonderfully clear night and remarkably calm for most everyone but for guards, a few mages and menservants, the rest had retired for the night. Unfortunately it was for a reason all but the disloyal despised. He sealed a letter and watched the light from the candles flicker over his desk. He knew that eventually the door would open. It did.

"I was lost forever in this miserable castle, cousin. There wasn't a single servant around to ask for directions, either. You need to train them better." The emperor strode in. "Hmf. You're not surprised, are you?"

"You're too grand to be a surprise," Cassius said.

"I just thought I'd drop in for a visit. I just got back from Cambiga. There are some girls that you can have if you want. I brought them with me."

Raven's clothing still bore blood stains. Cassius rolled his eyes. "Yes, I see that you've just returned...In fact, I would enjoy the girls. I'll send a servant for them." He undoubtedly stopped at every village on the way back as well. The message of his visit came many weeks ago. Unfortunately Cassius couldn't be at every village.

"Done." The emperor smiled. "I heard your conquest was successful."

"Yes." Cassius watched his cousin pull up a chair; it would need to be burned later.

Raven leaned forward, almost like he was discussing a secret. "I heard your armies were led by a girl."

"You've already heard so." The baron waited for the nonsense.

"Is she pretty?"

"Oh, I suppose. If you like that type." He watched Raven coolly; he was one of the few who didn't fear the emperor, but he'd known Raven for centuries.

"Whatever do you mean? Do tell." He had that look, the one that made so many unfortunate souls tremble with fear.

"Well, to put it pleasantly, she has the personality of a harpy. And..." Cassius made a face of disgust.

"And? Tell me."

"She has hair in the most disagreeable places. And warts."

Raven looked a little horrified and sat back in the chair. "You can keep her."

Cassius nodded. "I can't blame you. *I* wouldn't touch her. But she's a fairly good with a sword." He shrugged and sent magical tendrils throughout the castle to make sure all the doors were locked, physically and mystically. His servants would not be tormented. Raven always tried to appear he was there for a political visit, but it was never the case.

"Y-yes. Well, I'm going to take a romp through your castle, maybe I'll stay for a while," the emperor said cheerily, and rose. "Then I need to return to Ravengate to prepare for the party."

Cassius smiled and nodded and waited for him to exit. A while to Raven usually meant a month or two. The baron frowned. They would be short staffed for however long he stayed. All women, certainly servants and otherwise vulnerable women, were encouraged to stay in hiding. If they disobeyed their baron's orders they took their safety into their own hands. The mages and nobles were capable enough decide what risks to take.

***

Gellia sent the dormeuse and two knights back to Tintagel, carrying with her the paperwork and any other necessities. The vehicle had been nice, but its slowness was making her nervous.

As they moved along there was no talking, only the sound of armor, and the horses' rhythmic breathing as they galloped. The faster they left Myste the happier Gellia would be. Luckily they *did* have bond horses. Regular horses would never keep up the pace. Some of the company had been in the area before and said there was a small fortress ahead of them. Gellia ordered that they would not stop moving until they reached it. The idea of showing up at court in Kaymaria half dead did not appeal to her. With any luck the fortress would have an inn. Even though they were accustom to sleeping standing up, she was sure the horses wouldn't mind the comfort of straw filled stalls.

Gellia was beginning to understand what Cassius meant when he told her Xzepheniixenze was savage. There was vast wilderness throughout, but it was *so* beautiful. She wished she had more time to see it all, but there was work to be done in these trying times. The Golden Age of Xzepheniixenze had long passed, the reign of Razhiede. She hoped it would someday come again.

At the fortress gate they were allowed passage but not welcomed. It was a town, really, not a massive castle like Tintagel or city like Candiem. It was similar to the motte and bailey style of lesser lords. Gellia looked around at the few shops that seemed almost to be built into the wooden walls, and the large castle-like house where the lord lived. This wasn't a wealthy population but they didn't seem starved either. Her seekers stood around her for a moment, surveying the area while the knights waited for her command. The four seekers disappeared to collect information. The lord of the fortress wasn't friendly but was too impressed by her flash to give them a difficult time.

The inn was dark and smoky place, the wooden floor was uneven and the boards were worn smooth from so many patrons. Gellia found a table to sit at and ordered wine. It was sour. The only food they served there was meat pie. What kind of meat she wasn't sure but it smelled awful. It reminded her of Fuarmaania.

Minstrels played on the other side of the dim room. After a few moments the Tintagel knights and two of the seekers entered, some seated themselves on the wooden stools; some started to socialize. A few girls appeared, and some of the locals. Before long the room was filled with people and talk and drink. Gellia smiled sleepily and decided to go to her room. Joining their revels would not be fitting for a lady, and after all, she was tired.

Her room was sparse, something like her room in Fuarmaania but with a better view. Any part of Xzepheniixenze was a better view. The straw mattress was less comfortable than sleeping in the carriage. As she lie there she wondered if she was worthy of the name Zapheny. Razhiede had reined over Xzepheniixenze for countless years. If he and his son had lived she would be the rightful heir. Imagine. But she had been in born Fuarmaania.

Maybe she was no longer a princess even though Cassius called her such, but she was more significant than she had been. Of course, Cassius probably called her princess more as a jab than anything. The moment she tried to push the thoughts from her mind she could hear ocean waves crashing on the shore, sea birds calling. She wasn't sure if she was asleep or awake. Her magic began to dance around her and shape itself into unicorns and rose bushes. Zenobia...

When the sun rose and woke Gellia she felt more rested than she had in weeks, maybe even months. She rose and went to her window and gazed on the snowy mountains as they rose up in the distance beyond the swamp. Upon concentrating with her magic she could sense or almost see old stone structures built high on the mountainsides, old towers that must have fallen centuries before. What happened all those years back? Cassius saw it, she knew. He was there. Was that why the land was so tormented beneath its beautiful exterior?

After she dressed and marched downstairs she found her men were already prepared for departure, they merely waited for her command. They looked rather fresh after only one night of rest. Soon enough they were once again on their way.

"We'll have to cross the swamp on a raft," one of the seekers told her as they galloped through the gate.

"How far?" Gellia asked.

"Not long at this pace."

"Good." She grew impatient. Maybe she could dig into one of their minds and find the memories of locations needed to build a portal. Portals were dangerous things. Gellia wasn't sure if she was ready to make one even if she *did* have the ability— she did, however, feel her magic start to weave itself if she thought about it for too long. Cassius had given her his knowledge, and it was a priceless gift.

It was true; the swamp was not far at their pace. They reached the edge of the great swamp in a few days of steady travel on an ever-downward slope. It seemed fitting that the swamp was in a depression. "What is this place called?" Gellia asked. It was full of mist, only the surface of the water could be seen, all of it shades of grey. The group waited on the wooden dock for the ferry. Fog surrounded them, made it difficult to see past their horses' ears.

"The Swamp of Sorrows, milady," the seeker said. She continued to look at him so he told her a story. "It was named a long time ago. I read a book about it once and it mentioned death and the city in the sky."

Gellia recalled that she had read something that also mentioned it. "City in the sky?" Amarynth crunched on his bit.

The seeker nodded. "Well, milady, I don't know if it was true, but there supposedly was a great city made from magic that floated around in the clouds where no one could see it... the ferry should be here soon." Her seekers were alert, using their gift to locate their ride. "It's not far off now, milady." Their horses' ears flicked to and fro, listening to the water. "We're only crossing a small section of it to get to the pass, it shouldn't take all that long."

Gellia reached her magic out like fingers, trying to feel the land. No living magic was in the area, just tiny notes of energy long since gone. In actuality it could be considered a magically dead area, if she were to need much power she would have to draw it from a great distance. Only because of her sensitivity could she feel the old traces. She closed her eyes and tried to listen to the forgotten voices and for a moment felt that Cassius was there with her.

It was the thudding and swish of the raft that brought her from her thoughts. Gellia frowned. Would it hold all of them? It wasn't much more than a huge timber raft with a spindly old man standing on it, and it was supposed to bring them across the swamp? The knights waited her signal. As they dismounted and filed onto the 'ferry' Gellia detected magic around their ferryman—he had some magic running through him, enough to push the raft over the water.

The raft lurched forward into the blinding mist. It was only moments later that the shore disappeared. How could anyone find the way through this? This was the shortcut to Kaymaria? A few old logs poked up from the grey water around them, a few rocks here and there, and a patch of mud high enough to be seen on the surface. Every so often she was sure the black spikes that rose from the water were more of a bone shape rather than branch. She thought she spotted an old wall peeking above the rippling water, and on several occasions she spotted what looked to be old archways through the mist. Perhaps there was another reason for the swamp's name, but Gellia felt a reason herself. Its gloom was enough to make anyone sorrowful.

Night came. The ferry still floated along, and only its presence in the water, and her companions' low conversations could be heard over the black swamp. It was so dark. She felt herself slip into a trance. Perhaps it was the melancholy of the land. There was so much more to Xzepheniixenze, and she wanted to know it all. But she felt it would be more of a rediscovering than learning. *I am this place,* she thought, *and Cassius with me. I can never leave even if I die. Perhaps even my mother returned as a spirit.* She drifted into sleep.

The next day, through the silvery fog, a dark object appeared before them and took the shape of a huge gnarled tree. The seekers were sensitive to its presence before it appeared—looked at each other and wondered. Suddenly Gellia sensed life in the swamp. It was easy to sense, everything else was so quiet and devoid of magic, but it was old magic.

Gellia studied the tree, she was not seeing with her eyes alone. The barge moved around its great roots. It *was* conscious. It watched them passively. It was thinking what it might do to them if circumstances were different. It saw that Gellia could hear it and she could feel it smiling at her. She shivered and goose bumps crept over her skin. The ferry finally passed it, but Gellia still watched as it watched her with its spirit, not its eyes. She felt the toothy grin, the taste of powerful magic and finally the faded signature of Cassius. The tree disappeared into the mist.

No one else thought enough of it to make mention. Gellia waited for something large to spring from the fog behind him. No noise but for their voices could be heard. The magic that gave her ability to see the life in the old bark drew away and only her memory of it remained.

It was dusk when they finally reached the edge of the swamp and the road to Kaymaria. They galloped towards an inn at the base of the mountains. One of the bond horses lived there before and knew where it was so they let the mare lead the way. From the inn it would be a day's ride to Kaymaria. Even though she was tired, she still had the energy to press on and noticed the Xzepheniixenze with her did not look tired in the least.

Nightfall came, the lanterns from the inn were easy to see, beckoning them to dry beds. The horses were taken the moment they stopped in the stable yard. Gellia gave one of the seekers money to get the rooms. She didn't feel like talking to anyone, including the innkeeper. But she was still given a fine room, much nicer than the last room in which she stayed. It had a carved wooden bed, a brass bathtub, a large fireplace and woven rugs on the floor. Of course, this inn was much larger and catered to travelers going to and coming from Kaymaria, few people traveled through Myste. In this place she could order a hot bath—which she did—and hoped that the others did the same to look their best the next day. It was beyond Gellia what would happen when she arrived in the city and she still scarcely believed she was doing it.

They saw the city in the distance, a jagged line across the wide plateau, the snowy mountains making a border between the city and sky. The seekers came in from around them.

As they approached, the damage to the city became more apparent, the outer wall was crumbled, the houses destroyed. The renegade army had burned everything. The main gate was still there, an enormous archway that stood alone with no walls to keep it company. The main road was cleared so they didn't have to pick their way over rubble. Side roads were still full of soot and rocks. They didn't see a single soul until they rode into the inner part of the city—the only thing that let them believe there was still life was the sounds of chisels in the distance. Gellia was astounded by the size of the community, taking up more space than Tintagel and Dournzariame combined. There were groups of people with oxen and horses trying to haul stone from one place to another.

Gellia and her band kept moving along the main road, looking over the extent of the damage and noticing houses were being repaired. Most of the buildings in the inner city were made of stone, but were only shells. She was amazed at how tall they were; the different stones used telling how they were built in stages over so many years. These skeleton buildings barely let light down from the sky, and one certainly couldn't see the castle from the streets. It occurred to her that the inner city streets were like great corridors with gates here and there, mostly likely built as a strategic defense that she could not appreciate. *I would love to see its layout from the air,* she thought. She could only imagine what sort of army could destroy such a place.

Finally the castle came into view. It must have been an architectural masterpiece like Tintagel, the remaining walls were thick and plain and there were several of them before the actual castle. Gellia supposed this would have been the place to run to for safety. Two outer walls, the inner one taller, then the castle, and judging from the rubble the castle must have been very tall. There looked to be more of the population wandering around the castle grounds with more work animals and stone boats, most paused to look at the guests. A few people came from the ruined stable and offered to show their horses to the stable and told them their leader was taking visitors. "I don't know if it could be called a formal audience, milady," said an older man who was not Xzepheniixenze. He looked as though he had lived a hundred years in a matter of moments.

Gellia nodded, keeping her regal manner. "Come," she said to her men. She didn't want to do this alone. Maybe the Azqebryne were loyal to Cassius but it didn't mean they would be loyal to her.

***

"No, no. We have to make our priority the *castle*. Once the castle is built we can work on the rest of the city. Everyone still here can live in the castle. We need every one *here*," Queen Azqebryne said to one of her new council. She surveyed her surroundings for the one-hundredth time that day. She was the queen of wreckage, but was thankful that so much of the castle withstood the damage from magic, even if it did reduce her to poverty. Every day she used what magic she had to help reconstruction—she could put a hundred mages to work, but the problem was convincing people to move there. In its prime Kaymaria swarmed with people, but now no one saw the use of it—it was too remote for them to bother. She remembered it was only years ago that people from all over the realm came to train there, to study there, to live in its crowded streets filled with ancient traditions. Her family was one of the greatest, their stories intertwined with those of the Celestial, but no one remembered those stories. Now all they remembered was the massacre, and how the streets ran red and were littered with bodies.

The royal court was bright, but everyone hoped it wouldn't rain through the space that used to be the ceiling. A group of counselors stood around her each complaining about different issues. The Tintagel envoy could be arriving any day; it wasn't like Cassius not to check up on things. Kaymaria didn't ask for help, but the baron of Tintagel answered their need. The queen suspected that despite Kaymaria's current situation he still saw its uses, not since the time of the Golden Age did any of her family expect any alliance to be beneficial.

One of her servants, who had been a peasant, walked through the crack between the giant doors as they hung half off their hinges. Rooves were more important than interior doors. "What is it?" She felt a presence.

He opened his mouth but didn't say a word, he looked mystified. Her suspicions were confirmed as the doors behind him lifted and were set aside and magic rushed through the castle like a river. Queen Azqebryne was not a stranger to magic. She froze. The peasant man jumped aside and the Tintagel party entered. At their head was a young goddess whose beauty and transcendent magic could make the strongest weep with the grief of knowing such perfection could never be attained but by *Zapheny*.

As they strode into what had been the great hall the queen knew by every bit of the woman's behavior that she must be the one who so many talked about. Not only did she have the look of the Zapheny of the old stories, but she carried herself differently than a Xzepheniixenze—this woman almost carried herself in the posture of a Zephron. Every move she made was regal. The Azqebryne clan was loyal to the Zapheny for as long as any of them could remember, only after the fall of Zenobia did they swear their allegiance to House Vazepheny, to Cassius, the one Razhiede named his heir apparent. It was a story passed down the generations in the city of Kaymaria, one they all knew well. Here was the lost Zapheny heiress who came as a representative from Tintagel. A whole new world was opening up to them. Nonette was old enough to see a vastly different future than she'd expected before.

…Gellia sorted through her memories and recognized the woman in the room as the queen, her aura was deep blue. She was a mage, but not a strong one. A child stood next to her, a girl of about twelve who looked just like her, whose magical talents were far superior. Gellia announced herself as queen's attendants scattered. She tried out a better name. "I am Gellia Zapheny of Tintagel."

The queen deeply nodded. "Welcome, Zapheny. I am the queen of this…" she made a motion with her hand and did not take her eyes off Gellia. "Although I doubt anyone in the territory I'm to rule would call me queen, for I never intended to rule. You can call me Nonette if you like or Lady Azqebryne if you wish to keep things formal. This is my daughter, Ozska… we've been expecting you." She started to turn. "Please follow me so we can talk about the progress or lack thereof." She motioned to Gellia.

Gellia followed Nonette through a rock cluttered passage. From the rubble Gellia could see how beautiful the castle once was. She wondered how much worse it was if seemingly so little was done for its restoration. "I'm sure you've seen how things are out there," the lady began, "that's how it is all over Kaymaria. Would you believe we were the home of the finest warriors in the empire?"

"I've heard of their legend."

"…they were all butchered. Karn holds great power, thousands of troops made of undead and monsters…"

They walked out through a doorway even though most of the surrounding wall was gone. The two of them sat at a table in the courtyard. Since the walls were no longer there they had a view of the city below as it wrapped around the castle and down the gentle hill, the snowy mountains in the distance. Nonette looked at the destruction. "Tell his lordship I'm doing my best. I know he wants results, but there has been more deserters than settlers here."

"How many of you are here?" Gellia asked. Nonette didn't want the throne; she was merely a decoration, Gellia realized. She never bothered to learn how to run things assuming that nothing would ever happen to the rest of her family. Gellia also recognized that Nonette knew more that she would ever reveal.

"Oh, a few hundred. We used to be tens of thousands at least. Many of the outer villages were destroyed as well, and the ones in the mountains. There were no survivors that I know of. To make my duty here even easier the emperor has attacked as well. He didn't seem to understand we had nothing left to take. I hid my daughter in a well and sacrificed myself. He is a foe far too great for the likes of my magical talents."

Ozska spoke. "Mama, may I go?"

"Yes." The two women watched the girl wander down the slope and move herself around the sword in mock wielding. Gellia felt there was something familiar about the girl's movements. "...Her father was not of royal birth. I liked him so I asked him to give me a child. He already had a child by a merchant's daughter, a son Ozska idolized. He was a brilliant swordsman even while so young. It was a shame to lose him..." She looked at Gellia. "You must be thinking I'm not fit to rule. In all actuality Lord Vazepheny should give this place to you. You have more strength flowing through your veins than I could ever hope to have."

Gellia smiled to hide her shock. It wasn't a statement for which she was prepared. "He doesn't always reveal the reasons for his actions. If you're still on the throne of Kaymaria, there must be a good reason for it."

"We've heard about you."

This was also unexpected.

"Bards and seekers tell us tales about a young woman who took charge of Tintagel and ran with the armies to destroy those threatening the people... You must be exceptional. Of course, I was expecting a girl, and although you have the look of someone so young, I can see that you are not young at all after sensing your magic." She smiled. "The Lorkiegn are bullies. If we didn't live so far away from them they would attack us as well, especially now. We don't have any defenses."

As Gellia surveyed the city she noticed the layout of streets and gates and hills. It seemed to her that the city should have been impregnable—just a few mages should have been able to defend the city from attacking mages. In the notes Gellia didn't finish reading Cassius mentioned the use of many foot soldiers of sorts in the attack and few mages. Apparently her liege studied the entire city for clues. She wondered if someone in the attacking army knew of ways around the defenses. "You have enough funding to rebuild?"

"Yes. More than enough. Lord Vazepheny has been most generous and for that we thank him. It takes time and manpower, and it is even more difficult with the constant threat of attack."

Gellia mind-contacted one of her seekers, who almost instantly appeared. "Do you know where our nearest army is?"

The man nodded. Leave it to a seeker. "The third army, I can locate it easily, milady." The seeker pulled out a pen and paper, almost reading Gellia's mind as he handed it to her.

Gellia started to write. "I want you to go to our nearest army and give this to them. I want them to relocated to Kaymaria to help rebuild and to protect the people of this city." She was surprised this hadn't happened sooner, and hoped that she was making the right choice. Other than her recent skirmish with Candiem, the armies weren't engaged.

"Yes, milady."

The third army was one of the more experienced and had several mages and healers she knew of, which would aid Kaymaria greatly. She turned to Nonette, who understood Gellia's train of thought.

"We thank you, your majesty," Nonette said.

Gellia smiled and read through the woman's mind a bit deeper. Nonette didn't know Gellia was there, but thought out her opinion: *I can't tell if you're there, Lady Zapheny, but if you are, you are more than welcome to look.* Another surprise was Nonette was loyal, even more so to Gellia. It was the lady's belief that the Zapheny would bring new life and fulfillment to those who were shined upon by her light. Nonette was not a young woman; she saw many things in her life and understood her clan's history and legends. Gellia tried not to look startled. Her family's alliance ran deep. Nonette would betray the House of Vazepheny if Gellia asked her to, for it seemed the Azqebryne were loyal to the Zapheny since the dawn of time.

"Will you be staying long, milady?" Nonette asked. "You are certainly welcome to do so, and it would be an honor."

"I have an appointment at Shahyrahara," Gellia explained. "But I will return at the first opportunity to do so."

Nonette watched the lady, remembered the stories she was told as a child. Cassius was shrewd indeed. "I have a room for you to rest in, it isn't much but there is a roof."

That evening as she looked at her sparse room Gellia wondered how she would get to her next engagement. She didn't know how to get to Shahyrahara and neither did any of her company. The residents of Kaymaria never heard of it. So how did Cassius expect her to get there? She sat on the bed with a heavy exhale.

I know how the way. But we're not bringing them with us, Amarynth said.

You're talking to me now? She was just slipping under the covers.

He didn't answer. She guessed not.

We're leaving tonight, he said.

We are?

You heard me. You can sleep on the way. You only have a few days to get there. People are already arriving.

How do you know that?

He didn't answer.

Gellia rose from her shabby bed and got dressed to go to the stables. As quickly and neatly as she could she wrote a short letter to leave with one of her seekers, explaining her disappearance.

"I think I should like a long holiday after all this," Gellia said as she entered Amarynth's stall with his tack. "I suppose we're traveling light."

He didn't answer.

Out in Xzepheniixenze. Completely alone. Once again the world seemed terribly big.

11

Amarynth jigged. Gellia woke. It was nighttime, but she wasn't sure how long she had been asleep. *Quite some time,* Amarynth told her. *We're almost there. You realize it's going to take you almost a day to make yourself look presentable.*

They were still climbing the mountain, the trees were sparser and the path was rockier. She thought that certainly at such high elevation they should be able to see Kaymaria, but all she could see were more mountains. How far had they traveled? She wasn't asleep for that long, was she? "Don't you ever tire? ...Oh Amarynth you're so sullen."

You're the first person to mention it.

It was almost a conversation, and she smiled. Perhaps it would just take longer than expected to get to know him.

The path they were on was narrow and winding with the underbrush covering it like a thick blanket. There wasn't a wheel track to be seen anywhere, not that the path they were on could support a goat-drawn vegetable cart, much less a carriage. She wasn't even sure if it was even a riding path, maybe just a deer trail. Leave it to Amarynth to bring them through the thickest part of the wilderness. She listened for any sounds of wild animals or attackers.

The moons were out, both full, Aeryane and Ylzanare. As she gazed at them she thought about what she'd read. Only the educated few knew their names. It was easy enough to call them by color, sliver and blue, or smaller and larger.

They reached the peak and cantered over the top, below them was a steep and narrow valley, almost like a pit. Gellia didn't notice the pit; her mind was locked on a glowing iridescent palace opposite them. Nothing else was around them but starkness in comparison to the beauty of Shahyrahara. "My *word* Amarynth." Gellia breathed. The flags that topped the towers were long and thin and floated on a breeze she couldn't feel. Not stark white like Dournzariame, Shahyrahara was almost a soft ice blue. Great domes of almost glowing blue, shimmered in the night. There were rings of walls around a center structure, pillars and arches, flying buttresses, swooping curves and not a single corner to be seen. It was larger than Tintagel, than the palace of Dournzariame; she couldn't imagine that people built it. Their surroundings were silent as a tomb. "Of all things divine."

Indeed, Amarynth said.

They were greeted by stable attendants when they arrived. They seemed confused when Amarynth refused to accompany them. He barely looked back at her as he started away.

Strange, Gellia thought. *What is this place?* she asked as he walked away.

What was *is more appropriate. It hasn't been anything but a pretty building for quite some time. You'll need to ask Cassius for older history books, or ask him.*

She appeared to be the last one to arrive. Carriages were tucked away, all the horses were settled in their stalls and were rested like they had been there for several days.

It was a living palace, she could feel it whispering. Gellia reached out with her magic again as she entered a main corridor, but before she could explore some servants escorted her to her chambers. She knew she wouldn't be able to find her way around this place so she didn't bother paying attention to where she was going.

…Its essence was deep, buried deep in time; she had difficulty finding the feel. This place was full of life and death and stories. It was lonely and sad. She wondered if others could sense it as well. It gave her the feeling that it recognized her, or her magic at least and she felt that Razhiede must have visited there at one time.

The architecture was curves and circles and archways each flowing into the next. Wrought silver decorations covered pillars and entrances; there were graceful gates, and fantastic sculptures of winged people. Everything was a larger scale as well, even more so than Tintagel.

The servants whisked her away to a large suite. About twenty more attendants appeared from nowhere each busy with their own jobs; she was pleased to see a few familiar faces. They started to work her over—bathing, scrubbing, combing...

With all this nonsense Gellia couldn't wait to see what she would look like when it was finished. If they were making that much of a fuss over *her* she couldn't imagine what they were doing for his wonderful extravagance. She dozed while they worked on her hair, it seemed the chair was built for it.

Gellia woke and her scalp felt tight. With so many hairpins her hair felt like a helmet. "I need to move," she told the attendants. She pulled her dressing gown around herself and went back into the empty and dim corridor for a quick walk.

It was nice to stretch her legs a bit so she walked down several amazingly tall corridors. All the walls were etched with picture stories. She could just follow the story back to her room. Did she hear music? Following the sound down the hall she discovered where the musicians practiced. She peeked in through the partially opened door. Her heart seized in her chest. Her breath stopped and she froze in the doorway. The number of musicians astounded her. Gellia felt faint. This was not the size of party she was used to, not when the orchestra alone had great numbers. She backed away from the door and saw several menservants approaching.

"Milady? Come with us please."

These are obviously Cassius' servants, she thought, under strict orders for they didn't just let her do what she wanted. I can't go through with this, Gellia thought, I'm not ready to go through this. All those people with their nasty looks, I have a difficult a time with just the mages.

"Let's go back to the room, milady." They walked her into her chamber, handed her over to the maids who fanned her once they had her seated. The men left her chamber.

Gellia held her head. "I think I should faint away when I go out there. You think his lordship will be too unhappy if I don't go?"

The servants seemed to ignore her complains. "Let's get you dressed," they said.

"I still don't want to go."

"It will be lovely, milady," one of the women said.

The attendants stood Gellia on her feet and put her into all the under skirting and foundation garments while one sparingly applied cosmetics. In moments the team of attendants was dumping a cloud of purplish satin over her head, which seemed to fall onto the correct places. Some arranged sleeves, some laced her up, and others arranged the huge train. It was flowing, simple and elegant, no ruffles or lace. There was some bejeweled accenting and it was certainly the most flattering dress she ever wore. Someone handed her a jeweled fan to match and someone else pulled a beautiful necklace that was made to go with her pendant, and matching earrings to finish the picture. Everyone stepped back to admire their work. The door opened and a woman ushered in Skip. Gellia turned to see whom it was and saw Skip frozen in his footsteps. Gellia felt ridiculous. "You look beautiful," he said. "Like royalty."

"I feel foolish." They brought forward a long and wide mirror for her to see herself. Gellia barely recognized the reflection and she could barely breathe. She was a picture.

"Don't." The servants pushed him towards her and helped him take up the long train. "I've seen a few people here and trust me, you are the most beautiful."

"You've already been spying?" she asked with a smile. As she started to appreciate how well he'd been clean up and dressed, she felt his beauty might rival any woman's.

"Oh yes..."

Her servants went through a process of making final adjustments. Dusk came. It was time to go. She was so happy to have Skip with her.

"Remember to breathe, milady," one of the girls told Gellia.

"Breathe," Gellia parroted.

They walked her down a maze of corridors, Skip holding her train off the floor—not that there was any dirt on the ground to soil it. Gellia held her breath then remembered to let it out again, and she couldn't feel her feet. In the distance there was a flourish of trumpets. The attendants prodded Gellia forward; she knew they were all under orders from their baron. Soon they could hear the orchestra and the hall became unlit. "Why are there no candles, no orbs?" Gellia hazarded to ask.

"So the guests don't lose their way. They can follow the light, milady," one of the servants answered. "Milady has a special path." The other attendants melted into the darkness, leaving only one to lead Gellia to what she thought would be her impending doom. Skip took her hand even though he was supposed to be behind her. She squeezed his in appreciation.

Finally they reached a very large curtained doorway where the servant smiled and left. Gellia almost went into a panic. She tried to remember all that Connylia taught her.

"Don't worry, while you were off gallivanting they were pounding etiquette into my brain, amongst other things, but we can talk of that later," Skip said. "He told me look after you."

She made a face. "I see how much faith he has in me."

"You'd be surprised." Skip hated to admit it but Cassius had more faith in her than she could ever realize, he just never said it.

"I think I'm going to take a look so I know what to expect."

"Why don't you just go in?"

"I can't. I can't run out there blindly."

"Not knowing might be better than knowing," Skip said. Gellia ignored him and peeked through a tiny slit between the curtains. He continued, "I can already tell you that there are at least six hundred people out there not including the servants. You've missed most of the party. Yesterday they had archery competitions and spent the evening in the theater, the day before that they had a smaller ball and a great feast..." He'd been busy those days, always near Cassius but out of the way, learning all he could.

Beyond the curtain was a set of wide stairs that led to the floor of the largest room she had ever seen. All sorts of Xzepheniixenze nobles were there talking and dancing. Mostly all she could see was swirling colors and black hair. She pulled away. "I don't want to go, Skip."

"Why not? They've been waiting for you."

"All the most important people in the empire are down there, all at once. And that man will say my name and they'll all stare at me."

"How can anyone not stare at the brightest star?" he said.

Someone else was with them, Gellia could hear skirts rustling.

"I'll take some of the attention away from you if you like."

"Conny! Oh you're here! I'm so happy! Oh dear I don't know if I can do this!" Gellia sputtered.

"You certainly can. Here, take my hand for support—no one will think it odd." The older woman smiled. "I'm thrilled right to death to be here. I used to love going to these parties…"

In the dim light she really couldn't see her friend very well but took her hand. Connylia raised their clasped hands as if presenting Gellia.

"Deep breath." She knew Gellia's training would come out, had faith in the teaching even if Gellia did not. "This herald has special instructions." She then spoke to the man just on the other side of the curtain. "We're ready."

Gellia did as she was told. The curtains parted. A man's voice rang out: "Empress Connylia Duvray of Zenobia and Princess Gellia Zapheny of Tintagel."

They stepped out onto the dais, their boys held their trains behind them. Gellia tried not to stare as the ceiling spiraled open to reveal the full moons. Connylia's dress lit up in the moonlight, and Gellia's shimmered with silver. Every head turned to look at them. A chalice shattered on the floor. Everyone down to the last servant was silent. Gellia glanced at her friend who smiled demurely, and they slowly walked down the long staircase. *I can't feel my feet*, Gellia told Connylia. Left foot, right foot, left foot… It was the largest and grandest room she had ever been in—one could house an entire army there. Ornate columns, giant windows, tiered balconies, several stair cases, even the ceiling with its magnificent oculus was a work of art. It was breathtaking.

You'll be fine.

Then Gellia looked at her friend again, an empress. Gellia knew from where she inherited her beauty.

Below them were all sorts of lovely people dressed in all colors, and some clothing was entirely made from silver or gold fabric. Many of them were a bit gaudy. Feathers, jewelry, flowers, everything was used to make the most extravagant outfits. Some turned to each other and whispered while others were mesmerized. Gellia didn't recognize a single person, and more strangers entered through the archways around the room, all came to look at her and Connylia.

What seemed to have been an eternity of stairs was lessening, pouring them into a sea of nobility. After the first step onto the floor, a path between the other guests parted before them, leading them to their host. Gellia was thrilled to see a friendly face and was sure her expression changed from fear to elation. Cassius took Connylia's hand and kissed it then did the same with Gellia who was quite impressed by how conservatively dressed he was. His doublet was made of the same fabric as Gellia's (but green of course) and there were a few jewels here and there but that was it. In a way he complimented her perfectly for their attire was styled similarly.

He led Connylia to the dance. Gellia realized that even amongst the grace of their people Cassius still shone the brightest. A nobleman asked Gellia to dance and she was too nervous to say no. She held her head up and smiled at the man. Skip arranged her train over her arm and stood aside as the man led her out.

For the first time in Gellia's life the random dance partner was not falling all over his own feet. He introduced himself as Baron Arioch of Myste-Wildgate and he loved to talk about himself. She heard this name before—in correspondence at Tintagel. "...I know that my city isn't large right *now* but since I'm allied to Baron Vazepheny then I'm sure to have my lands grow..."

"Yes, I am familiar with your holdings," she said. Gellia was sure she was familiar with this nonsense. 'I have a lot to offer and so forth, come be my woman...' Maybe it was a *little* different. This mortal man must have been in his mid-forties with no magic, but had a respectable past as a knight. For the time being he was loyal to Tintagel but if a better offer came along he would switch sides immediately. It was his goal to steal her loyalties away from Tintagel.

As Gellia danced and he talked she tried to think of things logically and take a tally of her information. Anything to help deal with the feeling of being overwhelmed. She kept her expression of aloofness, even as her partner showered her with compliments.

She was the ward—no the ally—of a baron. But not a baron of a few acres and a small manor house. No, he had a magnificent castle and this palace that she knew of, lands that spanned across the empire. He threw this party, one of the caliber of royalty. For what reason? She wasn't accustomed to thinking of herself as much of anything in this realm, yet she had the distinct impression this was to show her to the empire. And she wasn't just a pretty face, she had led armies and helped the people. The scope of his plans was becoming clearer by the moment.

Connylia's presence was also significant. She was a person of power of times long ago. This entire party was a power play. He revealed to his allies and enemies that he had all the connections, that he could keep secrets, significant ones. That he must be respected, feared.

Gellia started to feel better. She looked at her partner and searched him with her magic. He was not a threat to her. Perhaps to others, but not to her. As she spread her magical fingers to sift through many around her, she found most were not her magical equal.

It was a revelation that did her a world of good. He wouldn't have her at a party if he thought she'd embarrass him. He wouldn't have left her in charge of Tintagel if he thought she would bollocks up what he worked so hard to create. He was too calculating for that. He knew her well, and had faith in her.

As they danced she caught a glimpse of him and their eyes met. *Cassius,* she thought, but it was so much more than just the sound of his name. It was a connection in their magic. For just a split second his eyes seemed to soften to that look reserved for only her. Their exchange was as quick as a thought and over as they danced with their partners.

"...*You're* the one who took Candiem." Baron Arioch said.

"I suppose you could say that," Gellia said. "But I think the army did most of the work."

Arioch looked at her with amusement in his purple Xzepheniixenze eyes, and smiled. "An alliance," said he, "or perhaps you would consider me for the father of your progeny."

Gellia just looked at him and smiled. An appropriate answer came to mind. "Aren't you pretentious?"

He laughed.

Even though he was taller than she, she still managed to look down at him. "I'm going to keep my options open." The dance ended and someone else approached her. She took her new partner's hand with passion and twirled away with vehemence.

Across the dance floor her friends spoke. "By the look on her face someone just proposed a bit of strategic generating," Connylia said as she looked over her shoulder.

"He did," Cassius said, "a Zapheny who has never been heard of comes out of nowhere, acts out against the general rule of Tintagel, takes Candiem as her first campaign, and has mage talent would attract that type of attention. She has options never open to her before—she could have anyone and anything, any province she liked and they would willingly give it to her. What they seem to forget is, as Zapheny, she is unattainable. If she was the beguiling type, she could have most of the empire eating from her hand. Who in this world has better heritage that she? Who could possibly be her equal?"

"I would say, if anyone, it would be you... At least she's powerful enough that none of them are going to try and club her over the head and drag her off like a prize," Connylia added. Give in, she thought. I can see the connection that no one can understand. You'll have to give in sooner or later...

"But for our emperor."

Connylia frowned. Something in that statement held a painful truth. "You're right, of course. I don't know how I forgot."

"You live in Zephronia under the protection of your brother, it's easy to forget unsavory people like Raven. I often wished Raven would try something brainless like attack Zephronia, then I could watch him burn in Gallylya's fires." He smiled at her. "I suppose even *he* isn't that foolish. Gallylya and his Vega Knights are every Xzepheniixenze's worst nightmare."

Connylia smiled back. She didn't want to talk about her brother. "Speaking of nightmares, it just occurred to me that we had the same primary dance instructor—your mother. The countess and Razhiede had her disguised at the finishing school so I would have the best training."

He chuckled. "Is that right? Nightmare she might have been, but *very* effective."

Across the room Gellia was further astounded at men's forwardness. "...The nobles need to find more interesting topics to discuss," Gellia said and smiled. She could sense his fear deep within him, even when his city was a strong one.

The nervous prince started to panic and searched for the right words. "But *I* already have a good name. It would be beneficial for you to…"

"Perhaps you should rethink the way you proposition me." She swore if someone had the gall to touch her hair she'd have them assassinated. Gellia pulled away from the dance and sought the refreshment table, leaving the prince behind. No one screamed at her for being 'impertinent' here—it made her even more sought after. No one could take his or her eyes off her. She could even see through all those who didn't take the direct approach as this last man did.

Thankfully, some talked with her pleasantly, spoke of times and parties to come, spoke intelligently to her about history and courtly matters. It reminded her of when Cassius first came to Fuarmaania and fooled everyone with his charm. In that place sweet and silent women were desired, here only the strong were acceptable.

Skip appeared next to her. "This is part of my job," he said proudly, ordered wine for her. "Want anything to eat?"

"No, thank you." …Though the thousands of tiny delicacies looked absolutely wonderful. Gellia traversed the edge of the room, picking up pieces of conversation and watching people dancing. "Are you enjoying yourself, Skip?" Several people who she already danced with smiled and bowed as she passed.

"Well, I've learned a lot since you were gone. He said I'm going to be a great seeker. I can read people's minds and sense their thoughts from long distances and I can sense their auras." He quickly stuffed a pastry into his mouth hoping no one but she noticed. "Some of the people here have been following you, and trying not to look like they are, so they can watch you. Most say nothing of you to each other but I know they're thinking of you. He's definitely keeping an eye on you."

"Is that so."

Gellia was watching the 'he' of whom Skip spoke. Cassius was speaking with a nobleman whose aura she recognized. With her magic she sorted through all the thoughts and mind barriers to theirs. The lord was a mage and knew what was going on for his mental barriers were woven thickly, but unevenly. Cassius wanted in and was speaking with him but didn't want to make the scene of him tearing down the protective walls around the lord.

Gellia's mind snuck up behind the man, found a weak spot in his barrier and tickled it. He immediately went on defensive against her, but could not hold up against Cassius who ducked in, procured the information he wanted and was out again before the man knew what happened. No one around them would have ever guessed such an incident took place seeing only simple conversation. Gellia laughed at the lord's face as Cassius excused himself—he must have been confused since he knew Cassius was after something, but apparently just gave up. Her liege glanced at her and she flashed him a coy smile and hid behind her fan.

"You're doing something sneaky," Skip whispered.

"Maybe."

"I am the king of sneaky. You can't trick me."

Near one of the corners rested the emperor and his consort. "Good gracious, Mina, she is far prettier than you."

Mina, the 'empress' and the mother of the emperor's children smiled, knowing that Raven should have been more excited about Gellia's potential than her looks, or perhaps her weight with the commoners but... "Indeed," said she. But Cassius knew Gellia's real talents. She knew he did, otherwise he wouldn't have wasted so much time to elevate her from pauper-princess to goddess. Perhaps Mina didn't know Gellia when she was first out of Fuarmaania, but she could imagine how much work was involved—Gellia glided around the room like she was born to it, gave all the right smiles and looks...

"I think I'll have a dance with her later," the emperor said, but made no motion to do so.

If Gellia was lucky she would be long gone before he decided it was time, Mina thought. She knew what Raven was about; she had her reasons for being with him. "Think you need her to replace me?"

"No. She looks as though she would break too easily." He smiled at her. "She's just like him, spares people."

Mina rolled her eyes. "Yes. You burn everything, kill everyone, and leave the bodies to rot."

"Stop it, you're exciting me..."

Mina ignored him as he continued to talk as he always did. Gellia didn't see Mina observing her, but the little trainbearer did. The trainbearer looked strikingly familiar, but he wouldn't come into play until he was older. How droll, Cassius, she thought. Mina looked over to their host and back to Gellia. She recognized a look in Gellia's eyes and felt pity for the girl. The empress knew what it was like to feel that kind of isolation in Xzepheniixenze. Foolish girl.

Sheltered under one of the archways one of Gellia's old allies watched the party unfold. "Hey 'Lipse, I think that's the girl."

His companion rolled his eyes. "Don't call me that. What girl?"

"The girl who got me to this party. Remember, I saved her life in Candiem?" Griffin shifted his weight, adjusted his uniform.

"Gellia Zapheny."

"Yes. From Tintagel," Griffin said. "I told you she was beautiful."

"Fuarmaania."

"How would you—never mind. Think I have a chance with her?" He was partially serious.

"I've never seen you so insecure before." Griffin's companion watched Gellia through narrow eyes for a moment. "Not a chance in a million years. Not that you aren't worthy."

"That bad? Who's the jealous one?"

"I don't know that jealousy would cause trouble, but she's already involved." He watched for a few moments in silence. "She may not realize it yet, though."

"I don't know why I bother talking to you. You and your mind-magic." Griffin muttered. His companion had very powerful mind-magic, but he also had thousands of years of observation to aid him. However, he never seemed to give any real information when asked.

For Gellia it came to the point that reading memories and thoughts as a team was so easy she didn't even have to think about it. She could tell if Cassius wanted her assistance without him asking and she'd join him. Gellia lost count of how many of these transactions they went through. Meanwhile Gellia smiled at the proposals of wealth and power and bloodlines. She even had propositions from women to become allies—there were quite a number of powerful women in Xzepheniixenze—more than Gellia expected.

In Fuarmaania women were property. In Xzepheniixenze women were almost worshiped. Never denied power because of their gender, never being thought of as inferior in any way. Women had the power of creation as well, and in such an unstable political climate, heirs were desirable. Unless a man was immortal and smart enough not to be killed the only things to keep the place going were his children. And they couldn't have her. It made her want to laugh. She was the only master of her destiny. She saw the truth of it now.

"You're thinking something wicked," Skip said.

Gellia smiled and sipped the wine Skip brought her as she took a lovely rest. He was such a treasure. Someone near was thinking her name. She ignored an approaching man, for she was allowed to do so.

He spoke. "You have a similarity of your mother, but indeed you are far more beautiful."

Skip poked his head around Gellia's skirts and she turned to look at the speaker. "What did you say?" she asked.

He was a bit taller than Cassius, looked rather gaunt from wear. Perhaps at one time he looked more regal but not now. "I said you look like your mother, milady."

This was a new strange way to start a conversation, Gellia thought. Perhaps he was confused. "Lady Connylia?"

"No. Princess Bernedette of Fuarmaania."

Gellia wouldn't allow herself to look surprised, but her trainbearer stepped in front of her. She noticed Skip had a dagger hidden under his cape.

He continued, ignored the look Saquime gave him. "At first I wasn't sure, but now I know who you are... Bernedette was human. Yet here you are—and looking quite Xzepheniixenze. It amazes me that you can stand there so icily still while I still remember your mother's hysterical pleas."

First she was in anguish, but then she felt only rage, but kept her face void of emotion other than insult.

"I see that you do not recognize me. No matter. I am Baron Decius Iolair of Desobre and your *mother* is the reason for my misery. I am he who gave you Xzepheniixenze blood."

Her father. There he was, face to face with her and she was filled with loathing. She needn't be associated with him. He killed her mother and he would have killed Gellia had Bernedette not left her with Corrah. Yet there was part of her that wanted desperately to know him, why he did what he did. "We have nothing to say to each other," Gellia said. She turned her heart cold, as was the way of Xzepheniixenze. If she were forced to she would kill this man to keep him away, debated whether to draw on her magic or not. Such an act on her part would cause an uproar she didn't want to deal with. No, Cassius would have to clean up after her and then she would listen to him scold her for days.

Maybe Decius didn't have magic, but he was wise enough to know when a mage was winding up. After one last look at her he moved away. Gellia discretely let out her breath and Skip spoke. "I don't think his lordship likes him either."

"Why do you say that?"

"Ever since that Decius-man came over he's been hovering."

Gellia glanced found Cassius chatting cheerily with a lady only ten paces away. "You're quite the observer."

"It's…"

"Part of your job," Gellia finished for him. "You take seeking very seriously."

"Yes. He's been looking out for you all evening, me as well. I'll never be far away. When we have time I'll have to tell you about what they say in Tintagel…"

She looked at their illustrious baron again and caught his glance at her when the person he was speaking with motioned to someone else. It was then she noticed someone new.

Her heart leapt. "Griffin is that *you*?" Gellia exclaimed as the knight approached. "What happened to your—"

Griffin kissed her hand and smiled. "I know." He ran his hand through his coppery hair. He had a distinct white streak of hair in his forelock. "I'm sure you understand why I might dye it black."

Gellia nodded. It wasn't easy being a half breed. "You match your red horse now. She's your bond horse? Tell her I think she's very pretty."

"Yes, yes, and she already knows."

"And I like your uniform. It's very becoming." There was something about him now, something familiar, but not from her time in Candiem. Something she read once, perhaps. Skip peeked from behind her skirts and eyed the knight.

He laughed. "Thank you. It's just the dress stuff they give you when important people recognize you. Good grief I'm not used to all these compliments."

"You deserve it."

"Stop you're going to make me blush."

"Oh bilge. You're the only one tonight who isn't trying to gain favor." Gellia said and fanned her face.

"Well actually…" After he saw her expression he laughed. "Just a joke!"

She gave him a coy look. "Oh yes? What do you have to offer me that these others don't have?" she asked.

"Well, I'm talented."

Gellia laughed. "Oh?"

He grinned. "I came over here to ask if you'd have a dance?"

"Certainly!" She took his hand.

"I can't say I'm all that good at dancing though."

"Either am I. Don't worry, if anyone complains I'll just smite them." She laughed.

On the dance floor Griffin was no klutz even though he claimed to be. He explained to her that it was rare someone of his lowly rank was invited to such a party. He was certain it was because he'd saved Gellia's life, but she had a feeling there was more to it than that.

"So are you his mistress or something? Can't imagine why I would be brought here otherwise."

It was quite the forward question, but it was refreshing for someone to be so uncomplicated. "No. No, I'm his charge. He's my teacher." Her instinct was that Cassius wanted to have a look at Griffin, which was the real reason he was invited.

He raised an eyebrow. "Truly?"

"Oh stop. The subject has never arisen."

"He must be blind then... So where is himself? I've never seen him."

Knowing it would be useless trying to see him through all the taller bodies Gellia reached with her magic and sought Cassius out. "Over there, see? The one in the shimmery green ensemble."

"Oh yes I see him. I've only ever heard about him—wait a minute. I *have* met him. He's the one who told me to join the army. Good grief if I'd known it was him I think I would have behaved differently... He sees us I think."

"Of course he does," Gellia said, looking past Griffin's shoulder. "I touched him with my mind." She gave her liege a snooty look as they turned away.

"With behavior like that one or both of us could be killed."

"No. I think he likes you." She turned back towards Cassius. "So where did you get this?" Gellia ran two of her fingers through a streak of white hair in Griffin's forelock. The moonlight seemed to bring it out. "I've only seen mages' hair go white." She knew she took a chance by being so familiar, she knew that it was an obvious gesture of desire. She certainly wouldn't dreamt of doing such a thing with anyone else for they would either be completely offended or any number of events might occur, none of which Gellia wanted any part. Something about Griffin comforted her; perhaps it was his honesty, perhaps his soul. He was a landless knight, but for some reason she felt the need to win an alliance with him, one that would last the ages. She was even willing to do certain things to gain it. She could only imagine it was her magic driving her to do so.

Griffin looked at her curiously, something in his eyes changed. "I don't have any magic. I don't know. I was born with it. It's part of my strangeness I guess." He looked in the direction of her liege, then quickly to other parts of the room. "Isn't that your grandmother?"

"Where?"

Connylia stood near the wall with three men and a woman. It looked as though they were people Connylia knew. The women embraced. "I have no idea who those people are." One of the men looked very young, younger than Gellia but had silver hair like a mage and wore nothing but shades of grey. He watched her and smiled. Gellia knew him, this man in grey, she had never met him but somehow she knew him. She barely could keep dancing and almost tripped over Griffin. Connylia looked at them and the women smiled at each other. Gellia and Griffin turned again. Connylia and her friends watched them; some strange look crossed Connylia's face. Gellia had no idea why.

"Well the shorter dark-haired man is someone *I* know... yes, they probably *do* know each other." He shrugged. "I never would have guessed that you were related to a Zephron."

"And to make it all more amazing I met my birth father for the first time tonight. It's an eventful night." The man with the silver hair was gone. Gellia had all she could do to keep herself from chasing after him.

"I wish I could say the same."

Cassius saw Connylia head for the doors and followed her. "Are you hiding out here? Do you think the palace will come crashing down on our heads?"

Connylia leaned on the rail of the long balcony and looked at the stars—she'd only been there for a few moments. "Only *you* would joke about that… I have something to ask."

Cassius came to stand near her. "Yes, I remember that night very clearly."

"Even after all these years? You were a small child."

"Oh yes," he said thoughtfully. "It surprises me that it has taken you all these years to ask me about it." Gellia and the young knight twirled by the door for their third dance. It was a distraction.

"You know who he reminds me of…" Connylia said, but wouldn't continue.

"Kellenvoss… Thank you for confirming my suspicions. Gellia said she'd never seen anything close to his equal with a sword."

"He has Kellenvoss' smile," Connylia said thoughtfully. "…and his mother's eyes."

"Indeed."

Connylia wanted to continue about the young knight— she had so many questions—but she knew Cassius wouldn't allow it—it was a discovery too new. Perhaps at another time. "…What happened after that? Why did they send me back to Zephronia and not keep me with them?"

Cassius looked at her. He could lie and tell her he couldn't remember, but lying had never been his way. They didn't want her. No refugees, they said, no matter who it was. He still remembered the cold stares and how curious he was about it all. Remembered seeing his first Lunan in the Temple at Qenai as they made their way to Ellyndrien Rehara and beyond. "Some things are better left unknown," he finally said.

Connylia looked at him and said, "Cassius, I want to know what happened."

He thought for a moment longer before speaking. "It is my understanding that we made the journey to the Palace on Aeryane although all I remember of that trip was flashes of light and Lunans... She said there was nothing she could do, that they had no room for refugees. The unicorns tried to have us both under the protection of the Lunans, but she said you had to go back to Zephronia, for Xzepheniixenze was no longer the place for you to be. I think it was Azraphael or possibly Thisbe who convinced her to help you live. In retrospect it seems that if you'd stayed with them you would have died, and you wouldn't have had any safe place to be in Xzepheniixenze. Sending you home to your brother was the best place to keep you, and your unborn son, safe." ...He remembered how bright it was, how surreal the surroundings were and remembered being held by the most powerful of Black Moon Dragons, his first, brief, and only teacher.

"And they're not even alive to thank them for their kindness," Connylia said. She stared at the ground; Cassius waited for her to continue. "He would have been proud of how you've turned out. He made a wise choice by naming you heir... If you need me just call."

"And risk Gallylya's wrath?" They both laughed despite the seriousness of the threat. Gellia whirled past the door with Griffin again. "I wonder if she'll run off," he said. She fancied the young knight, which was obvious even without her intimate gesture. Gellia knew little about her half-breed savior, although her magic brought out even more interest on her part. It made sense that her magic would be drawn to him.

Connylia felt strange. Suddenly she was his confidant, adrenaline rushed through her veins. "No, she won't, certainly not entirely." She started to speak in a language she hadn't used in a long time, one he but no one else would understand. "You have two choices right now. You can deny what your magic tells you and forever be in conflict, or you can give in and walk through the door of a new world. It is dangerous, perhaps even frightening at times. Once in the Zapheny's power..." She shook her head. "I know better than anyone, Avarzael. Walk this path together and no matter how difficult, you will not regret it." She only gave him a split second to digest what she said before she changed the subject. "Oh but Cassius, I have to tell you something for my own peace of mind."

Cassius's eyes narrowed.

"I want to thank you for this, for giving me some dignity again no matter what reason you did it. My son was right…" She put her hand on his shoulder briefly. "I have to go back to the palace before Gallylya realizes the countess lied to him." She spun and slipped away into the ballroom.

Cassius hung back for a few moments. *Oh Connylia, he already knows.*

…The rows of people moved back and forth to the music. Gellia tried to repress her laughter as Griffin entertained her with exaggerating the Xzepheniixenze demeanor. Unfortunately Connylia was not there to see her teachings at work as Gellia remembered all the steps. Griffin didn't care. At the end of the dance Gellia flipped out her fan and cooled herself while trying to catch her breath from laughing so hard.

"I'm going to get something to drink, would you like me to bring anything back for you?" Griffin asked.

"No, thank you. And you don't have to do that for me, that's what Skip- ah, Saquime is for."

"Ah, your boy?" he asked. She nodded. "I'll be back in a moment."

Gellia watched as her friend disappeared into the crowds. She wondered if he would act on her gesture. Perhaps later. However, she was just a serene if he didn't. He was so cheery it delighted her, but a dark cloud rolled over her joyous mood, she felt it near, pass over her and surround her. She wanted to bolt. Her instincts told her to run, but she wanted to stay strong. She knew this aura before she even laid eyes on him.

"I don't believe we've met."

An alarm went off in her mind as she turned to face the speaker. "You know who I am," he said.

Gellia forced out a smile. "Of course, sire." She curtsied. He was different from what she expected, but wasn't that the way of Xzepheniixenze? He was beautiful, almost effeminate, although he had a man's shape. At a glance girls must have adored him from afar, but certainly they learned too quickly of his insidious intentions. He was dressed in beautiful crimson and black. Raven took her hand and led her out for a dance.

She didn't like him. Yes, she had said that before about Cassius but with Cassius it was a survival instinct from her Zephronian past. This was a dislike that chilled her. She didn't want him touching her, looking at her or even thinking about her because she could imagine what he was thinking from the way he was looking. His hand on her waist made her wish to crawl out of her skin, despite his good looks and the power that went with it. She could feel his physical strength as they danced, he easily threw her off balance for his own amusement. There was nothing this person could offer that would win Gellia for any purpose. Ever.

Connylia was on her way out when she heard a voice she hadn't heard in centuries. "Lady Connylia?"

"Hello, Xzelleminiya," Connylia said, using Mina's proper name.

"It's good to see you're well," Mina said, smiling.

The Zephron returned the smile. "It *is* good to see you," she said warmly. Her carriage could wait.

"And how is everything at the palace?"

"Good. Business as usual, really. And how are *you*?" Connylia felt a pang of sorrow.

Mina smiled but could not hide her true feelings from Connylia.

"I *am* sorry... For us both I haven't forgiven him ..." Conny stopped herself. "...Zyendel has turned out to be a fine young man, although he isn't *that* young any longer."

"What it is now, several centuries?"

"A log time. His father..." Connylia smirked, "is mostly himself... Sometimes I think he misses the quest, misses some of the people he's met along the way..."

Mina smiled a little. There was little that could be said, but Connylia's continuing rapport was enough.

Conny continued, "I think of you, my sister."

The Xzepheniixenze woman nodded. "It's more than I hoped for... I must be going, I'm sure Raven is chasing after Gellia... I'll help look after her if I'm able."

Conny smiled. "Thank you. She still has a long way to go before she becomes the woman I know she can be... there is still much that needs to happen, there are agendas yet to be complete by people from our distant past, even some from the grave. Always remember that." The embraced briefly, Connylia kissed Mina's cheek before they parted ways. In the solitude of the corridor Connylia wiped her cheeks as her tears flowed. It would only take a moment to recover from the sorrow...

A hand rested on her shoulder, the hand of a friend from long ago. *I understand,* he said into her mind. *I will do what I'm able.*

Griffin watched from under his favorite archway. His friend spoke. "I think you've lost your partner."

"Yes. There's one person who has more to contribute than Cassius or anyone else here," Griffin said. "I wonder if he wants something different from the usual."

"I doubt Raven has more to offer than Cassius does... Oh I'm sure he wants everything. Everyone does. I'm sure there's already talk of the Key of Zenobia, not that Raven was thinking of that. Raven has a much more simplistic and diabolical outlook on life." He looked at his young friend watching the dancers. "Were you going to take her up on her offer?"

"It would have been pleasant, she's positively intoxicating, but no... She doesn't think they're consorts, but he was keeping an awfully close eye on us. I have a feeling I'd be murdered before I arrived at her door."

His companion chuckled.

"Besides, I'm a landless soldier with nothing but a bond horse and a sword. People like her don't take people like me seriously." He shook his head. "What are you thinking about 'Lipse?"

"Ugh. That monstrosity. It's Eclipse for the love of the goddess... I was thinking that she is not for you, but not for the reasons you suspect. Her ties to Cassius deeply rooted... I don't know how I tolerate you sometimes, and furthermore, people like her should take people like you under her wing. But perhaps that's what Cassius plans."

"Cassius." Mina hoped he would speak to her and not stifle her with his banter.

The baron immediately came to her side. "Are you enjoying yourself, your majesty?"

"I'm enjoying myself as much as can be expected. I have needed to talk to you."

"I'm honored."

"Don't lie. If you have a moment there are a few things I think you should know."

"Indeed? So you've decided to assist me rather than hinder, finally realized you won't be able to take back your lands by yourself?" He swept up two glasses of wine from a passing servant and handed her one. "I'm always willing to assist one of my peers."

"Not quite." She took a sip. "That girl you found is quite extraordinary. I heard she visited Dournzariame?"

Cassius smiled broadly. "Ah yes. She has met our fine Gallylya. An indirect connection to him. Excellent. What is your fascination with birds? Raven certainly doesn't burn as brightly, does he? Although he does enjoy fire…"

"She must be exceptional if Gallylya didn't kill her being that she is Xzepheniixenze, and I don't have to mention the obscene amount of time you've used on her."

…Cassius knew Mina inspected him, looked for something. She was always a perceptive woman, even in her youth, especially when it came to surviving in their world. Their association had been a long one. "I see you haven't lost your powers of observation, or your army of seekers."

"I think you and I have come to an understanding."

"Oh really?"

He was ever watchful, she noticed, always kept Gellia in sight. "I know better than to trust you. My plans and yours may not fit quite the way we would both like. I have faith that Gellia will be of more support than you. I also know she won't trust me if I were to say this to her, but she is so naïve she'll believe you. Luckily for her it will be the truth."

"I see. Well, I'm glad you learned *something* while in our presence." Mina was correct, Cassius knew the empress' mind, but he never did understand her fascination with…

Mina watched the dancers for a few moments, saw the emperor dancing with Gellia and could tell she was doing well, but would not hold for much longer against Raven. Cassius watched her as well. "You think she holds the key, don't you?" she asked. "I would imagine you've already discovered the talents for wild magic in her."

"We know where the dragon key half is, and it isn't with her."

"That wasn't the key to which I referred. I'm referring to the one you and Quenelzythe searched for, the one everyone seeks without admitting it. The one no one understands and doesn't even really know if such a thing exists."

"Who do you mean, 'everyone'?" He knew Mina didn't refer to Raven, for their emperor never showed any interest in such a thing. Was she bluffing? Or did she know of someone?

Mina smiled and glided away.

"You enjoy the company of boys?" Raven asked Gellia motioning to the young half-breed.

"He is an agreeable person." Raven disgusted her. Unfortunately she had to feel out his personality. She did her best to stay composed. If she met him in Fuarmaania those years ago she realized she would be powerless against him, and even now after all the training it was difficult. Just his physical presence was stifling.

He nodded. "So where has my cousin been hiding you? You *are* the one who took Candiem?"

"I've been here and there, keeping busy."

"Busy doing what?"

Cassius was occupied with thinking and observing. It wasn't unheard of for a host to stand aside and watch the party-goers, and there were far fewer of them now. Unfortunately one of them approached. "Go away Decius."

"Leave it to *you* to…"

"Why are you talking to me? Did I not just tell you to leave?" Cassius said. "You failed. I didn't. You lost your senses to a human girl. What did you expect would happen? Did you think your prowess would boggle her mind and she'd come with you? Did you think begetting a child would have her father marrying you? No, you were outsmarted by a human girl. Twice.

Deal with your benightedness by yourself." Not that Decius would know what to do with Zapheny.

Decius flared. "I—"

"Need I remind you that I have the key to your mind in my hand. Leave my sight."

"Why don't you just kill me then?" Decius said.

Cassius smiled. "Ah, the begging begins—it's more effective on your knees, you realize… Not yet. I like to bide my time. Run along before I loose the hounds." Cassius' mind magic locked onto Decius, spun him around and walked him towards the door.

A moment later a seeker hurried to Cassius' side. "My lord."

"I want the fourth army moved to Desobre. Go." Cassius' thoughts were truly elsewhere, preparing to weave barriers around Gellia.

"...and he said you were a harpy."

"Really." She understood why Cassius might have said something like that. He was trying to protect her. Even though he held her in the usual fashion for dancing she felt he was too close, she was trapped. She tried to pull away a little but his strength was undeniable. His magic rose around her; she couldn't tell what he planned. She forced herself to remain calm.

"You don't like to talk much do you? How do you command armies?" the emperor asked.

"I don't like to talk to imbeciles."

"Well, they would have to be imbeciles to join his army." He smiled.

Gellia wanted to gag. "Not as ridiculous as some, I suppose." She could feel every slight movement of his hand on her body with alarming acuteness. "I wish I could kill such refuse."

"So would I."

"How interesting."

"Why do you say that?"

He seemed to be getting closer and Gellia felt claustrophobic. If she hadn't been so sickened by the thought of touching him she would have pushed him away. As it was she barely touched him with her fingers as his hand grasped hers. But Gellia could not let this opportunity escape. The emperor's mind was open; not thinking anyone would bother him and knowing he would see him or her instantly—but at the moment he was distracted by his lust.

Yes, his mind was open, like a melon dropped on the ground two weeks ago, all the putrid slop there for her to see. Raven was a creature of chaos; he thrived on it. He lived for destruction. The throne meant he could destroy as he pleased, but he didn't truly rule Xzepheniixenze. There was nothing but lust on his mind and Gellia detested him for it. He was fantasizing about how her screams would sound. He wanted to eliminate all civilization if he could, but he was smart enough to know that Gallylya would come in and take Xzepheniixenze from him if there was no organization. Gellia would go no further; no deeper into his mind but she felt him physically moving closer. She felt a shimmer in the air, magic unseen but by her as it blanketed her. She knew who it was, although the magic was undetectable to anyone but her—because…

"There you are, sire. I bring news to you." A woman pushed between them. "One of your counselors has declared himself ruler of Ravengate."

"What? We leave at once! Mina, come." Raven stormed away leaving the two women alone.

Gellia regarded the beautiful Mina coolly, not sure what to expect. Mina drew closer. "Yes, he is a fool but don't underestimate his power, Gellia, he is not an easy foe." She glanced around. "I don't know when else I can tell you this so I say it now. I am at your call if you chose. My loyalties are closer to your cause than you realize."

Gellia blinked a few times as Mina parted. Mina seemed blunt like a Zephron. As she watched her disappear Gellia realized that many of the guests had left and more were on their way out, it had taken all her concentration to thwart Raven. Griffin was nowhere to be found. She wished she could have at least said good-bye.

The fresh air on the balcony beckoned her. Perhaps that would make her feel better. Skip had disappeared. Gellia wondered if Cassius had sent him on a chase. As she walked onto the balcony the cool air embraced her, giving her a lift. She swore that the air around Raven had been stale. She dropped her heavy train and fanned the cool air to her face. A mind touch. Gellia swung around and saw Cassius standing in the doorway. "You."

"You're angry because I *didn't* startle you?"

"I'm not angry." She turned to look at the distant stars once more.

Cassius joined her.

"You invited my father."

"You were going to meet him at some point, it was better that it was on our terms. He's a toad, princess. It was about time you saw it for yourself. And now you don't have to wonder."

"I gathered that. I'm the daughter of a toad and a human." It was so late, she was too tired to become angry. "How did you know I was something better than some feeble half-breed? Why won't you answer me?"

He smiled. "I'm afraid if I say anything you might try to tear me a part with your bare hands."

"I was a horrid girl, wasn't I?" Gellia looked at him as she leaned over the rail. "How uncouth I was."

He nodded, still smiling.

Again she returned her gaze to the horizon. "I don't want to go back into Raven's mind."

"I wouldn't want you to. I certainly never asked you to."

"How kind."

"Hardly, I'm just looking out for my investments. I'm wondering what madness drove you in there… You were lucky he was so distracted by your charms to notice you. That would result in a most unpleasant confrontation. Xzelleminiya has been the only woman to withstand him, and you aren't to her caliber… Mina, Raven calls her."

She could only imagine to what he referred. "I like the dress."

He looked at the sky like he was counting the stars. "It doesn't overwhelm you. The others always are noticed by their clothes and not their faces. Like fine horses; flashy tack only takes away from their natural beauty."

This time Gellia didn't say anything, just smiled. It might have been a backhanded compliment, but it was a compliment nonetheless. If she acknowledged it he'd feel the need to take it back. Gellia watched him, almost playfully, trying to guess his thoughts. Not that she would try to read them again.

That night she had felt closer to him than she ever did before, as if he were her dearest friend. And she trusted him even though there was no other person in the empire who did. She knew that was probably the most dangerous thing she would ever do. "There were quite a few outrageous outfits, wasn't there?" she said.

Cassius rolled his eyes. "They're worse every party I go to. I suppose not everyone can be as perfect as I am."

This too. He wasn't being completely serious about his perfection. "You just have impeccable taste." She was finally learning his humor, but it wasn't from experience, it was from something else.

"A curse, I know.... So just how many men offered you their soul?"

She smiled. "I don't think it was their souls they offered." He chuckled. "—I lost count. I think just about every person I danced with but for his highness and Griffin." She looked at her liege and felt overwhelmingly timid.

"Griffin is that boy who took an arrow for you?"

"Yes." She stared at the moons for a moment. They were so distant, so mysterious. She didn't get to say good-bye to Griffin. She didn't know if she'd see him again.

"Going to take any of them up on their offers? There were some worthy nobles."

She shook her head. "What about you?"

He chuckled. "Most amusing."

"You haven't danced with me all night," she said.

"But we have, when you weren't entirely focused elsewhere."

Gellia did her best not to blush like a foolish human girl. He was right, they danced with their magic, and when she thought about it she realized it had been even more exhilarating than actual dancing. She remembered how she felt then, powerful, sensual, brilliant. It amazed her how his words had always affected her. "You're right," she said. "But still...."

He picked up her train and put it over her other arm and took her hand. She knew the dance, and she curtsied to begin. She barely heard the music, but her feet moved just the same as she lost herself in her magic. She could feel it rise around her in swirls and sparkles and entirely against her will. His silence was unnerving her. Only the orchestra and a few servants remained. "Will they play forever?" She asked.

"If I want them to, yes."

She tried to ignore all the feelings welling inside her, within her mind, body, and magic. "It seems strange to me that people travel all this way—weeks on the road—to spend such a short time here."

He smirked. "Most parties last weeks, but no one would miss an opportunity to visit a place they thought destroyed, especially a Moonkeep."

"Moonkeep?"

"Yes, such things are from a time almost forgotten. I think the only person to ever see an intact Moonkeep before was Connylia and myself. People, not dragons mind you."

While she glanced away, he only looked at her. "Dragons?" she asked.

"Oh yes, make no mistake, there were dragons here tonight. Dragons untouchable by Gallylya's hand. Dragons who should be dead but who survived by divine intervention." He twirled her, but more slowly than the dance dictated. "Very few knew it was they, probably just Connylia and I. I may own this place but we are all still here as guests." He grew distant.

Gellia felt the moment out. "You're talking with Julian, aren't you?"

"What of it?"

They promenaded, but again the pace was slow, and there was little distance between them. "I wish Amarynth was more agreeable."

"Amarynth is very old. He runs much deeper than the average bond horse, no matter how smart they all think they are. Don't take his silence as an affront." He went to one knee as she danced around him.

"You talk like you know him. Did you pick him out for me? Manipulate fate as you always do?"

He shook his head. "No, I could have never predicted it, not even dreamt it as a possibility. Whatever bond it is between the two of you is a mystery to me.... I know very little of bonds but for those with bond horses." He rose again and they circled one another.

Gellia glanced at the empty ballroom. "I don't think he likes me."

"Those who are bonded don't have a choice."

"Why?" She asked. Cassius seemed deep in thought, distracted even, but somehow intense just the same.

"Bonded are with each other forever no matter what they think of each other or how much they might like or dislike each other." He vanished into his own thoughts for a few long moments, and when he spoke it seemed he spoke more to himself than her. "It's amazing how some things become clearer after so many years." His gaze returned to her. "It seems I've taken some of your mortality."

"What do you mean?"

Then she saw the conflict in his eyes, something she'd never seen before. He didn't have an answer for her, not a clear one that he could speak. She tread carefully and was happy to do so. Together they were invincible. Their magic had been drawn together by fate. She wondered what would happen after she was gone. They stopped dancing but remained oddly close. The orchestra had stopped playing and was dispersing. "I don't want to leave you," she said.

"Were you planning on going somewhere? With the emperor perhaps?"

"No, no. I don't want to die."

"No one does."

"Yes, but I've grown rather attached to your foul moods. When I'm dead I can't listen you gripe about the state of things." She felt a chill, something calling her from far, far away.

"Who said anything about dying? Your life has been extended." He looked at the horizon.

"How?" She felt dizzy as some ancient force summoned her. It was Zenobia, an entity she barely knew and certainly didn't understand.

He spoke without his usual intensity. "Were you not paying attention? You're very distracted."

She cautioned one more remark. "Explain it to me."

Cassius' ire rose but his voice was calm. "Have you noticed how well our magic meshes? That teaching you magic has been a very simple process rather than a lifelong undertaking? And I can extract information from your ancestors through you?" He thought a moment and muttered: "Of course you don't, how could you? You're a child."

She simpered. "Well yes—are you telling me that isn't normal? And although I haven't counted my years of late, I'm quite sure I'm over thirty, an old maid by human standards." Gellia leaned against the railing and looked up at him.

"You are a Zapheny, and we together are an anomaly like I've never seen before. And you're very young." Gellia was hurt and it must have shown on her face for he continued. "The world was against us—Quenelzythe and I—and although we knew each other well and were exceptionally talented we could not perform magic together as you and I do now." He watched her for a moment. "I suppose it doesn't help that I barely understand it myself." He seemed to withdraw a little, and Gellia was surprised how it saddened her. "I think it would be easier to show you. I've done what research I could. Trust me, there isn't a single book in Tintagel that tells of such a thing, and other libraries' collections only mention it in fleeting moments…" He held out his hand and made his magic take a visible form. Gellia watched the familiar green energies flow around them to his palm and into a glimmering sphere. She felt the urge to do the same and once she started to draw the energy she felt it grow stronger, flow like a river to her as it formed at her command. Their magic did not make way for each other in the same space. Instead it seemed to swirl together. Gellia thought for a moment about their partnership and what he said before. And something Connylia said. Their magic. Their magic was woven together, unable to be unraveled by anyone. It took on a life of its own, bound by fate. It started the moment he woke her sleeping talents. It was now no wonder why using their magic together felt intimate. Their souls, their magic, and now only the physical element remained.

She realized they were not the only ones. It was in her lineage, he did not know it. It was not some spell that took Connylia from her people; it was out of her hands. Half of her was torn away when Razhiede was killed—it was not an act. Gellia started to feel a horrible appreciation for what Connylia experienced, so horrible she felt the tears well up in her eyes. Razhiede loved Connylia and she him. How would it be possible for Cassius to understand this? To accept it? Gellia knew she would never feel part of any culture, trapped between worlds for eternity. But with him, they were their own empire of magic.

Back in Fuarmaania when she had first thought they were kindred spirits her instincts were true. Their souls spoke to each other even when their emotions did not. Yes, her magic remembered this. It was a Zapheny trait. He didn't know how it happened and she couldn't explain it, but she knew her magic chose this course despite anything they felt. She felt her great ancestor was speaking to her. Together they would find the key to Zenobia. Don't be troubled, Cassius. She dropped her train and put her hand in his. He looked at her. Her magic swirled around him in purple tendrils. I am Zapheny, she thought.

A step at a time Gellia moved towards him until she could rest her head against him, hear beat of his heart. After a moment his arms encircled her.

12

It must have been late afternoon by the time Gellia awoke. The sun shone through the gossamer bed curtain. It was a cavernous room, arches reached up to the ceiling forming stars with their arms. There were giant windows with open drapes, the light shining through to the glowing paleness of the room. She took a deep breath and thought about what recently transpired. Even in her inexperience she knew their moment was not something experienced by others. With her newest awareness she could tell Cassius hadn't left the room. She sat up and after a moment, rose to her feet.

"Good morning," he rumbled. He was on the other side of the room looking over paperwork in his dressing robe. His black hair cascaded over his back and spilled onto the floor. As she admired him a servant helped her with a dressing gown.
She went to stand near him. She put her hand on his shoulder and he slipped his arm around her. "Good morning, milord," she said. It was afternoon, yes, but it might as well have been morning to her. Near dawn she recalled searching his soul through their bond. It hadn't been helpful. He loved her, but didn't know what it was, feared it, for it made him vulnerable. This was not an easy path, but they had no choice but to walk it. He feared his connection to her more than anything. It would cause him to push her away at times, yet he would not be able to escape. "So tell me, were you the one who sent the Claidheams to Zephronia while I was held there?" she asked.

"Yes, actually." He picked up another letter. "You can guess that I have no great admiration for them."

"I'm surprised they listened to you." He wore a small pendant on a delicate chain, something he never took off. She took it into her hand and examined it. It was an odd shape; like some sort of elaborate symbol and it was so wrapped in magic she couldn't tell what its magic was.

"They don't know my true opinion of them."

It was the most euphoric morning she'd ever had. Even with the conflict still in her heart, their completed bond would fuel her good and peaceful mood for days. He too was thinking of the conflict within. Neither knew exactly what this new world would hold.

In truth he was rather distracted, and hadn't left the room because he was still out of sorts as he replayed the night before, and apparently she was too. His magic was alive in ways he never felt possible. He knew she didn't understand the scope of what had happened, but it was something he was unable to fight. They had been two souls, two magical entities without heeding much their physical forms. He knew what she felt, even without invoking his powers to an active role. ...Her reactions had been so pure, so untrained. She was shy, nervous, which with any other woman he would find repulsive. But with her it was positively charming.

He was always acutely aware of his own mysticism, and for some reason he was just as aware of hers. This was so much more than he knew of the person who'd first come to his room. Her old, magnificent soul was no longer nervous or unsure, it was strong, lusty and wanton. She was much more of a woman that he'd given her credit.

...He'd kissed her lips, gently and without expectation. He knew she was gaining her senses again, and she was concerned he would be harsh to her. He would not be so cruel to her, not while she was so very defenseless, as he was.

He'd pulled her into his arms as he came to rest.

She'd never felt so tired, so alive, so safe. But what now?

I don't know, he said.

I didn't speak, she replied. Even her mind voice was tired.

I just knew, as you know me, he said.

Is this how it usually is?

You already know the answer, Gellia. I can sense it in you. You perhaps know even more than I. ...do not fear me, Gellia. I am part of you, and you me. We cannot live without the

*other, lest be a half. We are each other's vulnerability. I must
protect you as I do myself, if not more so.*

She'd contemplated their bond, and was enchanted he
said her name.

Gellia, he said. Her heart leapt. He chuckled and
tightened his embrace. *It's where you belong,* he said. *Standing
by my side, or in my arms.*

She started to cry. Her tears rolled from her eyes with
abandon and against her will. She was embarrassed for such an
outburst and part of her wanted to run away. He pulled her
closer, kissed her damp cheeks. *Gellia, this life we live in is not
as your idealistic heart wishes. I must do as I must.*

...Cassius realized he'd pulled a sheet of paper but hadn't
begun to write. The nib hovered just above the paper. He didn't
know how long he'd been frozen there. He collected himself
drew the nib across the paper. Correspondence could never wait.

***

Gellia stepped from her very own first portal and into
Tintagel. Tintagel felt different to her magic now, but not in a
bad way. She felt more a part of it than ever, for now she could
see her magic helped fuel its life-force. It welcomed her as if she
was its mistress. She felt she'd had another awakening.

Cassius stood beside her, offered his arm, which she took.
Their secret would stay between them and their bond horses, not
that anyone would guess in a million years. *Well done on the
portal,* he said. *I couldn't have made it better myself.*

You wouldn't have given me bad advice, said she, a smile
playing at her lips. If she was going to be an empress, she needed
to act like one. It was time everyone else knew it.

As they passed through the corridors she felt the usual
gazes of its residents but it was slightly different now, he was
with her. Always. She could feel his strength, his confidence.

Vellura appeared in a side corridor, seeming to look for
business. Gellia nearly scoffed. The courtesan still might find her
way into their baron's rooms, but she would always be lesser.
She was a small fraction of the mage Gellia was, and her family

❧ 224 ❧

was not as great. She would never have the connection nor influence of Gellia.

After all the experiences at the ball Gellia knew she was inferior to no one. There were only a few who had magic enough to oppose her and no one in the world was strong enough to oppose *them*.

"So tell me of your expedition," Cassius said to her after he organized his mages and sent them on their way.

"I moved the third army into Kaymaria. Lady Nonette needed people and the money was holding up fine," Gellia said. "But the queen was frazzled. I wrote everything down."

"Yes, well, she had it in her mind that she would be nothing but a lady of leisure and now she's the queen." Cassius started to pen a letter. "Moving the army there was a good decision."

"Thank you." She looked at the books on the walls. Perhaps she could convince him to let her read them.

"Yes you can read them, just don't take them anywhere… You ran into Cleomenes in the swamp," he said.

"Who? The ferryman?" She slid a book partially from the shelf but changed her mind and slid it back.

"No, the tree."

"Oh. Yes." She started to absent-mindedly weave her magic, for no particular purpose. It was so easy when she wasn't concentrating on it so much. Weaving, knotting, folding, spinning its forces into spirals. She felt it all around her, could feel his magic supporting her.

"That was Cleomenes. He could see me through you and you could sense him because of me. He was a 'ghost' dragon in a more interesting life."

"He's been stuck in that tree for a thousand years?"

"Yes. Again, the former career Gallylya hates me for. That, and he and my mother were bitter personal enemies." He eyed her for a moment and smirked. "Such confidence. We need to have parties more often, I see."

She smiled. "I never realized until then what you meant. I'm Zapheny."

He chuckled. "And we have yet to see all you have."

"You *lied* to me, Connylia."

She said nothing but stared at her brother with defiance. He'd sent one of his peers to the school to check on her. Unfortunately it was Rellyarna, the strongest mage of the order, and he was able to disrupt the illusion of Connylia. Her unicorns wouldn't put up a fight, the countess acted shocked. Connylia couldn't blame any of them. At least Rellyarna would keep it to himself other than telling Gallylya, which was why he was chosen to go in the first place.

Connylia had returned to the school tired and happy, only to find Rellyarna there waiting to bring her back to the palace. Now she once again faced down her brother: the Phoenix, the emperor, the shining legendary hero. Some would prefer staring down a dragon.

Gallylya paced across his office. "I see you're just as deceitful as you've ever been."

"She is my descendant, my blood," she hissed. "Remember? I had a son once. The boy you killed?"

"I did my duty to my country. Because of this blasted xzelki we will not have peace."

"He's never threatened Zephronia," Connylia said. "He's only defended his own land in all these centuries."

"*And* he's plotting to take the throne. How long before he comes here? I'm sure his ambitions are limitless."

She answered, "I don't think he ever would." She hadn't seen her brother this irate in many years, but she'd learned long ago how to withstand him.

"How many lives has he taken for his own benefit over the centuries? He probably killed his own family to take Tintagel."

Connylia trusted Razhiede's opinion. Despite popular opinion in Zephronia, Razhiede never held ill will towards Zephronia, and wished them to live in peace. Cassius would be good for the world, even with his malevolent ways.

"I forbid you to return there and if I have to put a magical barrier around the palace I will."

"Oh I see. Why don't you just lock me in a tower and call me crazy a little longer?"

He had considered it.

Connylia fumed. "I've *never* been a traitor."

The emperor glowered at her. "By allying yourself to them like this you *are* a traitor. For withholding information that would aid us against them makes you treacherous. I pray evidence is never openly found that proves your treason for then I will have no choice." She knew of what he spoke. There was only one punishment for traitors. But she was not afraid of death, had welcomed it for centuries. "For now you have an excuse— you're mad and unable to control yourself."

"Worried about another scandal?" she scoffed, then drew a weapon of wrath. "Luckily for you, *your* scandal ran away to save your reputation." Immediately she regretted saying it.

He was too seasoned to react. "No, national security. I will not lose Zephronia to ruin while there is breath in this body. Zephronia's safety is more important than your life." He watched her storm from the room and thought of a time when she was young, when she was the queen's handmaiden. There was a time when Connylia listened to reason, when she was obedient and loyal. Then the fateful journey to Xzepheniixenze condemned her to this shadow of her former self.

Prince Zyendel walked in. He'd been listening at the door. "I can't believe she did it," he said.

The emperor exhaled noisily and let himself fall into his chair. "It won't happen again." He rubbed his brow.

"She promised?"

"No. Not that I would trust her promise right now." People like that man could extract information from her without her ever knowing it—paying attention to the words she used, how she might avoid a question, her body language. Gallylya was sure of it, for that was how he always forced the truth from her.

Zyendel sighed. "There was a dragon sighting in Qenai."

No. He raised his head. This could not be. "What?"

"It could have been an illusion but no one knows for sure. As for what type—the description I was given didn't sound like anything I ever read about."

"Oh? I'll have to read the accounts." He hoped and prayed it was some fool with an illusion.

"Well anyway, Gellia has become one of his key people. He turned her loose and she's been taking over cities and making quite a legend of herself. Go into any tavern and you'll hear songs about her, hundreds of songs. The Lady of the Roses." Zyendel wasn't going to tell his father about the extent of how *he* admired her. "She has magic equal to people of the olden times. And Cassius doesn't rein her in. Apparently she does whatever she wants without asking. From what I understand, the people love her."

Gallylya snorted. "Yes, manipulating them to do his will."

"I don't understand."

"If Cassius gains the support of the people, the battle with Raven is already won. They'll fight in his armies, be his spies. Generations of them vowing to serve their beloved lord. Time means nothing; neither do the lives of peasants. Gellia is just..."

"She's an equal, but not malicious," Zyendel said. He was silent for a moment, trapped in a thought. He could feel his father's eyes on him. "The truth is, I find her fascinating, as if there is something about her I can't escape. I know you think she's as terrible as the next Xzepheniixenze but I don't know..." He shook his head. "I feel there is a purity about her, a purity of spirit."

"Well, it won't matter soon enough. If you fancy Gellia I advise you get her out of there. Perhaps she's still savable."

Zyendel did his best not to be too excited. "What? You think we can save her? What are you planning?"

"If she's the pawn you think she is, she might be... I'm going to destroy Tintagel."

"Wouldn't that start a war with Xzepheniixenze?"

"No. The kingdoms are still too divided. It might cause a power void, but that's it. He must be destroyed; perhaps it will flush out others of his caliber as well. The Vega Knights merely await my command." The task he started would be finished. Just as with Zenobia. Xzepheniixenze was an empire always balancing on the edge of chaos. Take out its support and it would topple.

***

"Greetings, milady."

Connylia froze. "Sir Alynderan. I didn't know you were in the area." She hadn't seen her former betrothed in many years, but he was handsome as ever. His wavy honey-blonde hair and cornflower blue eyes always attracted admirers. But why was he here? She forever felt a great sorrow when he was near; he was always so kind to her and she never returned his affection. He never did marry.

The Vega Knight smiled at her with his undeniable warmth. "Well I'm here to see your brother, as you would expect, but I'm happy to have the chance to see that you are well."

Connylia always wanted to confide in him, but would never want to put him in a position where he would be forced to keep something from her brother. Somehow though, Alynderan always seemed to know the conflict in her heart, feel her sorrow and wish only for her happiness. "How long are you staying?"

"As long as his highness commands..."

***

I'm not coming to see you unless you have a silver bridle. I know the other requirement is –well—shall we say, compromised?

Gellia smiled and chuckled. "You're not that type of unicorn," she said. "I have questions, perhaps about your master."

Oh all right. The black unicorn materialized and promptly changed form to a man. "I'm so happy you laughed at my jest, and he's not our master. I'm sure you have questions." He led her to their tree to sit in the shade. Gellia never tired of watching the hundreds of tiny flowers grow around him whenever he stayed in one place.

"Well yes."

"I heard you were stunning at the party."

◈ 229 ◈

She raised an eyebrow. Stable talk. Bond horses were worse than servants when it came to gossip, but it rarely strayed past the stable. "Some would say so."

"I have to tell you Currain is quite jealous of your attachment even when I tell him not to be so. He's a fostered creature, it's how they learn anything. Being temporarily with someone who doesn't need him will make him stronger for someone who actually does. It's just a different bond than yours."

"Can you explain it to me?" Gellia asserted.

Julian became a bit more somber, but his eyes still sparkled. "It's when two magics fit together so perfectly that they start to merge and souls entwine. Magic and spirit are very similar. No one knows when one will happen, and it's not something that be forced nor stopped. They're very rare." He smiled a little. "He's been fighting it for a very long time, and you've been trying to deny it. You have already guessed when and to whom the last one happened. You have so much ahead of you." Julian smiled broadly. "We've been waiting for so long, have so much hope. A new age is coming."

Gellia could only look at him.

Julian continued. "Have you looked in the mirror lately? Even in these short years you have changed in grace, in magic, started to develop into who we knew you could be."

"I don't know if I understand entirely," Gellia said. "I feel so coarse much of the time."

Julian took her hand. Something about him was familiar, something from the past. "You are a strong person," he said. "We've been watching you for a long time, Zapheny, your transformation over the ages. Magic never dies. Quenelzythe was unable to use his magic to the extent he wished, it was twisted by the death of his father, the breaking of his parents' bond, but you are the result of his choice to have a family and protect them with his life. He knew the magic would come again in time, come back to help heal the land. He knew his friend would be the catalyst, which is why we chose Cassius over Quenelzythe after we lost Razhiede." His eyes held hers—they were so ageless. When he spoke the old emperor's name she could see the sorrow deep within him. Roses started to grow around them.

"When I die it's going to kill him?" Julian pulled her into a world of nature and the mystic; their magic seemed to rhyme somehow. "He has to continue or this world will be lost." She felt herself float in her mind. "I do not wish to be the reason for its demise." So far that was the only downfall she could see to this. Everything around them seemed to brighten, and she sensed life everywhere. She was the only Zapheny, and magic needed her. There would need to be another.

Julian smiled proudly. "He is very strong. He will always continue. He has *us*...and perhaps another to help."

Gellia shivered. *The Silver One.*

"He may not be happy about it but we'll keep him together—of course, he doesn't always know when he's happy... Be contented in the years you have (and you still have many), enjoy his company as much as he lets you. And who knows, in this day and age as long as your spirit is willing death is often negotiable. Do not fear, Gellia, although it may not seem it, fate is on your side."

Gellia looked around the courtyard for a moment before speaking again. Julian watched her patiently. She found her voice. "So that other horse the children loved so much at the village..."

"My brother, Justin. We seem to have that effect on many." He smiled. "You should have seen the way the old queen of Zephronia used to fawn over Justin and Jutham."

"You lived with Razhiede?"

"Yes." He picked a rose that grew before him and studied it. "We were his companions."

She didn't want to sound demanding, but she knew she had to ask the correct questions since he wasn't volunteering anything. "Will you tell me about him? Perhaps now?" but she didn't want to fluster him. "I'm sorry, but, I—"

"Your wonder is understandable," Julian said. "But Razhiede is a story too complicated to tell." He shook his head. "So few knew him, even fewer could see beyond his brilliance for they were blinded by it. Perhaps someday Zenobia will share the story."

The way Julian said it—Zenobia—gave her a chill from head to toe. Zenobia was calling her.

***

Even with how many people she knew were awake, it was remarkably quiet in Tintagel. Gellia opened her eyes and stared at the canopy above her, it was made of green and black velvet, finished with silver ropes and tassels, the posts were huge dragons, their scales each made from emerald, glittering in the faint light. She snuggled into the wonderful softness of the bed, looked over at her consort—who appeared to be sleeping. She couldn't tell if he was or not for sure, most people look at peace when asleep, but he looked restless. Gellia was surprised he let her stay. She closed her eyes and thought of her magic.

An explosion rattled the very foundations of Tintagel. It terrified the sleeping residents and startled the awake. Sure that they were under attack, everyone was up in arms in moments and running through the castle. The mages searched wildly with their magic for their assailant.

Cassius loomed over Gellia. "How dare you!" he roared.

Gellia looked up at him from the floor where she sat, the wind from the open wall blowing past her—it was very cold. She knew better than to say anything until he calmed. The castle to her right and behind her was gone.

At least the green glow that surrounded Cassius faded. The look on his face hadn't. Julian whinnied a complaint from his courtyard below. Someone started to bang on the door and Cassius threw Gellia a blanket before the door was smashed in. His mood didn't change, he paced through the room. Several mages and servants peered in at them.

"Will you be needing us, milord?" Mephibosheth said, then seemed to calm when he saw Gellia.

"No," Cassius said, never taking his eyes off her, hand on hip. "I'm sure I can handle this myself."

Mephibosheth nodded and the knights behind him started to move away. The white haired mage eyed Gellia. She tossed her hair and stared haughtily at the mage. Perhaps with the right expression she could convince them it was planned.

"Carry on," Cassius continued. "I have something to tend to myself."

≈ 232 ≈

The door was magically restored. There was nothing but dim moonlight. She looked back at Cassius and instinctively started weaving barriers.

"You silly girl. As if your ability to create barriers would ever stop an attack from *me*," he hissed. "I know ever finite thread of your magic, I could unravel it with a thought. No, I could unravel *you* with mere *words*. I hope you don't need a demonstration." He muttered something about inferior humans.

"I didn't mean to startle you," she said. But he wasn't entirely just angry, he was afraid for her, and afraid of what he'd done.

Cassius laughed. "They wonder why I never let a mistress stay the night." She felt his magic speak to the castle, one of the benefits of having a living castle with magic of its own, it could heal itself.

Rubble started moving around, rebuilding until it was as it had been. It was very dark. Gellia still didn't want to move, but his anger subsided. Cassius went to the couch at the foot of the bed and sat to watch her. "If anyone asks tell them you thought it would be exciting. That way they'll think nothing of it. Wouldn't be the first time someone bollocks up a tryst."

Gellia wrapped herself up tighter in the blanket and said nothing as she sorted through her thoughts.

He rose and went to the table and poured himself some wine then sat back down. After a few sips he rubbed his forehead. "I was a wild talent as a youth with few allies versus the rest of the world. It was better to attack when in doubt. Some habits are difficult to change."

She understood of what he spoke. Her attempt to inspect their bond while he wouldn't be distracted from life was poor judgment on her part. "I just wanted to…"

He raised his hand. "Yes I know."

"Are you going to make me leave now?" Gellia said. "I'm sure everyone's still milling around."

"No, you don't have to leave. It's all about keeping respect. We should have a huge, dramatic battle then a bout of wild carnality, but I don't think either of us up for that." He shrugged. "They'll draw their own conclusions. All will be incorrect, most will be amusing."

"Why not have them think I'm being beaten or that you're going to kill me? You have the talent to do so. You could make them think anything."

He snorted. "How foolish. Perhaps that would have worked before your party but not now. They think I have a Zapheny, hoodwinked and leashed, which is a precarious situation. They need to believe that I will keep you oppressed and in my control, but otherwise unscathed. It is not your time to soar alone, not yet."

She nodded.

He thought for a moment, pushed his hair out of his face. Gellia rose to her feet, carefully tip-toed to sit next to him. Gellia knew better than to expect this gentle mood to continue.

"He's going to call us both to court, you realize," he said.

"He?"

"Raven, he's going to call us both to his court."

Gellia felt ready for this event, she was prepared to face the emperor in a more formal manner, was anxious to take back the empire.

"You barely know where these ambitions come from," he said, "how amusing that is... Don't ever do that again. We could have lost Tintagel and everyone in it. It would have been a terrible mess... Luckily control is a bit easier to attain these days."

Gellia just huddled in her blanket. After a little while she cleared her throat quietly. "We're in this together," she said softly. "I won't betray you."

Rising to his feet he said: "you already have," and walked away.

"We're still stuck with each other."

"I suppose we are," he said. "How unfortunate for me."

For the first time Gellia didn't envy him. She started to understand the mysterious friendship between Cassius and her ancestor. She and Quenelzythe were not entirely different. She wished Connylia would visit, she needed someone with a similar experience with whom to talk.

"Well now that I'm up I suppose I should be back to work," he said.

He was always working, she thought. Always talking to his generals, dozens of seekers and the like. Besides the letters she always saw him write she knew he must have been speaking to others through telepathy. Nothing could ever be left. There was no rest for him. She was determined to learn the ropes.

***

Gellia stood like the court mages on the sides of the audience chamber, helping Cassius dig through people's minds. Since he could rely on her, Cassius increased his speed of omniscience and the anxiety of those who would try to betray him grew to a fever pitch.

No mage was disrespectful to her, not directly. Finally the complex secret conspiracies began against her, but through seekers and the baron they were always hindered—but it wasn't until she found out about the first elaborate plan directly against her that she truly felt like a noble. It wasn't long, though, before the schemes stopped. Gellia made it apparent that those caught plotting against her were properly dealt with. Of course she had to act completely on her own but for creative suggestions from Cassius. Yes, some of the ideas that so nonchalantly rolled off his tongue were rather disturbing to her half-human sensibilities, but he came up with a clever solution. Hire someone to do it— that's what seekers and thugs were for, anyway. It worked. No one bothered her in Tintagel any longer. Many of the minor lords of Tintagel who she stood amongst kept their distance and tip toed around her as if she was their liege. At audiences visitors started to look for her as the rumors grew. She no longer lived in the lord of Tintagel's shadow. It's true, the party did her good.

With these changes also came letters and tribute from interested parties. She received all sorts of expensive gifts: jewelry, rare books, gowns, carriages, artwork, even exotic animals. Every day a few more things arrived. Quite often it made her laugh. Cassius wasn't pleased with the expanding menagerie, but he found appropriate places for each—mostly returning them to the wild if it could be helped.

…Someone mentally asked for her. After a quick glance at their liege she made her way from the room.

Vellura watched Gellia make an exit and scowled. "What is it, pretty?" Sian whispered to her.

"There's something very strange about this arrangement," she whispered back. "Have you ever seen someone, mistress or otherwise, treat him so informally?"

"You're speaking of the way she stands closer to him more than anyone else dares? The way she doesn't seem to appreciate his volatility like the rest of us? And for some reason he tolerates it?"

Vellura nodded. "Yes. Amongst other things."

"Perhaps you need to admit that she is without physical or magical flaw, perfect for the likes of him." Sian moved closer. "I realize he's the greatest prize you can hope for, but surely there are enough consolations here in Tintagel to appease your sensibilities."

"Are you suggesting I'm jealous?"

He smiled. "I'm one of the mages, I never suggest anything. Although I do have a proposition for you."

Vellura looked up at him and raised an eyebrow.

"You know all our plans so this should come as no surprise to you. I have a question about a certain white haired mage you stayed with last night."

Vellura's lips curled into a smile.

Sian smiled as well. "Name your price, Vellura."

Moments later the great doors of the audience chamber opened and Gellia strode through, taking the floor from the worshipers who were already there. Gellia bowed to Cassius, who waited for her to begin. He already knew, he was there with her, this was a formality.

"Milord, I have just been given word that the Iolair are moving on Tintagel," she said. "They left Desobre a day ago."

"How droll," Cassius said and nodded to the captain of the castle guard who quickly exited. "Sir Dallen."

"Yes milord?" Dallen appeared out of the crowd and moved into the open space.

"We're moving the second army to the castle." Cassius seemed to ignore Dallen's 'yes my lord' and continued. "Princess, you shall take control of that army presently."

Sealed papers appeared before Gellia which she took, nodded, and spun on her heel to leave. Cassius placed the exact specifications of the army into Gellia's memory. It wasn't the first time she'd heard about them.

The second army—it would be overkill for the Desobreans. These men were unlike the others she moved; they were seasoned soldiers with a general Cassius didn't trust. In fact, she heard the general mentioned on several occasions previously. Talented yes, but his loyalty was questionable. If he gave Gellia a bad time she would be forced to deal with him and whatever mess he might make. Other than that, she hoped everything would go smoothly. She was informed that Decius's ego was bigger than his army by a long stretch, which gave her hope. Being fathered by such an inferior person was embarrassing. She was happy she was seen as Zapheny and not of the Iolair. She let this give her strength, for some part of her yet wanted to know him.

Other information would come in as seekers reported, she was told. Their liege was not concerned about this conflict, she felt, there was something else that was more important. Upon her return she would have to ask him what it was—wasn't the fourth army supposed to already be in Desobre? And she thought the second army was much, much farther away.

Amarynth was armored by the time Gellia reached the stables in her own armor. As she put a foot in the stirrup Gellia began a thought. Cassius immediately responded, giving her the power and proper location to teleport into the camp before she was completely into the saddle. In a shower of green and purple sparks Gellia appeared just outside the camp. She laughed to herself at her entrance. Cassius always used a pillar of swirling light to accentuate his teleporting; *she* would use a little sparkle.

Gellia rode towards the camp, took them by surprise. She heard raised voices as their leader quickly berated whatever seekers came in just before her. "It's difficult to sense a teleportation," she said, dismounting.

A very large man approached her; he must have been General Vael. The armor he wore was elaborate and finely made; his bond horse who followed him wore barding to match. Judging by his hair Gellia picked him to be in his second century. He carried himself in the usual Xzepheniixenze imposing posture, but Gellia was not afraid. She watched his approach, watched how he pushed a seeker aside, noted his physical strength, but his magic was minimal. The seekers left again.

"What's this all about?" he rumbled from above her.

Gellia looked him in the eye. "I am Gellia Zapheny from Tintagel and this army has to move to intercept the Iolairs." She held out the written orders.

He didn't take the papers, only looked at her. "He sent *you?*" His brow furrowed.

She nodded. "That's correct."

Vael snorted, closed the distance between them. "Do you know who I am? It's insolent to assume you can command anyone you like."

The words of someone noble-born, or at least someone who had some schooling besides warfare. Her neck started to ache from looking up at him. "You're to follow the command, General Vael. It is an order directly from the baron." She flicked her wrist to remind him of the sealed documents in her hand.

He stiffened and raised his head. "I'm familiar with the name Zapheny. Perhaps to make you sound more useful than you really are."

"I see word does not travel as quickly as it should." Gellia's eyes narrowed. He was worth keeping. She could try to talk him into submission but she didn't have the time. One of his hands rested on his sword. Without taking her eyes off him she drew upon her magic to crush him. His armor was no protection against her. First he stiffened, then fell to one knee, his hand was still on his sword but he couldn't draw it.

"Drop your sword." Gellia said and enabled him to move his arm. Instead, as she suspected, he drew it and lunged towards her only to be forced to his knees. Gellia didn't move an inch. His hand crumpled and the sword dropped. It was very true that he would overpower her in a battle of physical strength, but he would find her magic undefeatable. He looked up at her angrily, trying not to show the pain. There were cracking sounds. "Do you yield?" she asked. For a moment all she received was glare as in his arrogance he still defied her. Pop. Pop. Pop. Gellia looked very calmly at him. "You have a few choices, let me clarify them for you. You can refuse and I can kill you right now, you can deal with my command for a short time then be on your way to live a productive and profitable life, or better yet I can imprison you and send you directly Tintagel as traitor and he can decide what to do with you. Yes, he already knows about your lack of loyalty. He wants me to point out that no one else would put up with your pompous ways and certainly wouldn't pay you as well." She released him and let him catch his breath. It wouldn't be long before his men came to see where he was—she didn't want them to see any of this. "What will it be?"

Vael righted himself but did not hold the pose with which he greeted her. "I'll tolerate you for now," he grumbled.

She smirked. It's what she expected. "Good. How well you work with me will determine the type of report I give his lordship. Keep that in mind." Her magic swirled around them, revived him from his sore state before one of his captains approached from the camp.

"We'll pack up now, milady," Vael grumbled.

"Excellent. We need to be moving by nightfall."

He glared at her.

"Nightfall," she repeated. Vael wasn't going to like this, Gellia thought. She had to watch her back. Although he didn't say anything, she knew that Amarynth would support her.

***

Cassius watched the distance for a moment. It would be one of the best times for Gallylya to make his move. *You have me, don't you?* Cassius thought. The baron couldn't afford to move all his armies to intercept an attack from Zephronia. His cousin could not be allowed to know their exact numbers. Gellia was wise to move the western army into Kaymaria for they could be disguised as Azqebryne and not Vazepheny. If Raven knew that Cassius' armies size rivaled his own then Raven's attention might move to Tintagel. Luckily Raven didn't care for details and ignored most reports. The one person he'd listen to wasn't telling Cassius' secrets.

If Gallylya killed Cassius the armies would scatter and Zephronia would be completely safe, for Raven would never attempt to attack Zephronia while Gallylya's light still shone. There had been too many near-deaths for Raven when he was younger and crossed the path of the Phoenix. The old bird had to know what Cassius' goals were. Not Zephronia at all, but one goal was the other half of the dragon key. He would do whatever need be to retrieve it. Gallylya was no fool... he knew the art of war, but his son was only a two-bit spy, a half-breed would-be seeker, a twit spoiled by the previous queen. Cassius laughed to himself. Zyendel would be easy enough to sway... But Gallylya would attack first. Perhaps Gellia needed to be sent away again, someplace Gallylya and Raven couldn't touch.

It was more likely Gallylya would send scouts, then portal his army through. If he chose to move them physically through Xzepheniixenze they would be forced to plow through many of Cassius' allies as well as Raven's armies. Portal an army. What a Holy War thing to do. But it worked so well, especially when the Vega Knights were involved. A small army of the best and most experienced knights. The land around Tintagel was stable enough to make it happen. "What a mess," he muttered. The second army would be a decent buffer, but would it hold against the warriors of old? No, there would need to be another approach.

***

"Cursed weather," someone said.

Gellia maintained poise even though she was drenched like the rest. She would not waste her magic keeping herself dry. At a trot they would reach Tintagel in two days. Despite their general's misgivings the soldiers seemed pleased to be moving. The exact reason why, she wasn't sure.

There were many mixed bloods in the army. It seemed with any Xzepheniixenze or Zephron blood in a human gave them longer life. (Which accounted for numerous mentions of blood drinking for immortality, but few humans ever wanted to try to kill a Zephron or a Xzepheniixenze, and the ritual's results were debatable). It seemed she would out live everyone she had known in Fuarmaania, including the babies that were born in her last days there... It reminded Gellia she should write to her friends in Sen Dunea and tell her how she was. How long had it been since she left them there? Years. Perhaps Gellia would tell them she had learned about Xzepheniixenze after so many days in Tintagel's library... it would be wasted on them though. Well, she would have to limit her correspondence to how she was doing and how pretty everything was.

"Milady, we should stop for a while tonight," said Vael who knew she probably wanted to trot on all night.

"Yes, but only long enough to cool out the horses. A few hours of sleep." Yes, she thought, she knew that not everyone had bond horses in this army, Vael. She was sure she heard him mutter something about the stories of old—comparing her to how the Vega Knights were rumored to drive their armies. This made her smile. From what she read the armies of the Vega Knights were some of the most effective and dreaded armies of all time.

***

"Here are Decius' people, right on time." If he knew Gellia, the army would arrive at any time, ahead of what everyone thought to be the schedule. "I suppose I should change into something more appropriate." Cassius left the window and strolled towards his room. He wondered if Decius really thought he had a chance without his benefactor. Perhaps it was merely a matter of pride.

It had been a long time since Tintagel had seen a proper siege attempt. Many of the residents thought of it as an amusement. In its modern history, Tintagel had been under siege many times, but had never been taken by an enemy. Such was its magic. Over the centuries Cassius had imbued it so intensely with power that primitive attacks were no match for it. Even with that, Tintagel was a rather large castle which housed slightly fewer than two thousand men in its garrison. The mages, their lord not included, were skilled enough to turn away attackers. Indeed, Tintagel was an island and had many mouths to feed from its stores, but supplies were only a quick portal or teleport away. For most, the big question was why Decius attempted it on his own. An attack with the force of such as Raven, and it would be a different situation altogether. It would be a shame that all those fools would be killed.

After he donned an ensemble befitting any emperor to remind Decius of Cassius' superior wealth, Cassius sat meticulously applying kohl. It crossed his mind to wear his favorite armor, for he hadn't worn it in a very long time, but decided to save it for a war, not this scuffle.

Vellura slid through the heavy door of his dressing room and tried to be subtle. "Since when are you allowed back in my chambers?" he rumbled. He wasn't sure what angered him more, her arrogance or her bad timing.

Vellura sauntered over with the idea of running her fingers through his hair, but he rose to admire himself in a longer mirror.

"I'm leaving Tintagel soon," she purred.

"Poor me." He straightened his doublet.

"I was just wondering if you wanted one last frolic..."

"Why in this world would you believe I would want anything from you? I allowed you to stay here for one purpose and very quickly you failed to live up to my expectations. Now why my mages continue to pay you for such inadequate services I have no idea. I could barely to stomach you when I first met you, what makes you think I would be interested now? You haven't been needed for some time now, why *are* you still here?"

"But..."

"I trust I don't need to repeat myself."

Vellura withdrew. Her charms were only briefly amusing, and that was a long time ago. Her ambitions were too pathetic for him to retain an interest in her. Oddly, it seemed there would only be one woman who would ever interest him again.

Cassius took one last look into the mirror. "Well, let's be off," he said to himself.

Outside the Iolair army was rallying itself. Most of the enemy shouted up to the stoic faces of the knights and the court mages, who stood on the foremost battlement and rubbed their chins. The Iolair army had grown since they last saw it and it seemed to be better equipped than before. Cassius stepped out onto the platform where his mages greeted him.

"They've been calling for you for some time now, milord," Sian said.

Cassius smirked and approached the battlements to look the army over. They chanted for Vazepheny but didn't pay particular attention to who just walked out. "You'd think I was a dignitary." Cassius laughed from under the large brimmed hat. (It was sunny out; he didn't want to ruin the natural steel-blue highlights in his hair) "They seem optimistic."

Behind him they discussed the number of people.

"What brings you out on this beautiful day?" Cassius called. He didn't shout, his voice was of a conversational tone, but it carried over the entire battlefield.

The chanting stopped and Baron Decius stepped forward. "Where's Princess Gellia?"

"She's not seeing callers today. Come back tomorrow," Cassius said. If the fool thought he would turn over Gellia he was certainly out of his mind. Gellia had her own will, and would certainly outmatch this cretin.

"Don't play games, Vazepheny! I mean business!" Decius shouted. "Send out my daughter."

Cassius leaned on his elbow over the battlement. "I don't think you have any say in whether or not I play games with you, old man." Not that Decius was a year over fifty. Decius yelled something about death. "Only boredom will be the death of me," Cassius called then spoke again to Mephibosheth and the nearby Sian. "Someone's funding them. They have a few mages with them." It seemed the smartest thing Decius could do would be to have another force hidden somewhere, a stronger one, but there was little evidence of it.

An onslaught of arrows began, but merely dropped as they neared the castle. Decius' mages started working their talents for the offensive.

Meanwhile Cassius was feeling for any sign of Gallylya. "Well," Cassius said, "he has more in the woods with a mage to hide them. But here's ours. We might be done with this before dinner." A section of Cassius' army flushed the others out of the bushes like a pheasant hunt while the main force thundered down the easy slope into the camp like a spearhead into the body of Decius' army.

"A pleasant diversion," Mephibosheth said. "Better than the theater." As many on the battlements, Mephibosheth was having refreshments.

"Quite," Cassius said. But he was watching closer than he portrayed. Gellia's inexperience was proving to be trouble. She'd entered the fray, been knocked off Amarynth. She wasn't using her magic, not wanting to hit her own men. Amarynth was right there, she should have been mounting back up, but she wasn't. Instead she was fighting hand-to-hand.

The mages watched the enemy mages, waiting to make a move. Cassius leaned on the black stone and watched Gellia. What was she thinking? *Get out of the way*! She heard him, but the rider thrust the javelin into her shoulder as she turned. As her attacker raised his arms in triumph Cassius straightened himself. "I've had enough of these games," he said. The mood on the battlements shifted with ferocity.

The bond horses on the battlefield were nervous, bumped into each other, unseated their riders. Something wasn't right, each told the next. The Iolair mages looked at each other, feeling a tingle under their skins.

…Cassius grounded himself and the castle trembled. Storm winds funneled past the castle, the trees swayed. Most of the mages bent to the wind but their lord stood firm.

The soldiers started to scatter. When the first hint of a green glow surrounded Tintagel and the first bolt of lightning struck, the Iolair mages screamed for retreat. People fled, the earth changed shape beneath them. Lightning began to strike all around, hitting several at a time; taking to the armor so many wore. Flashes of green orbs throughout the battlefield as Cassius' protection magic did its job. The enemy trampled one another as they tried to escape.

…Gellia heard the screams and felt the energies coursing through the ground. The earth below trembled as the magic was yanked through its depths. She wondered if even the humans could feel it—it was so strong. It felt like the end of the world sung in a magnificent chorus, and it was the only thing she could sense besides the pain. She was too injured to react.

Flashes of light. All went quiet. No voices, no weapons, nothing. There was nothing but his magic; it took away her senses as it ripped through the battlefield. She could even feel it to her core, through the bond that held them together. From where she lie she could see nothing but streaking light, and she couldn't tell if she was still on the ground or if she was suspended in the air, whether time had passed or not, whether she still breathed. For a moment she felt the life force of all Xzepheniixenze, the empire's heartbeat, until finally it was over. She understood now, why he was so feared.

...A torrential downpour began as the knights of Tintagel collected themselves and started to clear the battlefield. The court mages filed tiredly back into the castle, already soaked to the bone. Cassius took one last look to where Gellia fell. She was alone but for Amarynth, thankfully. A Zapheny's head would be a trophy for any soldier. *Julian, go pick her up.* He could already tell how badly she was wounded. Under different circumstances he would go himself, but with all who were present it couldn't be.

...It must have been over. Only noises of armored people shuffling about. Amarynth stood above her, peacefully looked around, his ears swiveled to and fro. She hoped he would protect her from any traitors or any remaining enemies. Gellia wondered if the pain would ever stop, it didn't feel like it ever could. She wasn't sure if she would vomit or faint. Maybe both.

She lie on her side, the spear just poking through her skin on the other side under her armor. Her arm was tired from holding it up, putting it down made her scream with pain. She tried to keep her thinking straight as the rain ran in streams down her face. There was no use moving, she tried that already and found that the pain almost knocked her unconscious, breathing was painful enough. She couldn't concentrate enough to use her magic. She was certain Amarynth was helping her retain her wits. There were people moving around her, she could hear them, perhaps they inspected the dead.

Someone must have approached with ill intent. She could feel Amarynth's energy change and it was terrifying. He seemed to brace, his ears flat against his neck. She was certain she heard a vastly deep growl come from him, a noise that horses don't make. She couldn't see who it was, but after a moment Amarynth returned to his normal detached state.

Then there was light. Julian was coming. She could feel his magnificent power nearing her.

Gellia tried to look over her shoulder, only ended up wincing, but she refused to cry. Julian in the form of man leaned over her. "No silver bridle," Gellia murmured.

"Hello Amarynth. Beautiful day," Julian greeted. "You look terrible, Gellia."

"Yes," she coughed.

"Let's see, let's see." Julian said, thinking Gellia looked very much like a day old corpse. "There's no way we can sneak you in with that think sticking out of you. It's enchanted too, so... you're not going to like me much, pet. Amarynth, could you assist?" If he used his own magic too much it would draw too much attention…

Amarynth's voice rumbled through her mind. *I'm assuming that question is rhetorical.*

"He said…"

"I heard him, dear. The two of us are old friends," Julian said. He bent to rip off her cloak. "Now bite onto this." He put a wooden handle from a broken dagger in front of her face. "I've done this a great number of times…"

Gellia wondered if it would be any worse than she already felt.

Julian braced his foot on her back. "Don't tense."

"Is it—" she meant to finish 'that bad'.

"Oh yes, pet. Here we go." Julian gripped the javelin and wrenched it, wincing at Gellia's scream. After a final yank and a horrible wet suction noise, Julian threw the weapon to the ground and wove his magic to keep her with them. "She's out. Do you… would it be completely strange if…"

Yes, Julian, I can carry you both. He lowered himself to the ground so Julian in his man's form could pull Gellia with him onto Amarynth's back.

"An honor, my old friend," Julian said. "So this is what it's like…" As they made their way through the quieter sections of forest and field Gellia continued to bleed all over them. Julian started to reflect once more. "I may miss the days of adventure but I don't miss having to pick up the pieces all the time."

I think I'm ready to settle down and have more offspring... Amarynth said.

Julian chuckled at the joke. "Oh Amarynth, it's nice to see not all things change …"

***

"...Yes, send Decius my regards," Cassius said.

"Three hundred wounded, my lord. Iolair forces were completely obliterated."

"Clean it up. Now be off. Why are you still following me?" The courtiers scattered as would mice, and he strode down a corridor he rarely traveled.

It wasn't long before what seemed to be hordes of servants rushed towards him, all babbled about the crazy man in Lady Gellia's room who wouldn't let the healer in when she desperately needed one. Cassius plowed through the squealing attendants and charged into Gellia's room without knocking.

Julian gave his goodbye by smiling at Gellia in a way that only a unicorn could. He made his way out the door, past their liege.

Gellia blinked at him, not quite conscious.

Cassius walked to the blood saturated bed. Gellia looked at him in recognition. "You *should* feel like a dolt," he said, reading her hazy thoughts as he leaned over her. "You are too reckless when you can't afford to be so." He peeled the soaked bandage from the wound on her back. "I'm sure you thought you could march right into Ravengate and pluck off Raven's head, well you're lacking something I cannot give you. You may be more powerful, and he may be an idiot but he has a thousand years' experience on you," Cassius growled. "Afraid? Maybe you *should* have some fear in you." He said something about sheltering her too much under his breath. Julian's magic had saved her from death, but there was still much to be done.

He started healing the bone and muscle and finally healed her skin to flawlessness. "It's going to take you time to recover." He rolled her over onto her back. She could tell he was furious.

"You *had* to be part the fight, didn't you? Now you're useless for who knows how long." He crossed his arms and glared down at her. "From now on when you lead an army around stay *out* of combat. Let the soldiers do the work for you. *That* is what they're for. Is that understood? And for the last time you aren't skilled enough with a sword to deal with these knights. Use your magic." Cassius' voice had the unmistakable tone of disgust, but he didn't speak above the normal volume. He tossed his hair back, his eyes narrowed as he read her face.

Gellia thought of how she wished she could say something back. She would have loved to fight with him if she was feeling better. He was *worried* about her. Genuinely afraid for her well-being.

"Don't you dare mock me, princess," he growled. "I am in no humor to be mocked by the likes of you."

Gellia, still too weak to say anything, she could only lie there and try to stay awake. She was nearly out again when she found him changing her into a nightdress. Apparently he'd cleaner her up, too. Didn't she have servants for that?

Cassius exhaled, his expression still brooding. He looked around at the scattered armor pieces, bloody rags and soaked bedding. "Well you can't stay here in this mess."

Gellia wasn't sure exactly what he meant until she was teleported into another familiar room. His room. He wasn't there. She quickly drifted to sleep.

"...If you remember *you* were reckless once, too. You are cruel to her," Julian said. He watched Cassius pace around the grassy courtyard.

"Are you defending her?"

Julian snorted. "Of course I am. I'm reminding you that she is your companion and you do wrong to treat her so. You're lucky she's strong enough to stand by you even when you're so temperamental." Just like Quenelzythe, Gellia was one of the few to unfairly receive Cassius' wrath. Quenelzythe had a knack for ignoring most of it but his feelings were not the same as Gellia's. Julian understood how Gellia suffered—it took a unicorn to recognize it in this place. "And those poor servants. I've never known you to be cruel to loyal servants."

"I brought them back," Cassius said. "They were a little confused but they recovered." He continued to pace, crossing his arms and uncrossing them.

"She'll never forget it," Julian said. "And she'll likely never forgive you for it."

Cassius stiffened. "I don't see myself as cruel to her. It is I who is tormented."

Julian sighed. This was the way of things, Mystic—the Silver One, told him once that it was so. And it was. There was still so much that had not yet happened. But the prophecy had proven true so far, whether one believed the light or the dark had a part in it. Julian could see it; he could see the plan unfolding now, the one that was set into motion almost three millennia ago. No one realized just how brilliant and wise Razhiede was. At some point it would be truly appreciated.

13

"My dearest friends, as you might have guessed I have joined Cassius in his homeland. I hope that your lives in Sen Dunea have been enjoyable. Xzepheniixenze is beautiful beyond dreams and its people are complicated as well as brutal. Cassius of course is just as I always thought he was: arrogant, ruthless, choleric and filled with loathing (and I'm not the only one who thinks so) but I like him just the same. He's a brilliant leader and oddly enough the people are fond of him. I myself have acquired a reputation for I have led several armies and won each battle I've gone into as well as helping save those in need. I live in a glorious castle with wealth beyond your imagination and am treated like a queen. I met my birth father, a most unpleasant person, but that is another story. But please, my friends, write and tell me of your lives and give my affection to the king and his sons. Yours, Gellia."

Gellia handed the letter to the waiting seeker. It was quiet after the battle and she took time to regain her strength. She mostly stayed in her rooms and avoided Cassius. It was a particularly lovely day when she finally decided to go out and visit Amarynth. As she crossed the great hall several servants entered with a surprise—Connylia. It was a joyous meeting.

She and Gellia entertained themselves by watching the knights practice, going riding or spending time studying in the library. It was only a few weeks before word came back from Sen Dunea that Cress had accepted Lucifer and was expecting her third child, and Alexandria was engaged to Mervric. Truly she couldn't have been happier for them. Gellia was surprised that much time passed. It had been that long?

"You miss your friends," Connylia said.

Gellia smiled. "Yes, a bit. I don't think I could tolerate living with them again but I do sometimes miss their silliness. It can be so dark and serious here. I'm so pleased they were able to marry so well."

Connylia smiled. "Well, they're your friends, and you're part of a great house of Xzepheniixenze. That would be enough of a tie to be an advantageous match for the princes."

Gellia laughed. "If you say so."

"What would happen if an enemy attacked Sen Dunea? What would you do? What would happen?"

Gellia smiled. "You're right." Gellia would mow down the enemy with a vengeance never seen before.

"Let's go out today, maybe it will clear your mind."

Gellia didn't argue. An outing was always good.

They rode a great distance; farther than she had ever gone on her own. The countryside welcomed them with its splendor, something that Gellia could no longer live without. She could never return to live in the Outlands—to Fuarmaania and the other tiny countries, not when Xzepheniixenze sang to her. No, the Outlands felt flat and dull. Every day she felt she was more a part of the realm.

A cool breeze blew over the hills. Conny smiled. "I'm so happy you made it here," she said, "that you escaped Dournzariame."

Gellia looked at her friend and silently watched her think.

"The magic is still out there, it isn't organized, but it still remains. It's said that the world will heal someday, that there will be a magic that will put it all back together. All the places ripped from the whole will reattach. Places like Yzelle and the Winterlands and the others. It was fortold that the world would be split apart and it was. But there is more. Not many people remember or pay attention, but I remember someone who took those things seriously for they are true even when no one wants to listen."

"What do you mean?"

She looked at Gellia and smiled. "I don't understand it myself to tell you the truth, but I was always told that Zapheny understand things when no one else does. It's part of your gift. Come now, I think there's a town nearby we can visit."

Gellia didn't pursue the topic; she didn't want to try to bring out something her friend didn't want to remember. Conny could keep her secrets if she wanted, Gellia wouldn't force them out of her.

They cantered down a long road surrounded by the shimmering evergreens in the twilight, looking ahead at the lights of town. As the two friends entered they saw the streets were clean and the houses well-tended; several residents strolled merrily to the local tavern.

Connylia jumped off Justin and waited for Gellia, her foot tapping on the cobblestone walkway. "Hustle yourself, we're going in."

Even though Gellia hopped off Amarynth with enthusiasm she wasn't sure she was ready to deal with a tavern. She had seen the bawdy crowds before and they never appealed to her. "Are you sure," she asked.

"Very sure, it will be fun." She smiled and took Gellia's hand.

And there was quite a bit to see. Villagers from all walks of life drank and cavorted amidst tables and chairs, held hands with the serving wenches and shouted to each other. It took a few moments for the locals to adjust to the newcomers, most had never seen the likes of Gellia and Connylia, but the two women won them over. Before Gellia could blink, her friend was dancing with them.

After a while someone offered Gellia a drink, which she dumbly took and handed over a gold coin—she wasn't sure how much everything cost but thought it would be enough. Several people swung by her, laughing and greeting her, some asked her name. Luckily before she could answer, one of the wenches scolded him. "She's a lady, that's all you need to know!" It made Gellia laugh.

Soon after she was swept up into the dancing and laughing masses with no idea of what she was doing. It wasn't so awful. Everyone wanted to dance with her and all of them were polite to their best ability. Gellia wondered if they expected her to snub them, ignore them or beat them because of their lack of refinery. She suspected any other Xzepheniixenze would only appear in such a place to cause trouble.

For hours they danced, showed the villagers a few new steps as well as learning new ones themselves. There was singing and drinks and laughter in quantities Gellia never saw before— humans and even the few half-breeds who were there seemed to enjoy themselves. Gellia found out that most had barely even seen a purebred Xzepheniixenze, some only heard tales. Most only knew that Tintagel was a magnificent black castle far away where their generous baron, and the famous Lady of the Roses lived. Gellia had hear rumors that she was something of a legend, but only believed now. No one was sure how that title started.

Some of the oldsters were sure they saw the Baron of Tintagel once before. Gellia found talking to the community elders quite interesting and informative. For as long as anyone could remember the village prospered. The stories of their good life were passed down through several generations and they called it a blessing or even a miracle.

None of them ever heard of the Golden Age or the Holy War or even the Dragon Wars. Dragons were myths. The only legend they knew from that time was a vague one about the Vega Knights and how they were heroes in a time long past. The two women sat with the elders and listened to what they didn't know. Connylia's mind voice visited Gellia: *I'm not sure how many hundreds of generations have gone by for them since those times, but they survive, they spread like wildfire. They'll always be with us needing protection. Cassius has done a good job.* She rose again and returned to the dance.

Gellia continued to send her thoughts. *Sometimes I feel that I know things but I don't know where these thoughts come from... I know Cassius causes much destruction and takes apart the network of Xzepheniixenze society on a regular basis but I feel in my heart that I know he does far more good for this realm than anyone realizes. Conny, there is so much he does that is unseen. Perhaps this is all common since I only have ever known him and no one else, but I don't think so. Through him I can see all the lands, feel how things grow, watch the magic as it swirls through the substance of the lands...*

I trust you, Zapheny. Conny laughed with her current dancing partner who was wildly intoxicated. *Razhiede seemed to see it in him as well, although I never understood it, I just trusted*

Razhiede. All I could see was that Cassius' mother was a frightening individual who was unpredictable and violent. The only way I felt safe from her was because Razhiede was alive or she was dead. But enough of that now, enjoy yourself.

At the end of the night the two women lounged at a corner table and enjoyed their refreshments as they watched the crowd slowly dissipate. "I used to go dancing when I was young," Connylia said, "when I was your age and didn't have many responsibilities—before I went to serve the old queen. There was a treating house in town I would walk to."

Gellia sipped her ale thoughtfully.

Conny snickered. "A few times I forgot to tell my parents where I was going."

Gellia smiled. "There really wasn't anyplace for me to go in Fuarmaania. I don't know if I would have gone, either. The best I had was riding, and I was more than happy with that."

"You were a princess. You would have been missed much quicker. Not that my parents forgot me, but I wasn't very good about coming home when I was supposed to. I had too much fun dancing and talking with people. 'Go fetch your sister, Gallylya,' my father would say. And Gally would come cantering up on Gabriel and scold me. 'Mother and father are waiting for you, you have to come home with me now.' And I would beg him for just one more dance." She finished her drink and waited for another to be poured. "He always did."

"Did what?" Gellia asked, finishing her drink as well and wondered how many she had before that one.

"Let me stay just a little longer." Conny looked sad. "Those were different times." She drifted her thoughts.

Gellia rolled the last bit of ale around in the bottom of her cup. "What are you thinking about?" Gellia asked.

Connylia shook her head. "I've haven't spoken of home since the catastrophe, not to anyone... But it's time for us to go back now, it's almost dawn."

"No one's missing us," Gellia said over her cup. "It's nice here, I'm not nervous all the time."

"That would be the amount of ale you've consumed," Conny said.

Gellia smiled and settled in. "What catastrophe?"

"It began a very strange time in my life, during the Wars. The community we lived in was destroyed in one fell swoop. Everyone was killed. Gallylya and I were spared because we weren't there. We had a very large family."

"I'm sorry."

Conny gave her a wan smile. "It was a long time ago and a story I don't feel I can tell. I know you understand." She went silent for a moment. Gellia let her organize her thoughts for she looked as though she would speak again. "Something rather strange happened recently I feel I should discuss with you." She set her glass down and looked at the table for a moment before returning her gaze to Gellia. "Perhaps it's nothing but I'll see what you think of it. Lately I've had a difficult time locating my brother. He hasn't been where I expect him to be. Not that I've ever kept an eye on him before so it may just be my imagination. Also, not that long ago someone from my past appeared again. Alynderan Kadomon."

"Who?" The name was vaguely familiar.

"He's an earl who lives in the distant mountains in Castle Aisling, he's also one of the remaining Vega Knights, one of my brother's best friends, and at one time we were betrothed. He stopped by to say hello. It seemed a little strange to me, he lives very far away and although I know he travels out into the countryside often, Dournzariame is not just over the hill. He couldn't have been there just to visit me, although perhaps it would have happened in the past."

"Your betrothed?" They did that in Zephronia?

Connylia shook her head. "We never married of course, it's a rather long story… I'm nervous that something is going on. He even brought his armor. Perhaps it's nothing. I hope it's nothing. There is nothing false about him. He's all honor and light and kindness."

Gellia was silent.

"I don't want anything to happen to you," she said. "I want you to be protected, even if it does make me a traitor to my own people—you have to survive no matter what. Since you are the only one, much depends on you. You don't have an heir to take your place, Zapheny. Cassius knows this too."

It was there with her, Gellia felt it, her magic. "No matter what others say, we all have to do what we feel is best. Right or wrong isn't always as clear as we all hope."

"Make no mistake, Gellia, you *are* a descendant of Razhiede Zapheny. You *will* take the throne of Xzepheniixenze if your time is not too short." She regrouped and stretched. "Well I need to get back even if you don't want to. Come then," she slowly rose from the bench and gave Gellia a good-natured shove.

"You're so strange," Gellia said once they were mounted up again. The stable yard was quiet, only a lone boy was there to watch them leave.

"Why do you say that?"

"I can't decide if you act more like royalty or—"

"I've never *truly* been royalty. Some called me the empress when I was here. Until I had a brother for emperor I was just another daughter of a knight. My father served the emperor as his father before and so on and so forth. We were noble but not royalty." She smiled and stroked the neck of her glorious mount, Julian's brother. "You know what we have to do now,"

"No, what?"

"We have to gallop back to the castle without falling off."

***

When she woke, Gellia was handed a note from her friend. Shortly after they had returned a seeker came with word that it was urgent that Connylia return home. Gellia tried to remember the name of Connylia's betrothed so she could tell Cassius, but failed and waited to tell him when she could remember the name. She rolled over and pulled the blankets over her head. It was far too bright in her room even with the curtains closed. Perhaps she would rise at some point in the day, but certainly not for a while.

In time Gellia locked herself in the laboratory, battling out her frustrations into the protected walls and trying to see just what her best magic looked like. Little did she know that because of her experimentations the rest of the castle thought they had an earthquake until they figured out it was her. Cassius decided that it was best for her to stay around the castle for the time being. She believed that he didn't trust her enough to let her out of his sight without Connylia. The toad.

This time Sian was with her, after so many months she found him to be her favorite magic sparring partner. Perhaps this wasn't exactly the experience preferred, but it was something. Sian was lightning quick with his attacks, weather manipulation was his specialty. Gellia had to jump and build barriers all over the place all the while making counter attacks. Her biggest problem with him was his continuing innuendos about others in the castle. He always had her thinking about this one or that one and what they were concocting. "You're truly quite powerful," Sian commented and dusted off his tunic.

Gellia didn't respond, she was too busy watching his eyes.

"Perhaps the most powerful in the castle." He smiled a little

She was no longer surprised at comments like that. Gellia felt confident he tried to turn she and Cassius against one another, so when Mephibosheth was finally out of the way she too would be disposed of, and Sian would rise to the highest position under their baron.

He started to cast a hailstorm on her, Gellia could tell by the pattern of energy. She prepared herself for the next move. There was a mental touch. What? Sian started to look over his shoulder but then disappeared. She could hear footfalls echo behind her. She spun and cast a lightning bolt, which was quickly deflected. Cassius had entered the laboratory. "How do you fight someone like me?" he asked.

Gellia balked and felt the air shift. He was serious. She teleported behind him but found he was already facing her. She scrambled to drop a storm of flame on him. The fire fizzled around him without scorching a single black hair.

"How do you suppose you should defeat someone who is protected from elemental attacks?" he said, smiling. "If I were seriously trying to do away with you—you would already be dead."

Gellia felt the jerk of magic through the ground and layered barriers around herself. The first blow he dealt decimated the first three layers and the force knocked her to the ground. She felt she was being crushed; the world around her seemed fuzzy. Her shielding was gone.

Cassius stood above her smirking. "I'm impressed by your weaving ability but you break down the minute any pressure is put on you."

She automatically started building shields around herself without a thought, but as she reached for more energy she felt it yanked from under her and she was forced to struggle for it.

"There are a few of us who have talents such as this."

If only she had more practice...

"Yes. I can get you through battles of all kinds, princess, but it won't be you in your head, it will be me." He released her. "Your weakness is not in your magic, but in your mind."

Gellia rose and dusted off her breeches.

"We've been summoned," he said.

Gellia froze and looked at him. She knew he had to be upset about something, and now she knew why.

"We're leaving for Ravengate." It was very late at night. "You're already packed."

She didn't even have time to dig in her heels.

***

"What am I supposed to say? How am I supposed to act?" She hesitated while Amarynth waited for her to mount. Her bond horse's patience wore out quickly and he gave her a mental prod.

"I'll do the talking. Don't act like a victim. You're staying with me, as well. I'm not leaving you alone in that pit."

Cassius teleported them a short distance from the eerie city of Ravengate. It was a drastic change, from the physical and mystical elegance of Tintagel to a land ravaged by its keeper. Everything seemed to be in a state of decay. Julian and Amarynth snorted, Gellia covered her nose and mouth. The city was larger than Kaymaria but was a giant slum. It seemed there were mostly filthy, skinny, almost naked children running everywhere; sewage flowed down the roads in which they played. Down a nearby street there were people in chains being bid upon by who could only be local lords. Buildings were blackened piles of stones; fires burned everywhere, some controlled, most were wild. "You see why I like him so well," Cassius said.

Gellia swallowed several times to suppress her gagging. "You couldn't have teleported us inside?" Nothing Cassius ever did was as dreadful as the way Raven treated his people.

"The magic is so off balance we would have ended up in oblivion. Difficult to believe this city was once beautiful. It was called Ealachanara then." He smiled. "Don't worry; there is more hope here than you can see. With assistance, many have escaped over the years."

"You?"

"No, I don't have the time to stay here and orchestrate it, but I assist when it suits me."

As they rode farther into the destitute city Cassius opened a door to her. "We were allies once. My brother and I, Quenelzythe, and Raven all went on exploits together. Then there was Xzelleminiya later on." They passed through a gate, then another within thirty feet of the last.

"Xzelleminiya?"

"He calls her Mina, so that's become her call-name, Xzelleminiya is her real name. Xzelleminiya Ealachan. Raven and Xyrnne left us after Quenelzythe and I decided to take on Gallylya and the rest of the world. We had a purpose, and he doesn't enjoy organization—takes too much work. So when Quen and I ran off to fight in the Holy War and to nearly lose our lives by Gallylya, Raven found other friends and started raiding houses, then villages and so forth. We were too busy casting dragons into rocks and plants to care about him. Eventually after Quen was murdered I took Tintagel from my father, and Raven had built a little army of his own. It was just like that for a very long time, for centuries. Raven did nothing but wander about and kill everything he could find. Genocide is a favorite pastime of his. The throne was shaky, as it is most of the time since the fall of Zenobia and stayed that way for many centuries. We went through dozens of rulers until one time he just happened to be in the right place at the right time. He doesn't like ruling, there's too much responsibility that keeps nagging him, but he enjoys the authority and always seeks more."

Gellia spoke. "You enjoy killing," she said.

Cassius laughed. "I refuse to waste my energy on killing without a reason."

"You killed your twin and your father," she said.

He laughed again. "You've listened. Xyrnne was Aurelian's pet, a swordsman like him. He also crossed me one too many times. Lord Aurelian Vazepheny was an old tyrant who didn't appreciate the way I went about things. I made him nervous as my mother did. He took her name by the way, being that it was the better. Not that he was every truly part of the family." He smiled brilliantly at her. "How do you think I took Tintagel? And I made a legend of myself and started the trend. I'm sure you've heard the stories."

Gellia didn't feel so guilty about not caring for Decius. "Would you kill your children if you have them?"

"Look, here we are."

Before them stood a great castle, larger than Tintagel and certainly not as symmetrical. It was made of grey and blacked stone with narrow towers, sword-like spikes seemed to protrude from everywhere. Impaled bodies decorated the battlements. A single tattered flag fluttered pathetically from the top of a tower. "Oh look, they've brought out the banners for us," Cassius said cheerily. "And it looks like they've done some cleaning."

As they crossed the drawbridge over the moat Gellia tried not to look down, but with a glance found it was filled with decaying bodies and sludge. Cassius created a wind to blow away the stench. She mentally thanked him. Their horses were none too pleased about being left in the stables but did as they must as Gellia and Cassius entered the main corridor.

Prepare yourself, Cassius warned.

Nothing could have prepared her for the first room they entered, the trophy room. As they came into the great room they were greeted by the staring glass eyes of a stuffed unicorn, its coat dull and mane falling out from years of standing on its platform. Gellia gasped and hid her face in Cassius' sleeve for a moment. Cassius' hand on the small of her back guided her onward through a room full of such things. Many were animals she had never seen or heard of. There was a griffin and a hippogriff next to each other. A manticore, a giant serpent, a minotaur. A centaur stared blankly down at them and gave Gellia the chills. Standing side by side were two people with wings, one looked Zephron with white wings, the other looked Xzepheniixenze with black and both looked as though in life they were strikingly beautiful. Their clothes didn't fit them correctly, Gellia noticed.

They were already dead when he found them. Cassius told her, *He could have* never *taken either one of them down... we came from a different time, he and I. Everyone was much more powerful then... Lunans and Solarans they are, races destroyed long ago. Pity. I do believe your Guardian of Qenai was a Lunan.*

Gellia stared at the pair of beautiful men for a moment longer, feeling unsettled. There was a horse type of creature with dragon like wings and horns coming out of its head. 'Jayde' the plaque on the base said. Then there was a winged horse and its foal. Some more animals she had never heard of before. At the end of the room stood another unicorn. *He prides himself with these since it takes virtue to catch them,* Cassius said. *Most others have been killed off by other people.*

Gellia touched the age-coarsened white coat of the unicorn and felt loathing bubble up from the depths of her soul. *Are there any left?*

Hidden.

You put them there.

They keep the equilibrium. There's none around here, that's some of why the land is in waste. It's been contaminated by Raven's disease. Wild portals have appeared in a few places, no one knows where they lead to and not even I would want to walk through them... they're something like a rift in this plane, having to do with the Holy War. I'm sure you've read it in the library, but the written words have difficulty explaining the exact situation. Perhaps I'll explain it to you at a better time.

They made it through the room and into the next corridor. Gaudy art and other nonsense seemed to be everywhere along with the rabble that lived there. There were even two people copulating down a side corridor, barely in the shadows. Gellia wondered how Mina ever tolerated it. *Oh look, theater...* *Xzelleminiya has her reasons for being here,* Cassius explained. *A shame she hasn't succeeded yet.*

Gellia nearly laughed at his sarcasm. It certainly helped lighten the mood. A servant hobbled towards them and offered to take them to their rooms. Cassius spoke. "Show us both her room first. It must be inspected for our standards."

Her room was nice by Ravengate criteria. It had what had been lovely pieces of furniture, but nothing was well tended and the window let in the smell from the moat. She looked at Cassius and shook her head. The servant led them away to Cassius' chamber, which was quite the distance from hers. *You see,* Cassius said. *He isn't intelligent, but he does learn. He wants us separated to better access you.*

Indeed Cassius' chamber was much nicer. It was very clean, well-kept and was on the back of the castle facing the river and the distant mountains. "I complain," he explained as he looked out the window at the fires and the smoke. "And I send off his disgusting servants by drove. Not that it's their fault, poor sods. And no, I don't bring my own. They could easily end up dead or tortured."

She joined him at the window. *Can we kill him while he's here?*

He laughed mentally. *It's not as simple as that. How like a young Zephron you can be sometimes. A battle like that here would be a situation in which I wouldn't want involvement. There's other factors to be considered like Gallylya and old man Zaphaniah, not that anyone knows where he is.*

You do.

He smiled at her. *So do you.*

I'm going to have to learn about him... He's not going to call us for audience until tomorrow.

You're right. The castle speaks to you, eh? Luckily this one doesn't know how to lie.

While he was in a generous mood... *How do castles become living?* Gellia asked.

Generations of spirits fuse into the very stone. Living castles tend to have personality traits of the collective spirits. His arm slipped around her. *Look at this waste. You don't know all*

*that I've gone through to protect all the things he likes to kill.
I've an island off the coast of Qenai were I've brought countless
creatures, then there's Demf—the forest is enchanted and keeps
all but me and those who need rescuing out. Many have gone
there to hide. It's much easier to keep the energy levels in
balance with all Xzepheniixenze's creatures intact. Over the
years it's slowly become more dangerous to use magic.*

Even with all the books in the library, there was much
information still not available to her. Most books with talk of the
Holy War were summations, and didn't involve much about the
mystical ramifications. She could imagine why battles with such
as Gallylya and Raven would be detrimental to the empires on a
dire scale. She wondered if Avenzyre was stable, if Cassius
would act with speed and fury. Somehow she doubted it. She
smiled. It would be too messy.

Eventually there will be war, he said. *But not yet, and I
hope not for some time.*

A war like that caused him unease, that was for certain.
How would they bring this to a head and remove it?

If only she knew all that she needed to know, then she
would be more help. There was so much more studying she
needed to do, it seemed infinite. The more she learned, the more
she realized she didn't know. Was she ready to go out into the
castle on her own? She wanted to. She wanted to be useful.

You stay here. I have to go out. He changed his clothes
with magic. *Under no circumstances are you to leave this room.
I'm locking you in, besides.*

That was her answer. After he left she had the urge to
leave the boring room and investigate the place herself.
Something told her to stay, not just the locked and magically
sealed door. There were things out there she didn't want to see,
she could tell from the screams.

***

What did you find out? Gellia asked as she applied
cosmetics in front of the giant mirror. He had barely stayed in the
room, but why would his habits change here? He was part

seeker, really. She would have liked books to read to keep her occupied. That would have been nice.

Cassius had just walked in. *Nothing incredibly exciting. He wants Kaymaria but decided against attacking again after finding out there were more 'survivors' than he realized. Almost ready to go?*

Ready when you are. She rose and took his arm.

They waited in the antechamber to the throne room; their company consisted of two guards and a man at the door who made appointments. It appeared no one ever came to Raven's court but for military officials and Cassius. Gellia tried to keep her breathing steady, but it was difficult in such miasma. She had time to look at the stone carvings around the room, most covered by falling drapery, many smashed, all covered with dust.

A few she recognized as swans, upon closer inspection she realized some of the carvings had rings of roses around their necks. There was only one reason for such art—the original ruler of this castle was once allied to Zenobia. She felt a rush. Someone came from the shadows. Gellia jumped, but Cassius was not surprised. "Greetings majesty," he said and bowed dramatically.

Gellia recognized her as the empress but did not bow. Mina looked so elegant, so regal.

"As always, Cassius," she said. "I hope our discussion was useful."

"Very, majesty. I do not believe you have been formally introduced to Gellia Zapheny of Tintagel."

Mina smiled with the aloofness of a cat. "Perhaps, but we have met."

Gellia noticed something she found very odd—Cassius addressed Mina the way the courtiers in Zephronia addressed Gallylya, he even bowed like the Zephrons did. She felt a mental tap; it was Mina asking permission to speak. Gellia cracked open the door to her mind just a little, braced herself to slam it closed if need be. Mina's mind voice was a soothing, pale nondescript color and had the qualities Gellia recognized as from someone of great age. *Your potential greatness makes it easy to take for granted all that this situation is, easy to forget your innocence. I can see it. It is why Gallylya didn't have you killed—but such a thing will be your death in this place—or worse. Don't depend on Cassius, it will only be a disappointment.*

Gellia didn't respond. It only took a split second, but Cassius noticed, he always did. "Well then," he said, irritated. "How is he today, majesty?"

"How is he every day?" Mina said coolly.

Cassius chuckled. "For being such a creature of chaos he's so predictable... must be terrible for you living in this degraded place, especially after having such light shine down on you for so many years. This must be like a tomb, I would suspect." He looked around. Gellia noticed Mina's exquisite control over her emotions. "But you really have to be dead to truly appreciate a tomb so actually you're more like an un-dead, aren't you? A wraith waiting to be destroyed by such as Gallylya Duvray."

"But I am still here, aren't I," she said, "and I will remain until I have what I want."

What does she want? Gellia asked Cassius.

To start with, an alliance with you, he answered. *We don't need her, but she could make things much easier.*

"...I would like to speak with Lady Zapheny sometime in the future, perhaps in private." Mina continued. "I have a proposition for her."

Cassius' smirk had a mordant edge to it the likes of which Gellia never saw before. "You are quite the lady, majesty. I must say I've missed the pleasure of your company. Perhaps majesty would be willing to honor Tintagel with a visit?"

"I would visit a greater castle if you find it," Mina said, and her lips furled into a tight smile.

Before Cassius could respond someone came from the other room and told them it was time. Mina watched them go. He spoke into Gellia's mind. *Much easier.*

But how can we trust her? Gellia asked.

She needs us. She needs you to identify with her; she needs me to do what I do best. By allying herself with you she has us both, knowing better than to rely just on me. Damn I miss her sometimes. She's brilliant, a fast learner, always so cunning, a perfect cohort.

Gellia was impressed and perhaps a bit jealous. Never had she heard him praise someone as he did Mina—she must have been the only person he ever respected.

Not quite, princess. I have a great respect for many people and for many people's talents. Gallylya is a prime example. If I didn't have great respect for him I would now be blind to the fact that he is most likely planning an assault.

The throne room was large and windowless, cobwebs hung like curtains from the ceiling. Not many other than Cassius, Gellia and the emperor were there. A few servants, a knight or two. No one looked to be paying much attention until she and Cassius entered the room. Cassius' mind appeared in her head and started an onslaught of information. *You'll know when he's going to draw when he looks like he's concentrating, once that happens his magic will come forth like a flood. His favorite magic is fire. The corridor will be impassable and the left hand side of the room, which is weaker, will fall out—keep that in mind. He can teleport, easily. Look with your magic, not necessarily your eyes. He also is decent with a sword; you're better off staying out of his range and using your magic. If he calls his guards it will take a few moments for them to arrive, there are always three in the corridor behind the throne, six in the main corridor and twelve down the side. He has three other mages in the castle right now who are loyal to him. I can find them the fastest if something should happen so you should deal with Raven until I've finished them. Should take only moments. Chances are he'll attack me first; send the guards after you for he'll want you as a prize. If that happens attack him directly or attack his focuses. He might even give you a moment because he'll be shocked, but it will be a short moment. Remember he'll want to take you alive. Keep your barriers strong, which will keep out the guards—ignore them if you can. I know you have the ability to disrupt the energy levels for I've given it to you. Do not use that ability. Do not open a portal inside the castle no matter what happens. Never let him get behind you. Just for starters... Always remember that you are nothing but high quality meat to him.*

In the past Gellia would have fidgeted, but now she was too busy absorbing as much information as possible. Cassius showed her images and scenarios. When she was done focusing though, Ravengate closed in around her, the stuffy air, the smell of smoke, ale and filth. Her feet moved but she could not feel them.

Raven greeted them genially and wondered aloud how his cousin always looked so good and how anyone could be as radiant as Gellia. He tried to search her mind and found that she knew exactly what he was up to and was looking back at him. "Dear cousin," he said, "I do believe you betrayed me." Gellia already felt violated by his gaze, his magic. He never took his eyes off her. She stood in defiance, but was careful not to overdo.

"I?" Cassius said. "Never. What gave you that silly idea?"

Raven frowned. "This is that girl I sent you to find."

"Certainly not. That girl in Fuarmaania was useless and was destroyed. I already told you that, remember?"

"Then who is this?"

"This is Gellia Zapheny. She knew of her magic when I met her so I decided to take her under my wing so to speak. As it turns out she's a decent mage." Cassius' voice was so cool almost unnerved Gellia, the hairs on the back of her neck stood on end.

"Aren't they one in the same?" Raven asked, trying not to look confused.

"No, dear cousin," the lie rolled of his tongue as easily if it were the absolute truth. "Gellia Zapheny was sealed within the body of Gellia Iolair and was released when I killed her."

Raven looked at Cassius for a moment. "So this is a different person."

"Yes."

"Then why didn't you bring her to me?" Raven asked, a little annoyed.

"You wanted Gellia *Iolair* but she had to be destroyed. This is Gellia *Zapheny*," Cassius said deliberately slowly.

"But I *wanted* the missing Zapheny."

"You told me you wanted Gellia of Fuarmaania, Gellia *Iolair*."

Raven thought a minute.

Cassius continued, "The girl you desired is dead. Maybe you should speak with your spy, Decius, because I do believe he was confused when he told you of his daughter. We all respect him but he really can't tell the difference between one person and the next—he is *old* and all. (Just between you and me, I think he's plotting against you.)"

Gellia could sense the exasperation in the air.

"No," Raven said.

"Oh yes, I wouldn't trust him. Didn't you see him speaking to Lord Gian at the party? I'm sure if you check your sources and perhaps use some seekers you would find he is indeed against you. He even attacked Tintagel which is a direct affront to your lordship since I am your devoted supporter."

Raven looked at Gellia for a while as he thought about it. Cassius realized the words he chose were too complicated for the emperor to understand. "She doesn't look like him," he said finally. Gellia did her best not to cower.

"She looks like Connylia."

"Yes, she does. She's the one who has been leading your armies around?"

"Yes."

"I thought you said she was like a harpy."

"Oh! Silly me, I thought you were talking about someone else. She—" he motioned to Gellia, "is very beautiful, very infuriating and quite icy."

Gellia smirked. Maybe he was just talking to Raven, maybe he was teasing her. It was difficult to tell, but it made her feel better.

"You're always so confused, cousin." Raven continued to look at her then finally spoke to her. "You're quiet."

"I have nothing to say," Gellia said. With Raven's focus on her she started to feel sick again. Mina was right. There were some things Gellia just wasn't prepared for. She fought to keep her composure once again.

The emperor was slightly surprised, but smiled at her. No one ever came into his throne room without telling him how wonderful he was except Cassius and now this woman. "Cassius," It was still strange for Gellia to hear someone calling him by his name, even if it was the emperor. "Are you sure?"

Cassius smiled sweetly. "My dear cousin, I know it may seem a little—strange shall we say? But remember when you first sent me off to Fuarmaania you were busy with that whole Lynor thing. It must have been very difficult... It could be in all the commotion I didn't understand exactly what you wanted, but as you can see this girl does not fit the persona you were seeking." Raven leaned back into his throne and squinted. Gellia was intrigued.

That's his son. He tried to kill Raven not long ago and it was quite a mess, Cassius told her quickly. *Raven couldn't imagine his own son taking after* me... *of course, it was with my help...* He mentally laughed. *Lynor didn't survive of course. See how he looks right now? He's confused and bored with all the words I've used.*

Why did he want me, exactly? Was it just for carnal pleasure?

That, yes, and one of his smarter advisors convinced him that a Zapheny would be a great weapon against whomever he chose. They would have only half trained you, made you a slave, and used you for as long as they could before letting you burn yourself out.

He seems as though he needs a smart advisor.
Indeed. One of my mages betrayed me.
Ohhhh, she said.

Cassius' mind gave her a sardonic smile. *You can imagine the consequences, however the damage was already done. I haven't had a traitor at that level since, though, and it wasn't enough to really threaten my plans.*

"Yes, you're right. Well, it was good seeing you again, cousin. Like what you did with Desobre, especially since he isn't loyal... I'm going to find some fun activity to do." Promptly the emperor rose and took one last, long look at Gellia before leaving the room. It went far better than she hoped. Cassius had her nervous to death.

He's not sure about any of it. He'll go molest some hapless girl and when he feels better he'll talk to his advisors and he may or may not listen to them. It's all nonsense, Cassius said. *He accuses me of having a dizzying intellect when it helps that he is completely dull.* "Let's be off, shall we?" *We have a land to quell.*

I was petrified, does it amuse you to make me so nervous?

I didn't do it to amuse myself. It's difficult to say what he'll do. He could have attacked us before we ever entered the throne room. I'm so unappreciated... On their way out he paused to smile at Mina, who ignored him.

"That was so strange. Why haven't you done this earlier?" Gellia asked once they were riding through the city again. Their visit was unusually and thankfully short. She knew he understood she referred to the plot against the throne.

"There hasn't been a need. I don't care who sits on the throne as long as they let me do whatever I want and leave things the way I want them, which has been the way through sixteen rulers, sixteen ages and better than a millennia and a half. You've seen that Raven leaves me alone, but doesn't leave everything else... he asked me to find a girl in Fuarmaania as a favor, it wasn't an order. Of course I accepted happily because I had no intention of ever giving you to him. Gallylya should thank me. Raven would really like to decimate Zephronia if he could, using you as the perfect weapon."

"And you aren't?"

"Neither. You as a weapon *or* taking over Zephronia. I don't want Zephronia, I only want Gallylya. If it's easier to lay waste to Zephronia to get to him than I'll do it. If Zyendel was a better leader who could take over the throne and rule properly, or if one of the Vega Knights was willing to rule in his stead then Gallylya would give his own head on a platter to save his people. But then again it's the half-key I want and he would rather have a war than give it to me."

Gellia almost liked Gallylya, despite how abrasive he was—she always knew where he stood. Her mind skipped to her first impressions of Cassius and realized that her instincts had been true. Yes, he was everything she thought he was even though everyone else thought he was more like a Zephron. How odd. "Gallylya told me about the dragon key half... is there any way not to kill him?"

Cassius paused to look at her, his eyes were intense. "You're defending him?"

Gellia felt it was worth the risk. "Yes. I feel that he is too important to lose. I feel it in my very soul. We may need him." Cassius waited. "After Gallylya and Raven, is there anyone else? What about Zaphaniah? If anyone else has ambitions, a mess like open war would seem to be a good time to set things into motion." She knew Gallylya was responsible for killing his friend and her forefathers, but he still had great value…

Cassius looked into the distance for a few moments and Gellia was hit by a wave of dread. She could feel him think, plans unfurled. He smiled. "Zaphaniah has always wished for the destruction of Zephronia and the rule of Xzepheniixenze." He started to laugh, a laugh that came up from his toes. "Clever girl!" he said.

"What are you planning?" She asked.

"I can't tell you, but don't worry, you are a part of it and I won't kill Gallylya, it *would* be a shame."

"Why can't you tell me?"

"You are friends with Connylia, she is the sister of Gallylya. I can't risk her finding out from you and somehow letting her brother know. Her mind is not as sharp as it used to be. Clever, clever princess. We must be going, much to do."

Gellia remembered. "Oh, speaking of Connylia, she made mention of something odd and I don't know if it's significant or not. I had forgotten about it, and I can't remember the names but…" Cassius gave her a look. "She said some man who was her betrothed," Gellia used the Zephron word 'betrothed', "came to visit her and she said he had armor and that it was strange."

Cassius looked stricken. "How long ago?"

"She told me the last time she was here."

"And you didn't tell me?"

"I didn't think it was that important." She started to feel foolish.

"Dammit, princess. Gallylya has called to the Vega Knights, undoubtedly keeping his sister in the dark because he knows she visits us. Alynderan couldn't resist speaking with her."

"Is this bad?"

"Any situation concerning the Vega Knights is dire when you're a Xzepheniixenze."

She felt a black storm cloud roll over his mood and a spear of dread pierce her through her core. Perhaps outwardly her liege didn't look much different than usual, but she sensed his deep hatred surge below the surface. "But no," he said, there was a ferocity in his voice, one that he held in check but she could sense. "Gallylya doesn't understand: if he crosses me I will bring Zephronia to its knees and barely lift a finger."

Gellia could say nothing. She didn't want to fuel this plot she already unintentionally created, and felt guilty she was part of it. Zephronians truly had nothing to do with their emperor's decisions but had to do what he ordered.

She felt him weave and tidy up the magic around them so it would be safe to use the local resources. He was so quick at it. It was astounding. His magic plucked them from the road and replaced them in the stable yard of Tintagel. Stable boys scrambled from all directions as the green magic swirled across the cobblestones. "I'm giving you a castle of you own," Cassius said and dismounted.

"Me? Where? Why?" Gellia jumped off Amarynth, never took her eyes off her liege.

"Yes you. I'm giving you Demf castle. It's a bit run down right now but it's a nice place in the security of the protected forest. It you want we can go there tomorrow."

A castle of her *own*? Could she do right by such a gift? Why now? Was he going to explode at any moment? Was this an exile? Was he sending her away because he wanted to hide something from her?

"It's not that great of an issue, princess." He didn't need to read her mind to sense her thoughts. They walked into the castle together, the courtiers flocking to them. "Think about it if you want. I won't force you to go."

Gellia recalled the first time she ever came into Tintagel when she was whisked off into the opposite direction and now she and Cassius were walking side by side amongst all the nonsense and babbling of their attendants. This was her home now, this was where she *belonged*—people here would notice her absence. She would go live at this Demf castle and make it habitable, but it wouldn't be truly home, and Demf was far enough away that she couldn't keep an eye on him.

***

They once more fell into their routines, one being holding audiences and listening to complaints and reports of all kinds. Gellia stood next to the throne now, wearing an impish smile. Together she and Cassius performed the mystical dance through the room, sifting through memories and thoughts, looking for anything interesting. A lord from the south pledged his loyalty; a city to the east had a group of children they wanted schooled at Tintagel. It was the customary day. A few mercenaries were causing trouble in a village, several lords came to renew their vow to Tintagel and brought gifts, several specifically for Gellia. The people worshiped their baron, but it was their beautiful Gellia who took their hearts. Several villages just outside Tintagel's lands came to join in alliance, their lords caring little for them and the legend of the enigmatic baron and the Lady of Roses grew. Gellia let her magic carry her through court as her mind wandered more with each passing moment.

With the name of Zapheny making its way through the minds of the natives, the stories of the Golden Era were revisited. Even Gellia made sure to do as much research as possible about her ancient ancestor—she wished she could ask Connylia, but that never accomplished anything. It appeared Razhiede was a great scholar and teacher, wise as even the oldest of beings. All books written about him were filled with flattery, adoration as best as Xzepheniixenze knew. They spoke of his ability to rule, his boundless charisma. Even his archenemies respected him. But nothing was written of his rise to power, his past before that. There was some mention of his empress, towards the end of his reign, of her beauty and grace. There was much written of the splendor of his home, the castle he chose to stay in for most of his life, but its origins were also lost. Zenobia. The written word told of white beaches and a great cliff the size of a mountain. They spoke of glittering towers and labyrinthine corridors, artwork, gardens. It was always under construction in one part or another, but it was so vast one never noticed the sound of chisels, so full of magic no one noticed the forging magic.

Some wrote it had a magic of its own, that even the mortal servants gained powers from it. The descriptions were often wandering thoughts of the writers, who in their overwhelmed state could not clearly depict a single space in the castle, but only the castle as a whole, the feeling they had during their stay. It felt as if it was a legend, a fairytale. But it wasn't.

If she closed her eyes she could see it—the castle she dreamed of even when she was in Fuarmaania. It visited her even here in Tintagel, never far away. Sometimes on the wind she could hear it, hear the ocean in the voices of the trees. Her great grandfather knew she would come one day. He knew the line would not be broken, that a Zapheny would return to Xzepheniixenze. She remembered a dream she had, being in the gardens and seeing someone. Someone at Shahyrahara reminded her. The Silver One.

The audience continued. The mages always watched her; she could feel their gazes. Perhaps they could sense her drift, but her magic held so they could say nothing. All they knew was greed. They too were relearning the name Zapheny, and what that might mean once more. What she didn't know as of the topic none of them would bring up to each other, only think in their secret thoughts: the idea that Gellia potentially had some sort of power over Cassius.

Gellia suppressed her smile. Most couldn't make the right decisions and never understood what their lord was really about. They were too blinded by their own nature. That was her human advantage. Part of their malevolent lord was a philanthropist and preservationist—they just didn't see it as such and couldn't react to it correctly.

They had to postpone their trip to Demf for a few days since the castle was in an uproar about rumors of Cassius' treason charge. That was when Gellia realized that very few, if not only her and their horses knew of Cassius' actual goals. Very few questioned his loyalty to the emperor. There were always grabs at power, that was the natural state of the empire, but no one suspected he would go against Raven's rule. Cassius of course spent a day or so erasing the memories of those who were too cowardly to stay in Tintagel if it was against the throne. It was better, he told Gellia, if everything was kept quiet. Rumors were like wildfire and either there might be a lot of dead Tintagel deserters or hordes of people coming to join up. All of it was too messy and would force Cassius to make a move before he was ready, and would give any other forces thoughts of coming in and making more of a mess. Cassius liked his conspiracies well organized and meticulous. Gellia spent those days in anxious wonder, while Cassius handled everything with calm and ease. "It's what I do," he told her. "It happens more than you might think."

"Why don't you just squash him?" Gellia asked more than once.

Cassius answered. "Who are you, Gallylya? He's too lucky to be killed in one shot and that magnitude of energy raging through Xzepheniixenze would cause wide spread disaster. There wouldn't be anything left to rule. The energy levels have to be stabilized before I go and 'squash' him. Understand?" He even illustrated it for her in her mind to drive home the point.

It fascinated Gellia, this way of communicating. The hundred or so minds she had visited worked similar to each other, thinking in words and sometimes a picture to go along with the regular thinking process, but Cassius was different. He thought with all senses; vivid images, sound, smell, even the sense of touch and taste. His memories were so clear that it was if he was there again and could share the few that he chose to with Gellia. Even the air had color and shape—the currents all recognized. The energy levels could be seen, all the thoughts could be heard and so on. But it all made sense and wasn't jumbled in the least when he showed things to her. She mentioned it once and he said he didn't know he did it. Maybe she *did* still envy him a little.

Gellia was studying up on different languages in the library when Cassius appeared beside her. They were off again, she already could tell. Away to Demf to see her new house. Cassius plucked the book from her hands and magicked it back to the shelf. They headed for the vast stables.

"You're taking Julian," Gellia said, surprised.

"He and I are more of the same mind and Currain needs a holiday. It won't be long before he's off to find someone to mentor." Cassius said, mounted the stallion. "And he could never keep the pace that these two can. Let's be off."

Julian lunged into a canter and Amarynth automatically followed. Once out the gate Julian tossed his head and squealed happily.

They traveled southeast along the lake until finally veering off down a narrow path, a road that no wagon could travel through the evergreens. The lake shimmered in the sun behind them and Gellia realized just how big it was, how far away from home she had been when she visited Qenai. Weeks' worth of riding away.

She spotted the remains of a wall in the trees, covered in moss. It disappeared into the ground sometimes, sometimes it rose higher and the shape of an obelisk appeared. Perhaps this was an ancient road, one that no one traveled any longer. The trees around them changed in color from deep emerald to gold in the rays of the sun that penetrated through the boughs. The air was fresh and crisp. After a moment Gellia remembered the times they rode through the forest in Fuarmaania.

They traveled for several days at the canter before leaving the evergreens and arriving at rolling hills covered with grasses and flowers. She may have been a little weary, but their mounts were not. Every few nights they would stop wherever they were and make a small camp, usually near water. Heaven forbid Cassius go without a daily wash up. Although she thought it interesting that he was willing to travel so lightly and camp in the wilds, being that he was so fastidious. Then she started to wonder why they were riding the entire way there instead of teleporting or making a portal. She wouldn't ask, though, she was enjoying the ride. And if they had a few moments before sleeping, and there was a body of water big enough, he was finally teaching her to swim. Apparently it was very amusing for him.

"My mental map tells me we're in Centaurs' lands," Gellia said. The rolling hills were breezy and bright. There was a forest in the distance.

"You are correct, very good. None are here mind you. Any that still live are in hiding, but this is what they called home at one time. Raven might treat them like unintelligent animals, but they are quite clever and are an asset to any army. They have their own society and traditions…" Cassius said as they passed through the old main road that had grown over a long time before. "However, you can't always trust them around women."

"Should we rest here? I slept in the saddle a bit but wouldn't our mounts like to have a break?" Gellia asked. It had been a day or two. It was difficult to say, really, one day blended into the next without the daily routine of Tintagel.

"Are you two tired?"

Amarynth tossed his head, offended. Julian snorted and laughed into her mind. *Back in the old times we used to travel for months with hardly a stop. I'm still in top form and I don't think Amarynth tires. Ever.*

The nights were cool, the days were warm and pleasant as they traveled on, and Gellia continued to fall ever more in love with Xzepheniixenze. They saw no one, as if they were the only two left in the world, there wasn't even any sign of seekers following them. Any road or trail they were ever on seemed deserted. She said little; lost in her own thoughts and he said little to disturb her. It took her a while, but she eventually noticed their horses left no trail through the grasses, their passing was secret as if nature enveloped them in its mystery.

After some time they came to a rather interesting place. The trees were prehistoric and beautifully knotted and gnarled but they entered an area where trees were much younger although still very old. It was a clearing centuries ago. Some of the older trees had odd over-grown scars on their trunks at the edge of old and new. Gellia had Amarynth stop for a moment so she could touch one. A single tower stood in the center, it was covered with vines. Amarynth's hoof hit stone and Gellia looked to find a flat, square stone sitting in the grass. They moved on. There were walls, one after another under moss and underbrush, nature reclaiming them. Stairs in the trees, flowering vines flowed down the worn stone like a waterfall. Columns here and there. They rode up the stairs onto stone and grass; trees had grown up between the stones. "What is this place?" Gellia asked.

"It was called Adularia at one point long ago. It was destroyed before I was born. Our mounts remember it, but very few books exist that mention it."

They climbed more stairs and found rings of broken columns and archways. At the center no trees grew but the grass and bramble and vines played across the cracked stone. The remaining tower was not intact; although it was very tall, its top had crumbled. Gellia dismounted and looked for stairs to the tower while Cassius untacked their mounts. *Yes, I remember when Adularia fell,* Julian said to his rider. *There was no helping them. What a tragedy. I think it was recorded in detail...*

Yes, by Razhiede. And exactly where would those books be? Cassius said.

In the library.

Yes. Lost. Unless you want to tell me where to find the key.

Still going on about that? I thought you moved on to different things. Julian eyed Cassius from under his thick forelock.

Cassius picked a boulder to sit on and started to furiously write in a book. He could hear Gellia moving through the brush, muttering as she slid and tripped over fallen stone. *Perhaps the key is not where we expect it,* he said finally.

Julian came to stand near Cassius and smelled the air. *After a millennium of looking, you've finally come to that conclusion. You're hoping the answer will appear from Gellia's magic. That was your primary reason for going to Fuarmaania.* Julian sighed and closed his thoughts from the rest of the world. *...And your excuse for the present if someone wonders. But things change, people change. To them she is only a means to an end. Let yourself believe that if it comforts you, but I know what really is.*

Gellia hauled herself across the rubble and over what was left of the stairs. Yes, she thought of using her magic but she wasn't sure how secret they were trying to be and she wasn't about to give them away. As she went she took note of the worn markings on the walls, some sort of writing that was vaguely familiar to her. There were nooks in the walls that looked to have held jewels at one time but were stolen long ago. She cursed as her hand slipped and was scuffed by the rough stone. At times she was sure marks here and there were from magic weapons from a great battle.

She came to a floor and continued up the spiraling staircase. It was so high. Carefully she pulled herself up the last of the broken stairs to look over the crumbling wall where the tower ended. Xzepheniixenze spread out before her for miles and miles in all directions, the flowering forest all around her. She looked down to find her companions and to see just how vast the fortress was in its glory. Ring upon ring of walls with towers and gates in each, the castle itself had been enormous. Somehow it was related to Shahyrahara, it was clear enough by the rings.

It was windy at the top; it gently pulled and pushed her as she held onto the stone. The final sun was setting. She could see tiny lights in the forest; she watched them for a while before she descended.

Cassius had started a fire. It was chilly.

"Was this a moonkeep?" Gellia asked.

"It was indeed."

Gellia leaned on Julian; they both rested near the fire, their lord on the other side. "I have something I've been meaning to ask you," she said.

"Oh?" Cassius continued to write.

"I saw someone at the party who I found rather interesting although I didn't have the chance to speak with him. You knew everyone there..."

Cassius looked up. He had a sinking feeling because it could only be one person—someone who wasn't invited. "Who?"

"I don't know his name. He was a young fellow, had silver hair like a mage and dressed in grey. I feel like I've seen him before but I don't know when it might have been. I think I would have remembered him."

Cassius rolled his eyes. "If you're lucky you'll never have to meet him, but I don't think anyone can be that fortunate."

"Connylia knew him."

"Of course she did, she's ill-fated. Pray you never have to meet him." He slammed his book shut and started braiding his hair. "Of course she knew him."

Gellia shut her mouth and rested her head on Julian's satiny shoulder and could hear his heartbeat. She twirled a lock of his mane for a moment before drifting off to a very peaceful sleep.

***

"I'd looked Demf up on the map, at this pace we should have been there by now," Gellia said. She shivered.

"We're making a stop someplace else first," Cassius explained. "A place you should see."

It wasn't until a few days later that Gellia sensed something different in the air—it had a different smell to it. There was the sweet perfume of flowers but it was accompanied by something else. Julian seemed excited and picked up a stronger pace. They crossed through a wall that was barely more than a long mound in the earth, and the breath was stolen from Gellia's lungs. Even though the surroundings looked the same as before, she could feel it, something pulling her in. The magic was deep and mostly dormant, would barely be noticeable to a garden-variety mage yet it to her swirled around, danced for her.

They galloped through an array of trees, across an ancient road, around endless moss covered rubble, up a great hill until they stepped out onto a rock ledge overlooking the most water Gellia had ever seen. Far below them the waves crashed against the cliff in a serene rhythm. Amarynth stood next to Julian, with their riders silently watching the birds glide over the waves. The sides of the great cliff sloped down until finally turning into sandy white beaches that sparkled in the sun. Gellia could barely breathe as she was flooded.

"This sea," Cassius said, "used to put me to sleep every night. You can see my island over there, just barely."

The warm wind smelled of salt and seaweed. Julian sniffed the air elaborately. "Where are we?" Gellia asked. Her heart thundered in her chest.

"*This* is where Zenobia once stood. The greatest castle ever created."

He didn't understand what she felt. He how could he? Suddenly she felt like she lived thousands of years in shelter. She could barely move.

"It may not be much to look at, nothing to look at in fact, but it *is* your birthright."

Gellia closed her eyes and tried to remember what it looked like. She couldn't feel her body, like it was made of air.

The castle had stood for a very long time; the Zapheny always lived there. Architecture from all ages was used in its creation yet it all fit together. Sparkling pale stone walls, shingles made from amethyst. Bright banners with the unicorn crest fluttered in the wind. Inside a maze of beauty. Windows that had gems set in the glass. Paintings and sculpture, etched murals in walls, mirrors hanging everywhere, curtains made of platinum strands. A river filled with candles, flowers floating on the water. Zenobia was what dreams were made of.

It had a past rich with color and light, carved from magic and time. It was twice a temple and always a home to thousands. And there were roses. Roses everywhere. She could still smell them. It was surrounded with mystery, even while it stood, even to those who lived there. Only Zapheny knew its truth.

There was a party, a great ball and everyone was there, even the lover of the goddess herself and his best friend, a dragon. Connylia, she was so young and fresh wearing a dress of rare satin, which Gellia recognized. So many important people, so much magic. Guests came and went. It was wartime. A woman with regal features ushered around a small boy, Zenobia's heir. But something was wrong and the castle knew it, its master felt so. Everyone ran and screamed in terror and panic. Razhiede watched Connylia as three young men tried to lead her away, the unicorns. The emperor, Razhiede, watched them go, the young silver-haired man standing near. Razhiede knew his life would soon be over. On the way out Connylia noticed the child standing next to a collapsed wall. She insisted they take him with them. The rubble had struck down the child's mother and he had no one to assist him. Once outside, the five stopped to watch the castle fall into the sea with a depth of sadness that soon would take over the rest of the realm. ...But Zenobia had hope, it wished for her return for well over a thousand years. Now here she stood, the two heirs returned.

He watched her as she gazed out at sea, could see how her conscious thought left her. Somehow he knew the magic was there, but it was not something he could sense—this infuriated him to no end. No magic was beyond him but for this. What was it to be a Zapheny? To be one of those who possessed the most transcendent magic? ...She had to know of the key, it was her birthright. If Zenobia truly was responding to her it gave him hope. *Damn you, Razhiede*, he thought. Before him Gellia seemed to grow in grace—if that were possible—she already had the undeniable beauty and mysticism of unicorns and goddesses themselves.

Cassius still remembered the last thing Razhiede said to him all those years ago. "When you understand, Zenobia will rise again." Zenobia and all its secrets, all its power. He asked Connylia about it once, a long time ago, and she told him Razhiede explained it to her but his mind and his magic was far beyond her understanding. Gellia would understand it. There were too many stories of Zenobia, what its true power was, what the great emperor stored in its memory. The story that interested him most was that it would stabilize the magic in the world. Perhaps someday it would... She had much in common with Quenelzythe, like his parents. Cassius believed his friend knew what the key to Zenobia was but refused to share the secret— allowed them to continue for a century looking for it. He wondered if she knew and if she would keep it from him as well.

Gellia dropped from the memory; the sea came into focus again. It *had* been part of Cassius memory, for he was the one Connylia saved, but it was the castle that told the story. Zenobia was happy to see her and wanted her to stay; it wanted to reveal its secrets. It wanted both of them to stay. It wanted something she didn't understand. It told her that Cassius *must* realize. It was something he was told many, many years ago. She could feel it tugging at her, a gentle pull, it wanted something from her but she didn't know what. *I don't know what you want,* she thought. Gellia finally pushed it away. "I had a dream once, of this place, and there was a unicorn in it." She said, remembering. It was so clear. His silver face flashed in her mind.

"Oh yes, probably an image of Julian or one of his brothers."

"No, he was dapple-grey like Tempest, but larger. He spoke to me."

Cassius looked suspicious. "Him again. You poor thing. What he said was probably vague and made no sense, correct?"

"If I think about what actually was said I suppose it was, but I understood him, like he was in my soul."

Cassius snorted. "Unfortunately I know of whom you speak. If he is a reoccurring theme in your dreams then with any luck we're on the correct path. He seems to be one of your favorite topics of late."

Gellia felt there would be no more talk of it. Path to what? Fine. He could keep his secrets. And whatever secrets she had from him she would keep to herself as well.

"You must remember this place," Cassius said in a grave tone.

Gellia whispered. "I will."

"It is most important that you do. We will meet *here* if you're ever lost."

"I'll remember. This is one place I'll always remember how to find." For it had always called to her, from the moment she was born she felt its draw, from the moment she set foot in Xzepheniixenze she felt it whisper to her. It would always lead her home. Soon. Not even the gods could keep her away. ...But why the concern? What was happening that she didn't know about?

***

The river led them south into the forest of Demf. It must have been the main entrance to the forest, for a road along the river invited them. There were no turns in the road; it only went straight into the shadows of the dense trees—leaving the river. She could feel the magic shift. It was easy as that. "Now that you have been accepted," Cassius said, "it will open up to you as well. To anyone else but me and now you this place is impassible, even to seekers or mages." Sure enough, the road behind them disappeared as they went, turning into more conifers and briar. "This is just the outer ring."

Eventually the dense evergreens lessened and the flowering trees appeared again, grass beneath them cropped short as if by grazing animals. They came across a place where a waterfall sprung from the rocks of a cliff, splashing into a crystal clear pool. The surrounding boulders were smooth and spotted with tiny flowers and moss. Julian whinnied, and from behind a nearby tree peeked a white horse face crowned with a single spiral that reached towards the heavens. Shyly the white unicorn stepped out but kept his distance from the visitors. "I might have saved them but they still don't like me very much," Cassius said, smiling. "Can't imagine why. However, they are attracted to our magic."

Gellia decided at that moment she would be happy to spend time there. The other creatures they came across as they rode included a pair of winged horses, one grey and one chestnut; a griffin, and several little grey creatures who skittered about Julian's and Amarynth's feet. "They're called gargoyles because that's what they look like," Cassius explained. "They're exceptionally rare. I think there are only five… six left, and they all live here. They have a difficult time reproducing."

The castle was set into a nook in the trees, its two towers on either side of the main keep, the stables on the left stretching towards them, another wing on the right. It was not large at all, even a bit smaller than the Fuarmaanian castle, but it was covered with ivy, not moss. Demf castle was finely made, just a miniature of a full sized fortress, but without the stockades. They rode into the open stable yard where blades of grass crept up through the cobblestones. Both dismounted to untack their horses so they could graze (something Amarynth probably wouldn't even do) and stood looking up at the facade of the castle.

"Shall we see what the inside looks like? I already know the gardens must be a fright." Cassius said, walking towards the main door. "Although it will only take me moment to tend the gardens."

Gellia followed him. She felt he was nearly a different person in this place. Once inside Gellia thought she would feel closed in after the immense roominess of Tintagel, but found that she was comfortable. The castle had about thirty rooms, all of them dusty and filled with covered furniture. "Who will be my servants?" She could hardly manage all this space on her own.

"Your magic and everything that lives here will help you," he said as he followed her through the castle. With a smirk he said, "perhaps you could try singing to them."

Gellia gave him a look and continued to wander. She lifted a cover off a chair to look at it. "Looks like something you would like."

"Of course. After the fall of Zenobia this place was deserted. Quenelzythe and I lived here for years, practicing our skills. It took a bit of work to make the forest the way it is, especially since he didn't like to use his magic. I haven't been here for centuries."

The master bedchamber was on the top floor of the castle and had windows covering most of two opposite walls. After opening the heavy curtains the room looked as if it could be rather airy and pleasant. All the bedroom furniture was there minus bed coverings, but including a large bathing tub. Gellia turned to Cassius after thoroughly surveying the room. "Why are you giving this to me?"

"You deserve it."

"And?"

His expression turned icy. She wondered if what she saw before her was just and after-image and he was already on the other side of the empire.

"Are you keeping me here like one of your other pets?" she said.

"If you don't want it you don't have to take it," said he.

Gellia measured the tension in the air around them and decided let this fight go. "I like it." It was the truth. Perhaps it was an exile, but she was sure he had his reasons and he certainly wasn't going to tell her about them. If his magic was solid as she thought it was she could live there unbothered by the outside world until the end of her days. As long as she had books she could be content to stay for a while.

"When you want to be away from Tintagel you can come here and not be disturbed."

"I'll have to go back there and get some things to redecorate. You'll come visit?"

"I'll be the only one who is able."

14

They stayed at the Demf castle for several days, Gellia explored all around the building and the grounds. There were beautiful little gardens that were mostly overgrown, a lily pond and a brambly rose garden. Cassius once more used his magic to restore it, and showed her how to manage everything with her power.

She found that Julian was quite comfortable in the stables in a stall that had been his for an extremely long time—the stable had only ten stalls and was roomy and light.

Gellia uncovered much of the furniture, discovered the small library filled with books about dragons and magic, and was not frightened by the kitchen and pantry although its vacancy for so many years could have made it so. Apparently the two youths were very tidy—as if she expected any less from her liege. But with no one living there it needed sweeping and the windows needed washing and she hoped she could come up with magic for it for she didn't want to do it manually. On occasion in her explorations she would see Cassius but not often, he left her alone.

After a time some of the natives started to follow her and sniffed what she touched and looked at her curiously. Although many of them would be dangerous in other circumstances, they seemed to be docile towards her in this place. She wondered how many more different creatures she would see as time passed.

Outside she tried to tempt the unicorns with clover but they kept their distance. She enjoyed watching them and sat on the grass and did so for many hours. There were four unicorns from what she could tell, and they walked through the castle grounds seeming content. They were so beautiful, so graceful.

Julian was not so unlike them although larger and of a different color. His size did not change his splendor—in fact his magic was stronger than the lighter of his kind. As she watched them move through the garden she felt Julian approach and stand by her, she stood up and brushed the grass from her breeches. *Let me tell you a secret,* he said, *they may seem coy right now, but give them time. You are Gellia—they will come to you eventually, no matter what you do with his majesticness.*

Gellia placed her hand on his smooth shoulder, under his heavy mane. *I'll have to be patient then,* she said. The light began to fade as twilight spread across the forest. Gellia noticed immediately the presence of whispers, thousands of them. It was a beautiful scene, the palely shimmering unicorns and the tiny lights bobbing through the trees and across the lawn. She thought she smelled a faint hint of roses on the air. *You remember Zenobia, don't you? You remember what it was like living there.*

His ears twitched and he sounded different from usual—perhaps tired or wistful, Gellia couldn't decide which. *Yes. I remember.*

It amazed her that such a memory could halt him, a unicorn, so. She heard him sigh and wondered if he was lost in a recollection. It was getting late and her stomach grumbled. "I suppose I should find something to eat. I'll see you inside, Julian." She started towards the castle.

That night when she dreamed of the ocean waves crashing on rocks, the roses of every color, and the sparkling white granite of the castle she was not surprised. These were not dreams at all but visions. *I will find you,* she said to the wind, *it's only a matter of time.* She stood in the immense throne room; its tall, ornate columns surrounded her. She smiled and twirled through its vastness. There was someone else. She turned to find a person who her dreaming mind could not decide between unicorn or man. She knew who it was. Razhiede. This was a more complete form for him—as a man he was much taller than she, his black hair streaked with grey, his eyes calm and gentle. As a unicorn he was black like Julian, had the weightless movement like he was under water. *I have so much I wish to ask you,* Gellia said, but he did not give a vocal reply, only looked kindly at her. Books surrounded them—aisle upon giant aisle of books. He placed his hand on her heart and smiled. His touch was warm.

Gellia woke and climbed from bed to look out the window. In the sky she could see the light of the layers grind against each other, it seemed so painful, she almost heard it cry.

The whispers floated through the gardens and the forest, the moonlight touching the foliage. She could smell roses on the breeze, watched the tiny lights as they started to gather in one part of the garden. Through the trees she saw a shape, silver flash in the night. She opened the narrow glass pane and leaned out. It appeared again, a large shape guarded by the undergrowth. Whispers floated all around it. She pulled herself back inside, threw on her robe and skittered from her room. At times she was sure her plummet down the stairs was inevitable, but she managed to keep her feet as she scurried to the lower rooms of the castle. Cassius was sitting by the fire looking at a book, but she said nothing to him as she hurried by. The cool night air hit her as she ran into the stable yard, the cobblestones cold beneath her bare feet. It seemed to take her too long to round the corner at the end of the stables where the cobbles ended and soft, dewy grass began. Gellia paused and looked around. The whispers floated in a certain direction. She followed them through the gardens as best she could. After struggling with the flower patches she paused to hike up her damp robe and nightgown, held it above her knees so she could continue her flight. The whispers were all around her as she entered the forest. It was so dark, but somehow she managed to see where she was going. There was no trace of what passed, and now she realized as she looked at the trees in comparison, it must have been a large thing. It was so quiet; she could only hear the sound of her panting as she froze.

Again. She saw it again, deeper into the trees. For once she wished she were a seeker who could move agilely through the brush for it creaked and snapped and rustled as she fought her way through. Twigs and stone cut at her skin and tore her nightdress. She paused and leaned up against what she though was a tree but upon touching it realized it was a standing stone. She moved away, deeper and deeper into the forest. She softly cursed when she tripped over a fallen branch and cut her shin. It didn't matter, Gellia continued on, following the tiny lights of the whispers. A bright light. The ground under her feet turned to a stone floor partially covered by moss and twigs, trees grew up through the stones, displacing them. Part of a wall, a broken pillar. The silvery light grew stronger and she followed it, the trees were not as dense and continued to thin out until there was nothing but brush. A great stone wall stood behind the light, tall pillars and broken archways. She continued towards it and saw it take shape—she knew it was not a person, she knew it was more of an equine form. He was surrounded by whispers as if he summoned them. His coat was dappled not with grey, but silver, his mane and tail white like the snowy mountains by Kaymaria.

Everything was silent, she could hear her heartbeat. This was the unicorn from her dream, the one who appeared in Zenobia. His light faded and the sky lightened until dawn stole his glory, and she was alone in the ruin as the sun rose over the trees. Birds chirped, other things moved in the forest. Everything looked different in the light. She approached the wall, the brush ended and nothing but moss and tiny flowers graced the center of the ruin—it felt good on her sore feet. The wall was something of a half circle and it had carved writing on it that was mostly worn away from time. She sat in the middle, looked up at the wall and wondered what it said.

"Sometimes I wonder if you have any dignity at all," Cassius said as he stopped next to her.

She hadn't heard his approach, nor did she feel his magic and realized how disheveled she looked. Her legs ached and her nightgown was cold and damp, not to mention it was full of holes. She probably smelled like wet moss besides.

"A fledgling seeker could have found you from the path you made," he said. Gellia looked up at him. Did she want to tell him what she saw or keep it to herself forever? Could he shed any light on it? Her joints ached as she pulled herself to her feet. He must have been appalled by the way she looked but she didn't care—her quest was too important. For a moment he took his gaze from the ruins and looked at her disdainfully, and in that moment she hated him again.

"Were you chasing a ghost? Or was a ghost chasing you?" he asked.

She looked at the ruins again. "Do you know what's written there?" she asked.

Cassius eyed the characters. "It is indeed a rare language."

"I guessed that. Do you know what it says?"

He looked at her and smiled. "You look positively haggard. Much like your peasants in the mountains."

She was not amused. Again she could not feel his magic unless she used their bond, but books appeared before him.

"It's parts of Demf," he explained, "for some reason certain sections of the forest masks my power. Even though I have those capabilities to do the same affect I am not doing so now. Strange, yes?"

Strange and unnerving, Gellia thought. After so much time working so closely with he and his magic it made her very uneasy—the magic that she usually took for granted was not there, a huge void surrounded him. It was like he didn't exist. She knew what it should feel like, him using his magic, but it wasn't there and she automatically looked for it, grasped for it. Was this was it was like to be completely human? To not feel the power of another? She watched him float the books on the air to read them, writing notes of his magic as he always did. She looked over his shoulder. "Here's the amusing bit, princess. I've been here plenty of times, as I have all ruins, and never have I seen this writing before. I don't know how long it will take to translate it. I don't know if it will *stay* long enough for me to do so, although there is no latent magic left here—other than mine and that of your blood."

The sun was high in the sky before they spoke again. Gellia stood silently by, trying to decide if he made progress. He leaned on the books as he worked; they stayed steady on the air as if on a table. He answered her question. "This was written with magic, not carved with chisel. It's formed like handwriting, some of the strokes are very similar to many languages—most are considered dead languages. It holds so many similarities it seems it might be an original language if such a thing existed. These are not ruins from my or my parents' time, we've always known that." He stepped back from the books and his notes. "It reads: *When that is found, a new era will begin.*"

"What does that mean?"

"It's part of an old legend. One I memorized when I was a child. It was often considered a prophecy, and was always a great controversy."

"I wonder why it was written here like this."

He rolled his eyes. "Obviously it was meant for you to find. My concern is who put it there. No traces of magic, no sign of passage but for yours, not to mention none can come in here without special requirements. So it brings me back to why you came out here in the first place. Look at you. Ran outside in your bedclothes, barefoot, unarmed but for your magic, pushed through an amazing amount of underbrush in the blackest hour of night to come here. What was it that put you into such a state of hysteria? What possibly could drive you from your bed, drag you out here and have the capabilities of that language?" The books and papers disappeared. She recognized his posture—irritation.

"I had a dream about Zenobia. Razhiede was there."

"And he told you to come out here?" Razhiede's spirit was possible. Or perhaps a goddess, but that was highly unlikely—goddesses barely still existed.

"No, no one told me."

"Then it must have been Mystic. You saw a unicorn, didn't you?" Her surprise was obvious. "I'm too irritated for it *not* to be him. I was hoping I would never see him again but I suppose it was a lost hope considering the company I keep these days."

"Add that to the list of things about me that irritate you," Gellia said. What was it that annoyed him so about this Mystic? She felt drawn towards the silver-dappled unicorn, not repulsed.

"Zapheny. I should have known," Cassius grumbled. Connylia used to welcome the unicorns to her chambers when he and Quenelzythe used to visit, mentioned on several occasions that Mystic was very good allies with Razhiede and was pleased he and her son were companions.

Mystic only appeared when it was convenient for him. What Mystic actually was besides a unicorn, and what he was up to was anyone's guess. But Cassius didn't have time for this nonsense. There was too much danger on the horizon, mainly from Zephronia, and Gellia was trying to veer off course.

"*...Yes, Cress, the food here is wonderful. And yes, I have dozens of servants and all sorts of lovely things. In fact, Cassius has given me my own castle. Someday maybe you all can come and visit me in my castle and we can tour Xzepheniixenze and see all the lovely things. Or maybe I will visit you for a while. All my affection, Gellia.*"

Gellia handed the letter to the seeker who swiftly left the office. Recently she received a letter from Skip who wrote that his bond horse finally appeared (he was concerned because he was not wholly Xzepheniixenze) but from what he told her his new mare was the envy of the stables.

For a moment she watched Cassius from her gilded chair as he sat across from her tapping some unidentifiable trinket on the table now and then. He was working through the information he picked up in court that day, through correspondence and what not. After a few more minutes he considered the bookshelves until his eye caught one of interest. Gellia looked up from the letter she read. He set the bauble on the desk to go fetch the book—it was a tiny, carved, black horse. It had always been there on the desk, just always in his hand where she couldn't tell what it was. She glanced at Cassius; he was leafing through the book and not paying any attention to her. "Oh yes, there's another letter there on the desk for you. It is quite a curiosity, which was why it was brought to me and not you."

Gellia looked and knew immediately to which he referred. It was on fine stationery, some of the best she ever saw, and was sealed with the crest of the royal family of Zephronia. "It must be from Conny."

"No, even in her deranged state she would know better than to send something traceable," he said.

Gellia picked it up and broke the seal it to find a letter neatly written in Fuarmaanian in gold ink. It was from Zyendel.

'*Dearest Gellia,*
I would like to extend my friendship to you, and as a friend invite you to stay with us at Dournzariame. In truth, I miss your company as well as fear for your safety

*while living with such a person in such a place. I beseech
you to join us here where you will be known as our sister
and where your magic and amiable disposition will be
greatly appreciated. I cannot express to you enough of
the dire circumstances in which you find yourself
involved. Please understand I send this to you out of my
undying devotion.*

Yours, Zyendel'

"Did you read this?" Gellia asked.

"Did the seal look broken before you read it?" he
answered. "It was delivered by a very brave Zephron who carried
it all the way here just for you. He was brought to me, nearly
frightened him to death when I was the one who accepted it. He
begged me to give it to you but did not stay to see it for himself.
Sloppy, really."

She looked at the letter again. "Did you kill him?"

"How uncouth. I sent him on his way with new supplies
and coin. …And all Gallylya needs is one more reason to come."
Cassius put the book away and pulled out another.

"How does he expect me to respond? I can't send one of
ours over there; they're apt to be killed just for being
Xzepheniixenze."

"Yes, but upon seeing the letter to their fine prince they'll
make the delivery."

"He wants me to go to Dournzariame, thinks I'm in great
danger."

Cassius looked over his shoulder and spoke in mixed
Xzepheniixenze and Zephron. "He probably has it in his head to
marry you. By the look on your face you don't understand
completely. He has foolishly given us the true reason why you
are in danger."

"What do you mean?"

"You live in Xzepheniixenze and you have ambitions,
you already know of that danger, he knows you know about that
danger unless he's insulting your intelligence. But no, dear
princess, he warns of a danger perhaps you don't see, one that he
knows. Why didn't he just invite you to visit on a holiday? He
covets you, wants to protect you against something he believes I
cannot—his father. Zyendel has warned us of an imminent

❧ 294 ❧

attack. How long ago did this messenger leave his home? How much was he set back while traveling through the empire? How long did he think it would take you to leave Tintagel? From the time he sent it, the attack was already set into motion judging from the urgency of his letter. He knew he had to give you reason to make you leave Tintagel quickly. I've been watching them. Gallylya is shrewd, he knows me, and has kept his secrets from me but also realizes I know *him.* Thrilling it is. I haven't had a challenge like this in a very long time..."

Gellia thought on this, the idea of marrying Zyendel. What a strange concept. What did the prince think she would do with her life in Zephronia? Of course the more important matter was his father. This was the first time Cassius mentioned their imminent attack. And Raven watched them. All the while she knew the world suffered with its old wounds, the majority of its people oblivious to the danger all around them.

"Oh yes, Raven wrote us a note," Cassius said.

"Yes?" Her mind returned to something Cassius said while they were still in Ravengate. He would bring Zephronia to its knees if Gallylya crossed him. Was he so sure?

"Most of it is a subject you certainly don't want to hear."

She nodded. "What else did he say?" All those lives lost because of hatred between two men...

"He's going to lock Decius in a tower for treason as soon as he can find him."

Gellia shook her head and tried to bring herself back to something closer to the topic. "...You know, I feel sorry for Mina," Gellia said.

"Why? Because she couldn't have me?"

"You conceited—what is that supposed to mean?"

"It's a long story, really. She was looking out for her future—especially after that whole fiasco..." He stopped. "I'll save that story for later... Raven couldn't resist her pretty face. Don't feel sorry for her, she knows what she is doing. She also knows how to handle herself around him."

Gellia's thoughts were already onto something else. She only half paid attention to what he said. Something that would change the face of Xzepheniixenze was on her mind. "I want to rebuild Zenobia after we kill Raven. I want to set the world right." Perhaps if she could bring peace…

"Mind if I live with you? I rather liked the place… it won't be an easy place to rebuild. People have been trying to do that for centuries with little luck…"

She smiled and wondered if he was mocking her. "That's because they don't have the key."

Cassius looked at her in a way she had never seen before, distrustful, curious and a bit of something else. "Where did that come from?"

"I don't know. It just came out… why, *is* there a key?"

"You Zapheny are all alike," he muttered.

She shrugged off the tension and decided to leave. Her mind was in a whirl. There was much to take in. She needed to respond to Zyendel's letter. She already knew what she would write and she it wasn't something she wanted to share with Cassius. "If you want to live with me you can. I certainly don't know enough to run a country." She rose to her feet and straightened her tunic. Gellia did her best to suppress her thoughts on Zyendel. "I think I'm going to go soak in a bath now. That spar with Sian nearly did me in."

"Oh?"

"I think he's getting better at what he does."

Cassius eyed her suspiciously.

"He's always been tolerable." She shrugged. "He's been the only one to practice with me. Maybe someday he'll be on the level of Mephibosheth."

Cassius snorted.

"You're so cruel to them. Maybe a few are worth your time."

"I thought we already cleared this up. I'm nice to battle fodder, not this lot who are out for our ruin if they were capable."

"Not—"

"Oh no, Sian is only after a more secure place in the way of things. Oh yes, I know he vies for Mephibosheth's position, and how he tries to win your alliance. In his small mind he wishes to have you himself. Know this, princess; I do not share my mistresses with my mages. I hope you haven't become attached to him." His face was shadowed by bitterness as he glared at her.

"What if I have?" No, she was not attached to Sian; she couldn't allow herself to be attached to anyone. He was respectful but not a friend. But Gellia fought because she didn't want to admit she was foolish enough to have feelings for the likes of Cassius. Anyone who found out would laugh her to her grave. She couldn't believe she was so happy he kept the bauble. She wanted to believe that he at least enjoyed her company. Sometimes she thought just maybe—but he was such a scoundrel that she could never let herself believe much of anything. The light she chased after was sometimes too deep for her to find.

"You're starting to trust him, it isn't healthy. Can't you see the real issue? Are you even listening to me? You shouldn't allow yourself to think of them so."

"Why can't I?" She felt the dark weight of his anger, but would not be crushed beneath it. "Why can't I let myself be so?"

"Only a half-breed would come up with such nonsense. You should know better. I thought you were more intelligent."

"*Everyone* is expendable," she said.

"Yes," he said. "That's *exactly* it. Get out of my sight."

Did he really mean it? She didn't allow herself to show her hurt. But what about their bond? Did it mean nothing? She backed away and left the office. It seemed there were more seekers than usual in the corridors; it would be easy to find one to take a message. On her way to her rooms she was halted by a glimpse of someone familiar. One of her old servants. Gellia hailed her. "You," she said.

The girl curtsied. "Milady, I humbly apologize for being seen in the corridors. Please forgive me."

Gellia was frozen in her tracks. "I thought you were dead."

"No milady, we were merely transferred to another part of the castle. I beg forgiveness, milady."

"No need. Carry on." Gellia watched the girl hurry away. She was beginning to think she'd never understand him.

Once in her chambers she pulled out stationery and had a servant find a seeker who was willing to take a message to Zephronia. If she were obvious about it, perhaps Cassius would dismiss it as her snooty response to Zyendel's letter. That wasn't quite the case. Gellia sipped some tea and stared out at the lake for a few moments, remembered what the ocean sounded like. *Julian,* she thought quietly.

Yes, pet?

She did not in any way think he would respond and certainly not that quickly. *I,*

I'll keep him distracted.

I don't want you to be in trouble.

His laugher bubbled up through her mind, it echoed of giggling children. It made her want to smile. *Don't worry about me, dearest. There's a package on the way, just to let you know...* He started to sing into her mind, some enchanting song in a language she hadn't heard. She smiled and started to write.

'*Prince Zyendel,*

I thank you for your kind thoughts and words. Indeed there is danger, but is it not everywhere for those like us? Be assured I will face all danger willingly and without fear as much as I'm able. Know also that this letter is not to agree to come to Zephronia, nor is it meant to give you the impression of feelings I do not have for you. I do feel it necessary to warn you. Do not attack Xzepheniixenze. Do not attack Tintagel. This is not a threat. This is not some odd form of concern for you. This warning is out of concern for your people. Think not of pride or base attacks or conjectures of your father, think only of your countrymen. Perhaps some other compromise can be reached. If an attack on Tintagel is made, I cannot fathom what catastrophic repercussions will follow. You must not underestimate Cassius Vazepheny.

Regards,
Princess Gellia Zapheny of Xzepheniixenze.'

A knock at the door made Gellia jump. A servant answered it and delivered a small box to his mistress. The box abused and worn, tied with a strand of raffia. Carefully she opened it and took out the bit of fabric to unwrap the treasure. It was a seal. An old silver seal with the crest of the unicorn on it.

A letter like that deserves a proper mark, Julian said. *You don't know how long I've been saving it.*

Gellia smiled and sealed the letter. The seeker arrived. She recognized him as one of Cassius' favorites. He grinned at her. "Take this to Dournzariame if you're capable," she said. "Tell them it's in response to the prince's letter." She didn't like it one bit, but she didn't have a choice.

"That's where I'm headed anyway, milady." The seeker took the letter, bowed and exited.

Again Gellia was plagued by the heaviness of her heart. A walk would do her good.

She headed towards the rose courtyard. There didn't need to be feelings for a bond to exist. How could she let him destroy her with a few words? It wouldn't happen to a pure Xzepheniixenze, only someone like her, or humans, would ever be devastated by such a thing. Zephrons ignored what Xzepheniixenze said for it is all lies, so they too were cold. They all hid in a hard shell to protect themselves and for some the frozen exterior had gone straight to their core. Did she truly want to become one of them? One of the Xzepheniixenze who felt nothing? *You are Zapheny,* Julian said. She didn't mind that he was still with her.

Gellia stepped out into the sunlight amidst the rosebushes and sat in the center of the courtyard. Better she stay out of his way. If there was to be a confrontation she shouldn't be there to distract Cassius from what he was doing. A whisper floated by.

She thought of her choices. She could go live with Connylia, perhaps make peace with her uncle and live a productive life helping the Zephrons—but she would always long for Xzepheniixenze. It would be a slow death. She could go out on her own and risk Cassius coming after her; especially if she joined forces with someone else—and there were so many willing to accept her talents. He probably *wouldn't* follow her, he would let her rot until she was miserable in her new situation and was forced to go back to him. She could try to raise Zenobia by herself, how she wasn't sure, she didn't have any money, but she could live in the wilderness with Amarynth. He would not let her go. No one but perhaps Gallylya could and would protect if she made Cassius her enemy. And she didn't want to leave.

"You cannot raise Zenobia by yourself, no matter how you try," a small voice said. Gellia looked around and saw no one. She was hearing voices now. "Such a thing as you feel unhinges his soul, that is why he hates you so," the voice said.

"What do you mean?" Gellia whispered.

"It is their curse," it said.

Gellia continued to look around. "Who are you?"

"You know who we are."

There were several whispers now, floating around her.

* * *

"...And I know you don't take children into Tintagel but we're willing to pay you any amount if you could..." The lord explained his situation as he stood before Cassius. The audience was boring as usual. Gellia stood regally next to him and didn't show her restlessness. Something wasn't quite right. There were no games that day but Cassius seemed to be in a slightly lighter mood. She wanted to ask him if there was any news on Zephronia's approach, and hoped he would just volunteer the information instead.

Earlier the announcement was made to everyone that Gellia would be leaving for a holiday that afternoon, so beginning her exile. She'd packed her belongings and books that would be undoubtedly would need to be teleported or portalled into Demf. And although it might be an exile, she was happy to have a holiday and live quietly for a time. When she was ready to come back, she would, and no one could stop her.

Perhaps he didn't want her around to see what he planned, or wanted her out of the way for fear she would mismanage a war. But Gellia was pleased she could sort out a few things in her head. There was so much to take in, and lately she'd felt overwhelmed and unable to escape her thoughts. Demf was peaceful and Raven couldn't find her.

Then it finally dawned on her—she let her doubt of Cassius blind her from what truly was. He was genuinely concerned for her safety, otherwise he wouldn't have revealed his childhood secret hiding place to her. It was the only way he knew to keep her safe—send her to live with the unicorns. She wasn't ready to face the likes of Gallylya or Raven in battle, but she would undoubtedly stay by Cassius' side if she was near...

"...So your lordship, if you would consider..."

Gellia felt a hint of something strange. A shiver ran through the castle. She saw Cassius start to tense; for the first time in the history of audiences he looked something other than wintry. The great doors burst open and everyone on the floor jumped and stepped aside. Gellia wanted to shout across the room but couldn't break expression. Something was dreadfully wrong. Connylia charged through on Justin, his brother Jutham was also with her. Their shod hooves sent sparks across the stone floor.

Connylia slid out of the saddle and was barely able to keep her legs under her. One of the horses exited while the other stayed for a moment to act as a crutch. Cassius rose to his feet. Gellia felt a horrible pang in her stomach and did her best to calmly approach her friend.

"What's wrong?" Gellia whispered. She took Connylia's hand and decided she didn't care what the others thought. The look in Connylia's eyes scared Gellia right to her core. "What happened to you?"

"N..not me... Gallylya... he's coming... you have to... escape," she heaved. "I came...as soon as I...found out." The other horse trotted away as Connylia leaned on Gellia. "A portal... and the Knights..."

"What? What are you talking about?" Gellia asked. The room echoed with voices.

Cassius' mystical senses went wild as multiple portals were grounded outside the castle and began to open. The energies boiled up around Tintagel. His lips curled into a languid smile.

Everyone scattered. The castle shook with the first blow of Gallylya's attack. Mages pulled their magic, began defenses. The sky beyond the windows was red with fire.

Cassius smirked. No doubt they engaged his army still stationed outside of the castle. He suspected Gallylya started his magic before his forces were entirely out of the portal.

Connylia took both Gellia's hands in her own. "I came as fast as I could. He brought the other Vega Knights. You have to escape. Tintagel will be rubble. He'd infiltrated Xzepheniixenze with his agents months ago through the Dragonlands."

Gellia remained calm even as the floor beneath them shook. Parts of the castle started to fall from above them. *Stop your attack!* Gellia projected at Gallylya. *If you value the lives of your people, desist!* She had to try… Cassius had invited this. He had goaded Gallylya to do this with barely any effort.

People scattered in every direction and panic started to take hold. Gellia held Connylia and looked for Cassius for guidance. What should she do? Should she use her magic? Should she run? Should she attack Gallylya? Help Connylia? Cassius still stood across the room. He looked calm even though people fled all around him. Gellia felt cold. Cassius' magic was at rest. He was waiting for something, letting his treasured Tintagel fall. The castle shook from another blow. She needed a command.

"Connylia," he said. His voice could be clearly heard above the sound of falling rock.

The Zephron looked up.

"I need a favor—do your best." He hadn't sent Gellia away soon enough. She looked for some sort of direction. There was none to be had. Connylia knew of what he spoke, he could see it in her eyes. She knew what to do. "Wherever you put her, I'll find her."

The two women skittered out of the way of falling rock. Gellia wanted to say something, but the words still wouldn't come.

Gallylya was able to build a portal and transport an army in a few moments—any other place in Xzepheniixenze would have rejected such magic but not Tintagel. It was the most stable place in the realm because of Cassius' work. Cassius watched the rubble fall from the ceiling. It was so familiar. He summoned his magic, all that he could, all the untested. Such magic would distract every mage within all of Xzepheniixenze. Distract Gallylya long enough for Cassius' plan to take hold. And like anyone else, Gallylya could be used.

"We have to go, hurry!" Connylia said. She grabbed Gellia's arm.

Gellia didn't want to leave. The rumbling was deafening. She wanted to say *something*. Cassius watched them coolly and smiled. "Don't worry, Gellia Zapheny. Remember all I've taught you."

Connylia dragged Gellia through the door as she still watched Cassius until the wall caved in and blocked him from view. "We've a long way to go!" Conny shouted, dragged Gellia between fallen stone, she was positive they would not get out in time, much less make it through the battle raging outside... This was the favor Razhiede spoke of and she was determined to do it. It would take all the power she had. Connylia had made peace with herself. Rest was coming after so many years.

***

...Cassius stood alone, feeling the death all around him. The castle pulsed as it reclaimed energies. "Come now, Gallylya," he said, the thread of his magic moved unnoticed through the torrent of blue energy, unnoticed with the rest of his magic surging through the ground and up to the heavens. "Oh, Gallylya, there will be so many regrets from this day." He felt Connylia engage her magic—a power that was forbidden by her people.

***

Tintagel crumbled around them. The two women skittered through the castle, but only met dead ends. Gellia was too mystified to use her power, too distracted by the rainbow of magic that surged through every particle of castle. She could feel the emerald power gush all around them, but it wasn't doing anything other than raging. What was happening? Gallylya's magic raced through the corridors in blasts of flame. Others joined it, signatures she didn't recognize. Connylia dragged her down a few more passages before Gellia was knocked down by falling debris. Their hands slipped apart.

This was as stable a spot as Connylia could find. Her magic took hold. Gellia gazed at her friend from where she lie on the floor. Connylia suddenly looked as she must have a thousand years ago, grace reclaimed her. She gathered the last remnants of magic she possessed and tried to save the last Zapheny; her breath rasped as the magic ate through her. Her magic was wispy white arcs through the blinding color. It was beautiful.

Rubble fell around Gellia, and Connylia could feel that she was no longer there. Her hands and knees met stone as she fell amongst the rocks and dust. Connylia rested on the floor, feeling nothing. She had lived this all before, but finally… "Gellia, daughter of my heart," she said hoarsely. The stone was cool against her cheek. The thunder of the falling castle faded from her ears and dust started to cover her. All she could see was light from all the magic, so many colors until it finally faded.

"Not Gellia," came a voice. "You have saved her, saved another piece of Xzepheniixenze's future."

Connylia was lifted to her feet. The face she had not seen in a millennium appeared before her, she could feel his warmth. She could hear the ocean crashing on rocks, could smell the roses and the salty air. Weight from the years of sadness was lifted from her shoulders. Razhiede looked as she had remembered him. Now he was here with her once again. It was as it had been, the two of them in Zenobia, but without the tension of open war. "It's time for you to come with me;" he said softly, "for your journey has ended. Come with me to Zenobia for eternity."

Connylia smiled and took his hand. Finally.

***

Gallylya watched the black walls crumble into the lake as if it had surrendered. Snow began to fall from the amounts of magic ripped through the land. Trees smoldered all around them and the lake was dark with ash. The green magic finally faded to nothingness. He held out his hand to catch a snowflake. It was a long time since this part of the empire Xzepheniixenze last saw snow. Tintagel gave a few more pulses of magic; even the aftershock was powerful enough to fell a hundred more men. You have lost, Cassius, Gallylya thought.

He had no physical proof yet, but he was sure he felt his sister's magic in the mess. When he looked to his old friend,

Alynderan, the emperor noticed that he too sensed it. The sorrow was apparent on the earl's face.

She was all Gallylya had left. Zyendel was not to be trusted. "Perhaps with this Xzepheniixenze will finally fold," Gallylya said. Conny, why? His stallion, Gabriel, twitched his pert ears in response. The others of Gallylya's order stood by, their magic spent as well. Seeing Tintagel fall gave him a feeling of satisfaction, unlike Zenobia. Gallylya thought of the letter they intercepted, one destined for Zyendel from Gellia. He thought of how eerily similar it was to so many letters sent by Emperor Razhiede Zapheny before Zephronia joined the Holy War. What did she hope to accomplish? And most importantly, what part did Cassius play in its writing? But it was all over now.

His men chased the ruminants of the enemy through the forest, magic set the trees ablaze. Cassius knew Gallylya was coming for him, had called his army to the castle, but it was no match for the Zephrons. You have finally lost, he thought again. He rubbed at a pain at his temple.

With everyone in Tintagel dead there was little threat of retaliation. The threat from Xzepheniixenze was now greatly lessened. Like all rulers in Xzepheniixenze, when there was one many followed, all an enemy need do was take the leader away and the rest would fight each other indefinitely.

Gallylya looked at the snow as it collected on his horse's armor. It took only a short time for the ash to settle into the rubble and cover everything with a grey blanket. He rode Gabriel to his comrades to speak with them. Something still wasn't right. Something gave him a sense of dread, more so than any dragon ever did. It hung in the air like the strange lights that now appeared in the sky.

About the Author

GB MacRae grew up with her family and horses in rural New England. She started writing stories from a very young age, and started writing novels in her teens. She has a bachelor's degree in Literature and Culture from a small Central New York college, and loves to research anything and everything.

Her home is near Lake Ontario in a rambling old colonial house with her family and beloved pets. You can find her on Facebook, Pinterest, Twitter, at gbmacrae.com, and occasionally at sci-fi conventions dressed in one of her many costumes. You might even catch her dancing.

Made in the
USA
Lexington, KY